Dickens and the Law

Michael Lynch

Dickens and the Law

A Hate-Love Relationship

Michael Lynch

Acropolis Publishing

First published by Acropolis Publishing, a division of Canbury Press, 2025
This edition published 2025

Acropolis Publishing
Kingston upon Thames, Surrey, United Kingdom
www.canburypress.com

Typeset in Athelas (heading), Futura PT (body)

All rights reserved © Michael Lynch

Michael Lynch has asserted his right to be identified as the author of this work in accordance with Section 77 of the Copyright, Designs and Patents Act 1988

This is a work of non-fiction

ISBN:
Paperback: 9781914487538
Ebook: 9781914487545

For Penny

ACKNOWLEDGEMENTS

I acknowledge with gratitude my great debt to the work of the many recent and less-recent scholars and commentators on Dickens - in particular Humphrey House, Professor Michael Slater and Peter Ackroyd, whose depth of scholarship and breadth of vision have enabled us to encounter Dickens the living author. Through their work, Dickens has not entirely vanished over time but remains accessible to us as a complex individual whose thinking and creative imagination continue to add interest and vitality to our common life.

I also remember with gratitude my grandparents Tom and Lydia Frost whose set of Dickens was my early introduction to this remarkable author, and to my parents John and Margaret Lynch for stimulating my curiosity further.

I wish to thank Barnaby Bryan, Beth Flerlage and Marie-Elena Nash of the Middle Temple Library for their informative exhibition of material on Dickens held by the Inn, Jenny Smith for her valuable assistance in preparing the manuscript and my son Philip for being such a reliable guide through the benefits of digital access and communication.

The link to the Middle Temple Dickens exhibition is: Charles Dickens' Legal London

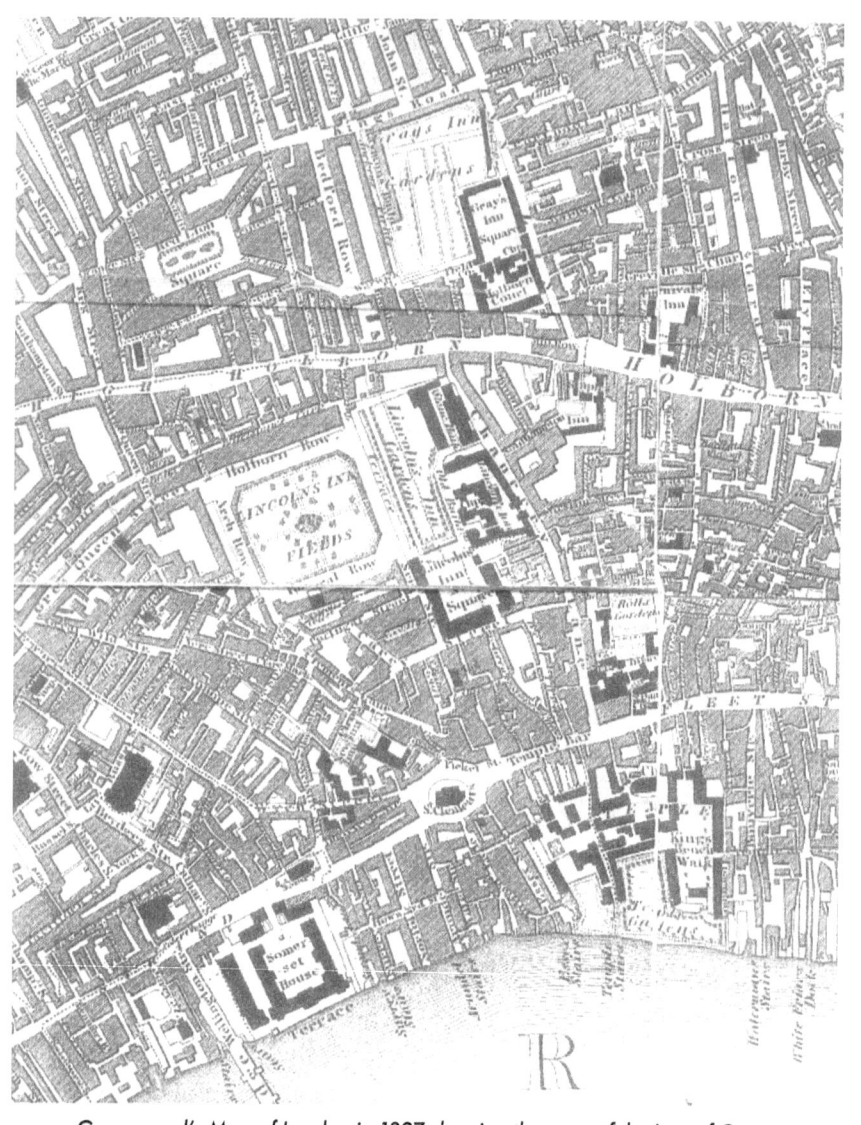

Greenwood's Map of London in 1827 showing the area of the Inns of Court

Contents

Acknowledgements	7
Introduction	11
1. **Decency v Arrogance:** The Pickwick Papers	25
2. **Childhood, Crime and Virtue:** Oliver Twist	39
3. **Squeers and the Power of the Law:** Nicholas Nickleby	62
4. **A Scary Legal Dummy:** The Old Curiosity Shop	78
5. **Prejudice, Populism and the Constitution:** Barnaby Rudge	92
6. **A Law-Abiding Society?** American Notes and Martin Chuzzlewit	126
7. **An Unlikely Partnership:** David Copperfield	154
8. **A Troubled Dream of the Law:** Bleak House	178
9. **Recte Numerare:** Little Dorrit	208
10. **The Lion and the Jackal:** A Tale of Two Cities	234
11. **Illusions and Evidence:** Great Expectations	242
12. **A Lawyer Learns to Love:** Our Mutual Friend	261
Notes	272
About the Author	276

Dickens posting his first work in the Editor's box

INTRODUCTION

This well-known drawing (opposite) by the Victorian artist J Stephenson captures the mixture of hope and apprehension with which the youthful Dickens posted the manuscript of his first article or 'sketch' in the Editor's Box of the Monthly Magazine in the autumn of 1833.

In early December of that year, returning to the same shop in Johnson's Court off Fleet Street, he bought a copy of the magazine and saw that his story had been published. He had entitled it '*Mr Minns and his Cousin*', but it appeared as '*A Dinner at Poplar Walk*'. Dickens relates in his preface to the first edition of *The Pickwick Papers* how he was affected when his work appeared 'in all the glory of print':

> I walked down to Westminster Hall and turned into it for half an hour, because my eyes were so dimmed with joy and pride that they could not bear the street and were not fit to be seen there.

If the young man had simply wanted to avoid the crowds, however, Westminster Hall, adjoining the Houses of Parliament, would have been a surprising place to go. It is almost a mile and a half away from Johnson's Court, Fleet Street – about half an hour's walk through the thoroughfares which Dickens says he wished to avoid. In early December of 1833 the Hall itself would have been full of people because at that time of the year – towards the end of the Michaelmas Term in the law's calendar – it was the active, beating heart of the English legal system.

From medieval times until about eight years before Dickens' visit in 1833, three courts had carried on their proceedings in Westminster Hall. Two held their sittings on the dais at the far end of the Hall – the Court of the King's Bench on the right-hand side of the dais and the Court of Chancery opposite on the left-hand side. The Court of Common Pleas occupied a space nearer the north entrance door, on the right-hand wall.

By 1833, when Dickens visited, there was insufficient room in the Hall itself and the three courts were held in adjacent buildings in St Margaret's Street, while the ancient Hall continued to be used as the meeting place for lawyers and their clients. On the day the young Dickens slipped into the Hall – as he says for some relief from the public gaze – the courts would have been in full operation and the Hall crowded with lawyers, their clients, witnesses, court officials, sightseers and customers buying food and other goods from the stalls lining the sides of the ancient building.

We will never know what prompted Dickens to seek out that place at that time. His decision seems to show, however, that at that happy moment of his first publication he wished to seek out surroundings associated with the law in its most ancient and time-honoured setting.

The judicial role of the Hall represented a remarkable example of continuity. In this Hall, built by William Rufus in 1097, kings from William onwards had sat with their advisers on the dais at the far end to hear petitions and do justice as monarch. Three Courts had evolved from the original King's Council – the King's Bench, the Court of Chancery and the Court of Common Pleas. The first two courts had, when not 'on eyre' or on circuit, occupied the same positions on the same dais since they had separated from the King's Council in the late twelfth century: a decree of Henry II ordered that five judges from the

King's household were to remain and hold court at Westminster when the King was elsewhere.[1] The King's Bench derived its authority from the King's delegation of his power to specific royal councillors acting as judges and the Court of Chancery in effect derived its authority – as Dickens tells us in *Bleak House* – from the Lord Chancellor's possession of the Great Seal of the Kingdom.

As to the third court, Magna Carta provided in 1215[2] that the Court of Common Pleas should 'be held in some certain place', which was inevitably Westminster Hall. It was there that all three courts continued to sit for over six hundred years until they moved to adjacent buildings in 1825 and then to their present site of the Royal Courts of Justice in the Strand in 1882.

Dickens' impulse to link the most ancient traditions of the law with the happiness of achieving his first literary publication sits somewhat unexpectedly with his later heartfelt condemnation of the legal system. Dickens as a campaigner attacked a wide range of abuses and injustices, including those in education, the provision of poor relief, the financial system, Parliament and the Civil Service, but the most frequent target of his criticism was the law itself.

Less than three years after his visit to Westminster Hall we find Dickens recounting Mr Pickwick's unfortunate encounters with those sharp legal practitioners Dodson and Fogg. His fiercest attack, however, is that directed at the High Court of Chancery in chapter I of *Bleak House*:

> This is the Court of Chancery; which has its decaying houses and its blighted lands in every shire; which has its worn-out lunatic in every madhouse, and its dead in every churchyard ... which so exhausts finances, patience, courage, hope, so overthrows the brain and breaks the heart; that there is not an honourable man among its practitioners who would not give ... the warning, 'Suffer any wrong that can be done to you, rather than come here!'

And in chapter 39, where we visit for the first time the office of that pitiless legal parasite Mr Vholes in Symond's Inn, Dickens sets out what seems to be the fundamental principle explaining all characteristics and anomalies of the law:

> The one great principle of the English law is to make business for itself. There is no other principle distinctly, certainly and consistently maintained through all its narrow turnings. Viewed in this light it becomes a coherent scheme, not the monstrous maze the laity are apt to think it.

Dickens' use of legal characters and settings nevertheless reflects a close and continuing interest in the law as a social institution, and such attention is certainly not uniformly negative. A Dickens reader will soon notice the author's use of legal settings in ways which appear quite incidental, but which actually indicate some form of sympathetic engagement. Sir John Chester in *Barnaby Rudge*, Tom Pinch in *Martin Chuzzlewit*, Pip in *Great Expectations* and even Eugene Wrayburn in *Our Mutual Friend* all at some point find lodging in the chambers of the Temple, even though that Inn of Court has no particular connection with the plot of any of these novels.

Other apparently arbitrary allusions are made. In *The Pickwick Papers* Mr Pickwick, looking for his solicitor Mr Perker, is prevailed upon to attend an evening harmonic meeting of lawyers' clerks at the Magpie and Stump, where Mr Jack Bamber tells gloomy stories about the Inns of Court:

> What do you know of the time when those young men shut themselves up in those lonely rooms and read and read, hour after hour, and night after night, till their reason wanders beneath their midnight studies...

though Dickens describes them as pleasant places at other times. In *Martin Chuzzlewit* Ruth Pinch meets her brother Tom in Fountain Court of the Middle Temple. Tellson's Bank in *A Tale of Two Cities* is placed at Temple Bar, then the formal gateway to the City of London at the west end of Fleet Street, named for its proximity to the Temple, and it is that way that Cly's funeral passes, watched by the grave-robbing Jerry Cruncher. When in *Our Mutual Friend* young John Harmon approaches Noddy Boffin hoping for work as a secretary, they happen to step aside from the street into the doorway of Clifford's Inn, one of the twelve or so then-surviving Inns of Chancery, to continue their conversation. This ancient Inn seems to have some special claim on Dickens' attention. In *Little Dorrit*, Amy Dorrit gets her brother some months' employment there, and when in *Our Mutual Friend* Mr Riah refers Alfred Lammle to a moneylender, it is 'Melchizedek, of Clifford's Inn'.

Woven within this wide legalesque tapestry, moreover, we can discern figures of indisputable virtue who actually achieve some success within the system. Mr Jaggers is a highly effective defender and much sought after, though he washes his hands throughout the day to remove the taint of the law. Sydney Carton gains the acquittal of Charles Darnay by a dramatic demonstration of forensic skill on the question of identity and later dies a hero on the Paris scaffold. In *David Copperfield* Tommy Traddles, who stands up so stoutly for David at Mr Creakle's school, grows up to become a barrister. Even the financially inept but determinedly honest Mr Micawber, after playing his key role in defeating Uriah Heep, becomes a well-regarded magistrate in Australia.

In a kind of real-life parallel to these creations, Dickens' own son Harry (Henry Fielding Dickens) joins the Middle Temple with his father's encouragement, is knighted and achieves high judicial office as the Common Sergeant of London.

Dickens, a member of Middle Temple

An indication of his serious interest in legal institutions at an early stage in his literary career is that Dickens does not just describe them, he is thinking of joining them. In November 1834, while he was busy setting up his first independent home and rescuing his father from once again being imprisoned for debt, he wrote to the Steward of New Inn – the Inn of Chancery linked to the Middle Temple – enquiring about chambers there, saying, 'I intend entering at the bar, as soon as circumstances will enable me to do so'³. Five years later, on the day after Boxing Day 1839, Dickens carries out that intention, writing to his publisher and friend Edward Chapman of Chapman and Hall to let him know where to go to sign a bond undertaking to underwrite Dickens' expenses at the Middle Temple:

> 'The place where you pledge yourself to pay ... is the Treasurer's Office of the Middle Temple, the new building at the bottom of Middle Temple Lane, on the right hand side. You walk up into the first floor and say (boldly) that you come to sign Mr Charles Dickens' bond – which is already signed by Mr Sergeant Talfourd.'⁴

In 1847, at the age of 35, Dickens sent the first few pages of an autobiography to his lifelong friend John Forster. In them he described his experiences of being sent, aged twelve, to work labelling bottles of shoe-blacking in a ramshackle warehouse by the Thames. There, he said:

> I ... felt my hopes of being a learned and distinguished man crushed in my bosom.

One can easily imagine a connection between Dickens' heartfelt early hope of becoming 'a learned and distinguished man' and his wish to join an Inn of Court. Apart from the fledgling University of London then being established in the neighbourhood of Gower Street, the Inns of Court could at that time be said to be the only institution of higher education in London. When a young man of 16 – 17 in his first job as a clerk in solicitor's offices first in Gray's Inn and later in Lincoln's Inn, Dickens would have been close to the communal life of the barrister members of that Inn in their dining hall, library and chapel, though without being able to participate in it. To such a young man, that communal life would have seemed to offer – at least at its best, if not always realised – a companionship of learning and an accepted social status that Dickens must have felt his own family background only partially supplied.

The prospect of social status and intelligent companionship is by no means the whole explanation, however. In a strange way, the life of the Inns stimulated his imagination and energised his creative writing. For Dickens, the buildings of the Inns of Court and the practices carried on within them were in a very real sense an outward manifestation of the system of law they were created to serve. For this reason they intrigued the young author and seemed to offer an opportunity to explore from within a legal system which at the same time repelled and attracted him.

So, in 1840 Dickens began to eat dinners in Middle Temple Hall, as student members are still required to do. This was an experience he described, though in relation to Gray's Inn, as:

> ...having a frayed old gown put on in a pantry by an old woman in a chronic state of Saint Anthony's fire and dropsy, and, so decorated, bolting a bad dinner in a party of four, whereof each individual mistrusts the other three[5]

He remained a member of the Inn for some fifteen years, finally withdrawing his application to the Bar in 1855.

With Dickens, social observation and literary creativity were never kept in separate compartments, and this is particularly true of his observations on the law. Dickens is in one sense a social reformer with the straightforward aim of using his literary work to expose the abuses and iniquities of society and so help to bring them to an end. The interplay between Dickens' views on social problems and his creative work is however both strong and complex. For instance, a speech which Dickens gave to the Administrative Reform Association in June 1855 on the government's disastrous mismanagement of the Crimean campaign clearly anticipated the theme of *Little Dorrit*. As K J Fielding[6] writes in relation to this speech:

> It is wrong to look for any of the themes of the novels *simply* in the author's activities in real life, since life and fiction were both closely twisted round the core of the writer's personality. (My italics)

Another contemporary, Percy Fitzgerald, who worked with Dickens on the magazine *All the Year Round* perceptively noted[7] that the abuses which Dickens saw in society seemed not simply to fire his indignation but also to stimulate his creative powers. They:

> ...supplied him with a certain dramatic stimulus, or motive power. Once started, and furnished with something real or living to work on, his imagination kindled; fancies rushed upon him, and he put the topic in all sorts of forms. It supplied him with characters and situations.

Dickens the social reformer?

For some critics Dickens is seen primarily as a social reformer, albeit not an entirely convincing one. Dickens' comments might be honest and penetrating as social observation, they say, but they are not sufficiently constructive to bring about any actual programme of reform. Though an admirer of Dickens, George Orwell made his most telling criticism of the writer in his essay *Inside the Whale and Other Essays* in 1940:

> The truth is that Dickens's criticism of society is almost exclusively moral. Hence the utter lack of any constructive suggestion anywhere in his work. He attacks the law, parliamentary government, the educational system and so forth, without clearly suggesting what he would put in their places. ... It would be difficult to point anywhere in his books to a passage suggesting that the economic system is wrong as a system. ... Hence that recurrent Dickens figure, the good rich man. ... He ... is is always a superhumanly kindhearted old gentleman who 'trots to and fro, raising his employees' wages, patting children on the head, getting debtors out of jail and in general, acting the fairy godmother'.

Few would feel they could disagree with this criticism at first sight. While in fact we don't usually expect creative novelists to produce worked-out social solutions to the iniquities of our society, we feel somehow that Orwell's criticism hits the mark with Dickens. On reflection however, we can see that this is not because Dickens fails to offer a solution to society's problems. Most novelists fail to do that. It is because Dickens actually does offer one – the good rich man – and the solution he produces is so clearly an inadequate remedy for the abuses he describes.

In aiming at Dickens' 'good rich man' as a target, therefore, Orwell was taking something of a cheap shot. Over the totality of his work, Dickens in fact goes further than most creative writers in attempting, in legal as well as moral terms, a wider structural assessment of society's shortcomings and in providing at least an intimation of where solutions might be sought.

Dickens' treatment of the legal system as a target for his satire is different in an important way from his treatment of other topics. His attention to the various aspects of the law is both emotional and intellectual in character. It is directed not just to the shortcomings and abuses of the law but also, perhaps more importantly, to examining the problems which the law is attempting to solve. People's failure to meet their contractual obligations, the problem of indebtedness and the endemic crime of the so-called rookeries for whose inhabitants a career of crime is virtually inevitable, all these are the subject of long and thoughtful attention.

In *Bleak House*, for instance, as well as the devastating criticism of the Court of Chancery which is the framework of this powerful novel, we also have a continuing concern with how to ensure that people meet their ordinary contractual obligations. In *Little Dorrit*, as well as the moving account of the evils of debtors' prisons, we are brought face to face with the problem of how to treat truly unrepentant debtors. In *Bleak House* again, and in *Our Mutual Friend*, we find, among the endemic crime of the rookeries of St Giles and the rough waterside districts of Wapping and Limehouse the calm, methodical and occasionally, in Dickens' eyes, almost magical operation of the newly formed Metropolitan Police.

Dickens and legal self-help

This interest can lead beyond mere discussion of abuses towards, in fictional terms at least, a real righting of wrongs. In three, arguably four, of his novels Dickens does actually allow matters to be resolved through use of the law but, significantly, not through recourse to the court system. In these novels, the complicated, expensive procedures of the courts are kept at bay and matters are satisfactorily resolved by operating a kind of home-made justice.

This can be seen partly as a reflection of the fact that at least up to the 1830s the burden of initiating the prosecution of a crime rested with the victim, who not only had to ask for help but often also to provide sufficient evidence before the matter was taken up by the authorities. In *Oliver Twist*, Oliver is eventually redeemed by Mr Brownlow and his aptly-named friend Mr Grimwig – who we are told had been 'bred to the law' – who act together to defeat the claims of Oliver's half-brother Monks. In *Nicholas Nickleby*, Ralph Nickleby and Squeers are defeated in their fraudulently legalistic attempts to seize back Smike. In *David Copperfield* the schemes of Uriah Heep are exploded by Mr Micawber and the recently qualified barrister Tom Traddles. In *Martin Chuzzlewit*, the exposure of Pecksniff and general righting of wrongs is achieved in chapter 52 by Old Martin in Tom Pinch's room in the Temple.

In his narration of these informal but law-related procedures, Dickens puts to creative use both his condemnation of the law and his continuing interest in it, which in turn reflects his own view of the common law.

As it is usually viewed, one essential aspect of the common law is that it is ultimately based on the customary practices and values of ordinary society. As the commentator AWB Simpson puts it:

> common law is seen to be the expression or manifestation of commonly shared values and conceptions of reasonableness and the common good[8].

Another equally essential aspect, however, is that, as the seventeenth-century legal historian Sir Matthew Hale famously wrote:

> ... men are not born Common Lawyers, neither can bare exercise of the faculty of reason give a man sufficient knowledge of it, but it must be gained by the habituating and accustoming and exercising of that Faculty by reading, Study and observation to give a Man a complete knowledge thereof[9].

In the way key problems are so often resolved in his novels, Dickens seems to be reflecting on a conception of the English Common Law which recognises the origin of its rules and principles in the settled, accepted manners and conventions making up the common life of the people. He nevertheless also recognises that in order to have its independent existence and force the common law has to have a distinctive system of rules, to understand which a legal training is required.

In his fictional and therefore somewhat idealised use of the procedures in *Oliver Twist, David Copperfield* and *Martin Chuzzlewit* Dickens contrives to bring together these two aspects – the closeness to common values and everyday virtues, together with the specialised training and experience needed to make the complex system work – while keeping safely away from the frustrating and cumbersome procedures of the courts.

Elsewhere in his work we see individual lawyers working within the legal system but at the same time not being fully 'of' it. Mr Jaggers in *Great Expectations* scrupulously washes his hands after every case. Sydney Carton in *A Tale of Two Cities* is a very able lawyer but somehow stifled and unable to exert himself in his profession. Traddles himself, at the start of his career in *David Copperfield*, has rooms in the highest attics of Gray's Inn where against all the rules he maintains a joyous household with his wife and her sisters.

Contrary to Orwell's view, Dickens' novels overall do not suggest that our only remedy is the benevolence of a few good rich men. Human kindness is always an important element in any society, but it inevitably acts in a random manner. Dickens intimates that another powerful factor is available to us, one which can operate not randomly but as part of social structure. So often in the novels the English common law glimmers, intermittently but with a kind of dim encouragement, suggesting that there is within it a redeeming element, long suppressed and choked by the weight of legal fictions, self-serving practices and complexity of procedure, which could nevertheless emerge as the means of fostering personal responsibility and sustaining the bonds between individuals which enable us to function as a society.

Mr. Pickwick and Sam in the Attorney's Office

Mr Pickwick visits the offices of Dodson and Fogg

1.
THE PICKWICK PAPERS

Decency v Arrogance

The years 1836 – 1839 were probably the busiest period of Dickens' life. In 1836 his 'day job' was as a Parliamentary reporter for the *Morning Chronicle*, but the success of his Sketches by Boz published over the previous three years had made him, at the age of 24, something of a literary celebrity. Over the next three years, he would write three books in monthly editions – *The Pickwick Papers, Oliver Twist* and *Nicholas Nickleby* – as well as editing and contributing to *Bentley's Miscellany* and revising the *Sketches*.

After his early success with the *Sketches*, Dickens' real 'breakthrough' was in February 1836. William Chapman of the publishers Chapman and Hall had noticed a sketch – *The Tuggses at Ramsgate* – which Dickens had written for their magazine[1] and he now asked the young man to write the text to accompany a series of illustrations of '*Cockney Sporting Life*' by Robert Seymour, a well-known illustrator. Dickens suggested the title – *The Pickwick Papers* – based on the name of a coach proprietor, Moses Pickwick, which appeared on the side of his vehicles.

Dickens' pay for his monthly contribution of *Pickwick* text together with his salary from the *Morning Chronicle* and the royalties from the earlier *Sketches* provided enough for him to get married. On 2nd April 1836, he married Catherine Hogarth and the couple set up home in

Furnival's Inn – in a slightly larger set of rooms than those he had occupied earlier with his brother Fred.

The plan for *Pickwick Papers* was however suddenly disrupted when Robert Seymour the illustrator committed suicide at the end of April. Though a young man called Hablot Brown was eventually recruited to provide the illustrations, the project could not continue quite as before. Dickens had earlier suggested significant changes to the work, but now he had the initiative – he was no longer supplying words to accompany Seymour's drawings, but originating a text to be illustrated by the artist Hablot Brown. The basic structure of the project, however, remained as a series of only vaguely connected events – a duel, a cricket match, an election, a Christmas gathering, an elopement and so on.

If the book can be said to have any continuous theme it is the story of Mr Pickwick's unfortunate misunderstanding with Mrs Bardell, his widowed landlady, and the subsequent case – urged on by the scandalous solicitors Dodson and Fogg – of breach of promise of marriage.

The story of Pickwick's legal misfortunes has a kind of a curtain-raiser – the chapter 24 incident in which Pickwick, in error, goes to bed in the Ipswich hotel room occupied by 'the lady in yellow curl-papers', which leads to his being challenged to a duel. As duelling was by then illegal, he is consequently apprehended by the officious town constable and brought in triumphant procession to the local magistrate:

> The shopkeepers of the town, although they had a very indistinct notion of the nature of the offence, could not but be much edified and gratified by this spectacle. Here was the strong arm of the law, coming down with twenty gold-beater force, upon two offenders from the metropolis itself; the mighty engine was directed by their own magistrate, worked by their own officers; and both the criminals, by their united efforts, were securely shut up, in the narrow compass of a sedan chair.

Pickwick fortunately talks his way out of that situation. The main action, however, takes place in London and concerns the famous trial of Bardell v Pickwick and the events leading up to it.

The fourth monthly number of *The Pickwick Papers* was written in June 1836. Following the death of Robert Seymour, Dickens now had the greater responsibility and had introduced the character of Sam Weller. In the following number, we have the fateful scene where Pickwick, who is intending to take Sam Weller into his employment as a valet, asks his landlady whether she thought that two could live as cheaply as one and imagined that in the future her little boy would have a companion. To the admiring Mrs Bardell, this seemed to amount to a proposal of marriage. She faints in Pickwick's arms and the scene is witnessed by Pickwick's friends Winkle, Tupman and Snodgrass, who enter the room at that moment.

Six chapters later, when Pickwick receives Dodson & Fogg's letter informing him of Mrs Bardell's unexpected claim he takes the direct, no-nonsense approach of returning to London and visiting Dodson and Fogg in their offices. Pickwick asks to see either of the partners, and from behind a partition a voice is heard to say:

> 'Mr Dodson ain't at home, and Mr Fogg is particularly engaged.'
>
> 'When will Mr Dodson be back, sir?' asks Mr Pickwick.
>
> 'Can't say.'
>
> 'Will it be long before Mr Fogg is disengaged, sir?'
>
> 'Don't know.'
>
> Here the man proceeded to mend his pen with great deliberation, while another clerk, who was mixing a Sedlitz powder under cover of the lid of his desk, laughed approvingly.

The approving laugh of Dodson and Fogg's clerk here is one of the most important moments in the whole of Dickens' work. It establishes the whole tone and feeling of the way the law can treat ordinary people. Its echoes can be heard throughout the subsequent legal proceedings, though Mr Pickwick's sense of his own rightness remains undiminished. When Fogg eventually appears, Pickwick, articulating the view the lay person might hold but never express, begins to describe the proceedings as rascally and disgraceful. Fogg immediately calls his clerks to witness what Mr Pickwick is saying and invites him to make further accusations. Pickwick is saved from this potentially disastrous course only by the intervention of the worldly Sam Weller, who forcibly leads his master away.

In many ways, this is simply a frank and happy comedy, showing those failings and anomalies which provided Dickens with material for his most entertaining satire. Just under the surface, however, is a strong, dangerous current of injustice. The benign sunshine of comedy gives way to threatening clouds as Mr Pickwick's encounter with the legal system unfolds. By bringing Pickwick's character of almost imperturbable benevolence into confrontation with the institutions of the law, Dickens is able to amuse and entertain us while he reveals some of the most frightening aspects of the legal system.

This creates a highly successful dramatic sequence. Certain of his own moral rightness Pickwick refuses, as far as is humanly possible, to play the legal game. He never tries to evade his obligations but insists on dealing with the law as if it were a rational system operating under the rules of ordinary civilised behaviour, and the resulting encounters are at the same time funny and disturbing. Pickwick never wins, of course, but he is not defeated either. The result is a stand-off each time.

When Pickwick is told that Sergeant Snubbin has been retained as counsel, he first asks where he lives and then asks to see him. This request, perfectly reasonable in the context of ordinary life, has here almost the same astounding force as Oliver's request for more gruel in the workhouse.

> 'See Sergeant Snubbin, my dear sir,' rejoined Mr Perker in utter amazement. 'Pooh pooh, my dear sir, such a thing was never heard

of, without a consultation fee being paid, and a consultation fixed. It couldn't be done, my dear sir, it couldn't be done'

Dickens here, incidentally, gives us a picture of members of the oldest Order of English legal advocates at work in the years of that Order's decline. Sergeants-at-Law had existed in England since before 1270 and were the senior and most distinguished members of the legal profession. Their position began to be weakened by the appointment of Queen's or King's Counsel from the 1590s onwards and in 1834 – two years before *Pickwick* was written – they had temporarily lost their monopoly of pleading in the Court of Common Pleas.

As Mr Pickwick has the power that money confers, he is shown into Sergeant Snubbin's chambers in ten minutes, despite Perker's earlier protestations. The ensuing remarkable encounter appears to take place between inhabitants of two different worlds, conducted through a glass wall. Snubbin never speaks directly to Pickwick, only to Perker.

Snubbin puts on his spectacles, looks at Pickwick for a few seconds with great curiosity and begins to smile slightly. He asks Perker if Pickwick has a strong case, at which Perker shrugs. 'Has any witnesses?' 'No'. Sergeant Snubbins' smile then becomes 'more defined'. He 'rocks his leg with increasing violence, throws himself back in his chair' and 'coughs dubiously'. As Dickens observes:

> These tokens of the sergeant's presentiments on the subject, slight as they were, were not lost on Mr Pickwick.

Pickwick therefore now also 'settles his spectacles' and proceeds to make a series of observations about people viewing the Bar as being suspicious, distrustful and over-cautious. Snubbin cannot be seen to be affected by these remarks. In order to preserve the invisible barrier between himself and Pickwick, he simply sends for his junior in the case, Mr Phunky, and asks him to 'take Mr Pickwick away' and listen to anything he wishes to say.

The humour is mixed with real indignation. Dickens depicts the blank, impenetrable wall of etiquette and procedure by which the law protected itself from any genuine contact with members of the public. It can be argued that this enables a dispassionate, objective view to be taken of a case. Mr Pickwick, however, finds it to be a thick, protective plate against which ordinary emotions and affections beat themselves in vain.

This is certainly true of the trial in Bardell v Pickwick. The trial described in chapter 34 is undeniably funny. The opening words of chapter 34 refer to 'The eventful morning of the fourteenth of February' which indicates that this breach of promise of marriage case was heard on St Valentine's day. Other references suggest it was heard on the first of April – All Fools' day. On whichever of these significant dates it took place, we can enjoy the lilting cadences in which Sergeants-at-Law Buzfuz and Snubbins attempt to bamboozle the jurers as when, Mrs Bardell being the widow of a customs officer, Sergeant Buzfuz smoothly proceeds to relate that:

> ... the late Mr Bardell, after enjoying for many years the esteem and confidence of his sovereign as one of the guardians of the royal revenues, glided almost imperceptibly from the world to seek elsewhere the repose and peace which a custom house could never afford.

He then continues in smooth, rhythmical prose and at great length to assert, even though he is not in the witness box giving actual evidence, that Mrs Bardell is a grieving and vulnerable woman while Pickwick is a predatory monster.

We can be entertained by Sergeant Buzfuz's terrific ability to create evidence out of nothing – magnificently shown by his use of Pickwick's completely innocent and irrelevant notes to his landlady:

> 'They are not open, fervent eloquent epistles ... they are covert, sly underhanded communications, but fortunately, far more communicative than if couched in the most ... poetic imagery – 'Dear Mrs B – Chops in tomato sauce, Yours, Pickwick.' Gentlemen, what can this mean? ...

'Chops! Tomata sauce! Gentlemen, is the happiness of a sensitive and confiding female to be trifled away, by such shallow artifices as these?'

Buzfuz's simple question, 'What can this mean?' is masterly. Again without producing any evidence, Buzfuz leads the jury to believe that the words 'chops and tomato sauce' must have some other meaning beyond the obvious one, too mysterious to identify but almost certainly reflecting badly on Mr Pickwick.

This piece of humour seems to be not entirely of Dickens' invention. It appears to have been inspired by the similar use of evidence in the case of *Norton v Lord Melbourne* in which Melbourne's extremely informal notes to Mrs Norton were interpreted in court in much the same way as Pickwick's notes to his landlady.

As so often, Dickens' humour contains the bite of cruel reality. His account of the Bardell trial shows not only the techniques used by sharp lawyers to impress the jury and confuse witnesses but also the mistakes made by complacent or inexperienced counsel.

In *Bardell v Pickwick*, all the sharp techniques are ably deployed by the Dodson and Fogg team – Sergeant Buzfuz and his junior Mr Simpkin. Mrs Bardell is brought into court in an apparently bemused state, starts at the sight of her own child and asks where she is. As if to emphasise the pathos, Dickens even introduces an 'extra-sized' umbrella.

We have seen Buzfuz's effective but unsubstantiated rhetoric in his opening speech. Mr Simpkin, Buzfuz's efficient junior, then begins the questioning and asks Mr Winkle whether he is a friend of Mr Pickwick. Winkle begins, 'I have known Mr Pickwick now, as well as I recollect at this moment, nearly...' and Simpkin interrupts him by saying, 'Do not evade the question'. Winkle has not evaded the question but Simpkin has already started to discredit him in the eyes of the jury. Later, questioning Winkle about what he heard when on the stairs outside the room where Pickwick and Mrs Bardell were speaking, Simpkin asked him whether he was 'prepared to swear' that Pickwick had *not* spoken the compromising words. Winkle could not say he was prepared so to swear, which to the jury suggested that it was more likely than not that Pickwick had spoken the words in question.

Mr Pickwick is less fortunate in his representation. Sergeant Snubbin, so disparagingly dismissive of Pickwick during their consultation, seems very slow to recognise a forensic opportunity. When Sam Weller had been asked by Buzfuz whether anything particular had happened on the morning in question, Sam had said that he had had 'a new fit out of clothes' which was 'a wery particklar and uncommon circumstance'.

Had Snubbin learnt enough about the case to cross-question Sam on this point, he could have easily evinced evidence from him of the entirely innocent explanation for Pickwick's question to Mrs Bardell about two living as cheaply as one, ie that he was contemplating taking on Sam as his valet, the new outfit of clothes being his new livery on taking on this position.

Sam hands the chance to ask this question to Snubbin on a plate:

> 'Would any other gen'leman like to ask me anythin'?' inquired Sam, taking up his hat and looking round most deliberately.

The great Sergeant Snubbin, however, fails to see the point, describes Sam as a witness of 'impenetrable stupidity' and asks him to stand down.

The fatal blow to Pickwick's case is, however, struck by Snubbin's junior, Mr Phunky. Phunky had, we are told, been at the Bar for eight years but had had little experience in court. The advocate's job is to know the answer to his question already, and get the witness to give it as evidence to the court. Phunky asks Winkle an open-ended question about Pickwick's general behaviour, to which almost any answer is possible, with the result that Winkle refers to 'one trifling occasion'. Buzfuz then of course pounces to question him on this 'occasion' and the Judge himself orders Winkle to relate the embarrassing incident of the lady with the yellow curl-papers to the scandalised ears of the jury.

In modern terms the case actually makes no sense at all. It has often been observed that there has been no evidence that Mr Pickwick actually asked Mrs Bardell to marry him, nor any evidence that, if he ever had done so, he later refused to marry her. The two people best placed to shed light on this are of course Mr Pickwick and Mrs Bardell themselves, but they do not give evidence. Dickens' account of the case faithfully illustrates the state of the law at that time, which did not allow anyone who had an interest in the outcome of the case, and certainly not the parties themselves, to give evidence, on the grounds that this would present them with a temptation to tell an untruth, ie commit perjury.[2]

The outcome is that the jury awards Mrs Bardell the substantial sum of £750. Pickwick makes it clear to Dodson and Fogg that he has no intention of paying either damages or costs. He then goes off to Bath and nothing happens in the case for some two months.

Dickens takes us further into the dark machinery of the law when Pickwick surrenders himself to the Fleet prison rather than pay the £750 and Dodson and Fogg's costs that had been awarded against him.

Pickwick is taken to the Fleet rather than that other debtors' prison with which Dickens was more familiar, the Marshalsea, perhaps because Dickens wished to distance himself from the painful memory of his father's imprisonment in the Marshalsea some twelve years earlier.

That memory remained strong, nevertheless, as indicated by the description of the Marshalsea in chapter 21, where old Jack Bamber, at the gathering of lawyer's clerks at the Magpie and Stump, tells the tale of the Queer Client:

> It may be my fancy, or it may be that I cannot separate the place from my old recollections associated with it, but this part of London I cannot bear. The street is broad, the shops are spacious, the noise of passing vehicles, the footsteps of a perpetual stream of people – all the busy sounds of traffic resound in it from morn to midnight; but the streets around are mean and close; poverty and debauchery lie festering in the crowded alleys; want and misfortune are pent up in the narrow

> prison; and air of gloom and dreariness seems, in my eyes at least, to hang about the scene, and to impart to it a squalid and sickly hue.

This seems like Dickens speaking of the memory of his own experience rather than old Jack Bamber's recollections. Certainly, his thirteen months or so in 1824-25 working at Warren's Blacking factory, pasting labels on blacking bottles while his father was in the Marshalsea and the family broken up was a traumatic experience. The much-examined 'autobiographical fragment' which Dickens gave to his friend and biographer John Forster over twenty years afterwards describes that time:

> 'No words can express the secret agony of my soul as I sunk into this companionship ... and felt my early hope of growing up to be a learned and distinguished man crushed in my breast'.

The mixture of shame and indignation Dickens felt and continued to feel as a result of those experiences – directed not only at the Marshalsea itself but also, arguably, at the legal processes which placed his father there – almost certainly provided the drive and energy which gave an angry edge to his account of the consultation with Sergeant Snubbin.

The impulse to 'throw a little comedy' over things that he found disturbing or threatening, which Dickens later confided to Forster, finds a remarkable creative expression in the character of Pickwick. Of complete integrity, consistently civil and unshakeably kind, Pickwick insists on dealing with a wicked world on his own terms. He is important not just because he survives the indignities and misfortunes he experiences but because he has challenged the things that have caused him to suffer.

He and Sam Weller are certainly comparable to Don Quixote and Sancho Panza, though while Don Quixote carried his lance against harmless windmills Pickwick challenges real evils. Pickwick does not succeed, of course, but this determined, imperturbable and physically rotund figure bounces back from his encounters essentially unharmed.

He cannot be said to have won his fights, but the malign forces cannot be said to have won either. Pickwick holds the contending factors in balance within his own imperturbable person, leaving us free to appreciate the irony and laugh at the comedy as Dickens intended.

The convincing detail with which Dickens describes the interior of the Fleet Prison gives us the atmosphere of the place as well as the layout. There is no record of his visiting that institution and he appears to have relied on a contemporary publication 'Scenes and Stories by a Clergyman in Debt. Written during his confinement in the Debtors' Prisons' for much of the factual information, but the mixture of ironic comedy and grim suffering is Dickens' own.

The clouds gather as Mr Roker, the turnkey, conducts Pickwick to his quarters.

> 'This', said the gentleman, thrusting his hands into his pockets and looking carelessly over his shoulder to Mr Pickwick, 'This here is the hall flight'.
>
> 'Oh,' replied Mr Pickwick, looking down a dark and filthy staircase which appeared to lead to a range of damp, gloomy stone vaults beneath the ground, 'and those, I suppose are the little cellars where the prisoners kept their small quantities of coals. Unpleasant places to have to go down to, but very convenient, I dare say.'
>
> 'Yes, I shouldn't wonder if they was convenient,' replied the gentleman, 'seeing that a few people live there, pretty snug. That's the Fair, that is.' ...
>
> 'My friend,' said Mr Pickwick, 'you don't really mean to say that human beings live down in those wretched dungeons?' ...
>
> 'Live down there! Yes, and die down there too, very often!' replied Mr Roker. 'and what of that?'

Later Pickwick looks through the open door of one of the rooms:

> Here three or four great hulking fellows, just visible through a cloud of tobacco smoke, were engaged in noisy and riotous conversation over half-emptied pots of beer, or playing at all-fours with a very greasy pack of cards.

In another place

> A young woman, with a child in her arms, who seemed scarcely able to crawl, from emaciation and misery, was walking up and down a passage in conversation with her husband, who had no other place to see her in. As they passed Mr Pickwick, he could hear the female sob bitterly; and once she burst into such a passion of grief, that she was compelled to lean against the wall for support.

Pickwick is shown a bed and manages to get to sleep, but is woken up by the sound of singing and dancing:

> On the floor of the room, a man in a broad-skirted green coat, with corduroy knee-smalls and grey cotton stockings, was performing the most popular steps of a hornpipe, with a slang and burlesque caricature of grace and lightness ... Another man, evidently very drunk, who had probably been tumbled into bed by his companions, was sitting up between the sheets, warbling as much as he could recollect of a comic song, with the most intensely sentimental feeling and expression.

The scenes on Pickwick's first night are rough and somewhat alarming comedy, but comedy nevertheless. The gentlemanly pretensions and smooth parasitic practices of Mivins and Smangle provide a steady flow of entertaining narrative, and Pickwick, protected by Sam, survives fairly well the evening of prison conviviality.

Graver notes are sounded when, in the 'poor side' of the prison, we meet Alfred Jingle and Job Trotter, the two confidence men who have imposed on Pickwick earlier in the book. They have pawned most of their clothes for food and are now literally starving to death. Jingle's statement, beginning on an almost comic note, takes us rapidly through the stages of the basically corrupt procedure by means of which prisoners' deaths are explained away:

> 'Everything – Job's too – all shirts gone – never mind – saves washing – nothing soon – lie in bed – starve – die – inquest – little bone house – poor prisoner – common necessaries – hush it up – gentlemen of the jury – warden's tradesmen – keep it snug – natural death – coroner's order – workhouse funeral – serve him right – all over – drop the curtain.'

We have not yet reached the limits of the law's destructive power, however. Its savage claw, in the form of Dodson and Fogg's clerk Mr Jackson, reaches out as far as the sunny tea gardens of Hampstead where Mrs Bardell and her friends are taking a holiday outing. Mrs Bardell has 'as a matter of form' signed a 'cognovit for costs', the effect of which is that she is bound to pay Dodson and Fogg's costs if Mr Pickwick does not pay them. Mrs Bardell is persuaded to get into a coach and is taken to 'one of our public offices', which is of course the Fleet Prison where, as she cannot afford to pay the costs, she discovers that she is now confined.

To bring the story towards a happier conclusion, Sam contacts Mr Perker who applies his mind to the situation with good effect. Having spoken with Mrs Bardell, is able to advise Pickwick that he can now free both Mrs Bardell and himself from prison by paying simply the costs of the case in exchange for her apology and her signing an undertaking for a release and discharge from damages. At first Pickwick remains obdurate and is persuaded to accept the compromise only by the pleading of the newly married Arabella Allen.

This is not quite the end of the story, however. Pickwick's kindness has led him to rescue his former adversaries, Alfred Jingle and Job Trotter, not only paying their debts but also fitting them out to go to new jobs in Demerara. In chapter 53, they come to Perker's office to conclude the arrangements. The two miscreants appear to be genuinely reformed. Full of remorse, respectful and grateful to Pickwick, they declare that they will repay the money from their earnings in the West Indies.

Their departure from the office is immediately followed by the arrival of Dodson and Fogg – Perker had forgotten that he had arranged for them to come and complete the payment of their costs. In contrast to the humble and reformed Jingle and Trotter, the predatory Dodson and Fogg show absolutely no sign of humility; they are as impertinent and confident as ever. Although Pickwick on their entry moves away to the window, they tease him as they produce their papers, saying they have no secrets, will make him 'pay for peeping' and with mock concern ask about his stay in the Fleet. Pickwick eventually dismisses them in a burst of indignation as a 'pair of mean, rascally pettifogging robbers' and predictably this has no effect whatsoever on Dodson and Fogg, who are hurried out of the door by the anxious Mr Perker. The result of the battle which Pickwick has waged with the forces of the law remains as it has been throughout the tale – a standoff.

2.
OLIVER TWIST

Childhood, Crime and Virtue

In January 1837 Dickens' career gained significant momentum. He was 24 years old. Two years earlier he had established his first independent home in Furnival's Inn, Holborn and he had married Catherine Hogarth in April 1836. Their first son was born the following January. Dickens already had a considerable reputation as Boz, the writer of the *Sketches*, and was writing *The Pickwick Papers* in monthly instalments. With the appearance of Sam Weller in the fourth instalment his popularity had soared so that he was one of the best-known young writers in the country.

Several strands of thought from his childhood experience and adult reflection seem to have come together when he began to write the story of Oliver Twist for the monthly magazine *Bentley's Miscellany*. The first instalment of 'Oliver Twist, or The Parish Boy's Progress' appeared in February 1837. It is set in the fictional town of Mudfog, widely supposed to represent Chatham, where Dickens lived until the age of ten.

The changes in the Poor Law introduced by the Poor Law Amendment Act of 1834 begin to be implemented during the second half of 1836 and it seems no coincidence that Dickens' Mudfog satire begins to acquire a sharper focus at that time. The first article in the February edition of the *Miscellany* has the title, '*Oliver Twist, or The*

Parish Boy's Progress' and the workhouse in which Oliver – 'the parish boy' – is born is set in Mudfog. However, the reference to Mudfog, ie Chatham, is explicitly deleted from the story when it is published in book form some six months later. This later opening begins:

> Among other public buildings in a certain town, which for many reasons it will be prudent to refrain from mentioning, and to which I will assign no fictitious name, there is one anciently common to most towns, great and small, to wit, a workhouse, and there was born, on a day and date which I need not trouble myself to repeat .... the item of mortality whose name is prefixed to the head of this chapter.

Dickens' own early childhood years in Chatham, where his father was posted in the course of his duties as a pay clerk in the Admiralty, were probably among the happiest of his life. His family was financially stable and there seems little to suggest a link between those times and the misery and brutality of the workhouse experienced by the young Oliver.

Another workhouse, however, this time a real one, does feature in Dickens' early life. It actually survives as the remaining part of the old Middlesex Hospital in London and stands on Cleveland Street, opposite the junction with Foley Street, just south-west of the Telecom Tower. It was the workhouse for the parish of St Paul's, Covent Garden. For a time as a child and later as a young man up to 1831 Dickens lived with his family at 10 Norfolk Street, which is now Cleveland Street. The family home was nine doors down from the Cleveland Street workhouse.

As a Parliamentary reporter during the summer of 1834, Dickens had a first-hand knowledge of the debates which produced the new Poor Law legislation of that year. Up to that time, the system of poor relief had been based on the Elizabethan Poor Relief Act of 1601. The system had been patchy and never generous but was essentially pragmatic and relatively benign, money being raised locally through the Poor Rate to provide food, fuel and clothing on the basis of need to people in their own homes. The Poor Law Amendment Act, brought in by Earl Grey's Whig government in August 1834, introduced a drastic change. The Act's key objectives were, firstly, to replace 'outdoor relief' given to people in their own homes with 'indoor relief', available only in the new workhouses where husbands, wives and children were separated, and secondly to ensure that the diet provided was calculated on a 'scientific' basis to be sufficient to maintain life, and nothing more.

The parish of St Paul's, Covent Garden was amalgamated with other parishes in the area to form the Strand group of parishes. The Cleveland Street workhouse, close to where Dickens had lived until 1831, became the central workhouse for this group, and the new law began to be applied there in June 1836, a few months before Dickens began the first instalment of Oliver Twist.

As the 1834 legislation aimed to deter all but the most desperate from claiming any relief, specific dietary tables were circulated to ensure that food relief provided was at the very minimum necessary level. By Mr Limbkin's reference to 'the dietary' in chapter two, Dickens clearly identifies this aspect of the New Poor Law as the focus of his attack.

While the official diet might perhaps be just sufficient to maintain life, some of the children did not even get that. Workhouse officials such as Mrs Mann, in charge of 'the house' for child paupers, 'appropriated the greater part of the weekly stipend to her own use, consigning the rising parochial generation to an even shorter allowance than was originally provided for them'. As a result, Oliver's friend Dick dies. Oliver's own survival might be seen as being due to his expulsion from the workhouse and being sent as an apprentice to the undertaker Sowerberry, where, according to Bumble himself, his consumption of broken meats gave him sufficient strength to punch Noah Claypole on the nose and escape to London.

The famous, or infamous, scene in chapter 2 in which Oliver 'asks for more' is often read and even played for laughs, as in the musical 'Oliver!'. This is easy to do as Dickens frequently adopts a comic-ironic style when approaching a subject he finds painful to address directly. We are tempted to laugh at Oliver's innocent daring and the horrified reaction of the Workhouse Master and the Beadle. Once again, however, the reality is that their reaction is absolutely serious. The authorities rightly see Oliver's timid request as a direct challenge to the whole spirit of the 1834 legislation:

> The master was a fat, healthy man, but he turned very pale. He gazed in stupified astonishment at the young rebel for some seconds, and then clung for support to the copper.

When Oliver repeats his request, he:

> ...aimed a blow at Oliver's hear with the ladle, pinioned him in his arms and shrieked aloud for the Beadle.

The Board is instantly informed of the incident:

> There was a general start. Horror was depicted on every countenance. 'For more?' said Mr Limbkins. 'Compose yourself, Bumble, and answer me distinctly. Do I understand that he asked for more, after he had eaten the supper allotted by the dietary?'

The Board orders Oliver's instant confinement, and the posting of a notice offering five pounds to anyone who will take Oliver off the hands of the parish. Until that happens, he is to be released only for the purpose of a daily public flogging before the boys. During prayers he is to be described as being, 'under the exclusive patronage of the powers of wickedness ... an article ... direct ... from the very Devil himself'.

In other words, Oliver is regarded as so inimical to the spirit of the new law that he must be instantly isolated and then expelled from the system. Dickens' tone is characteristic, an apparently light, exaggerated satire, but deriving a savage force from being far closer to the truth than the reader at first expects. Not for nothing did Dickens ask his illustrator, George Cruikshank, to have in the first number the illustration of the small hungry figure of Oliver making his devastating request.

Although the Cleveland Street establishment in London may in some sense have provided Dickens with a background for Oliver's harsh childhood experiences, he actually depicts Oliver travelling to London from a workhouse in some fairly distant town.

Oliver faces new and quite different perils on his arrival in the metropolis. We are now moving into another area of Dickens' concerns, and other considerations begin to apply. In the workhouse, Oliver had faced the physical danger of beating and starvation. In London, however, he faces the moral danger of sinking into the semi-criminal underworld.

We see a small beginning to the testing of Oliver's moral character as soon as he approaches London. When Oliver arrives in Barnet, near the end of his journey from Sowerberry's shop, he is met by the Artful Dodger who engages him in conversation and provides him with 'a long and hearty meal' of bread, ham and beer:

> 'Going to London?' said the strange boy when Oliver had concluded.
>
> 'Yes'.
>
> 'Got any lodgings?'
>
> 'No.'
>
> 'Money?'
>
> 'No.'
>
> The strange boy whistled and put his arms into his pockets as far as they would go.

At this point we simply see that, as far as Oliver was concerned:

> This unexpected offer of shelter was too tempting to be resisted.

The Dodger 'introduces' Oliver to Fagin, who soon sends him out on the pickpocketing expedition with the Dodger and Charlie Bates, in the course of which he is arrested.

Dickens often records features of the legal system which were on the point of disappearing, and the 'Hue and Cry' which followed Oliver and brought about his arrest is one of them. The duty on anyone witnessing a crime to join in the pursuit of the offender was created by the Statute of Westminster in 1285. It was formally abolished only in 1827, ten years before *Oliver Twist* was written, and probably continued as an informal practice for some time after that.

Oliver has already had a brief encounter with the legal process when he was to be bound apprentice to the coarse bullying Gamfield as a chimneysweep's 'climbing boy'. On that occasion the 'half blind, half childish' magistrate accidentally glimpsed Oliver's face and told the Beadle to stand aside while he heard Oliver's plea. He then refused to sanction his indentures. The law, albeit in an accidental, haphazard manner, had fulfilled its proper function.

The London magistrates' court in which Oliver finds himself after being arrested for stealing Mr Brownlow's handkerchief is a very different place. In his account of the proceedings Dickens, is directing his attack towards a real and very notorious magistrate, a Mr Laing, though that does not make it any less effective as part of Oliver's story. The court is a sinister pantomime run by a man who is essentially out of control. Oliver is never actually identified in court. When he faints and falls to the floor, no one dares move to assist him. No evidence is produced against him, he is not able to speak in his own defence and the alleged victim declines to prosecute. Oliver is nevertheless sentenced to three months hard labour. Only the arrival of the bookseller and his courageous determination to give his evidence saves the boy.

Interestingly, Oliver's case has a relatively fortunate outcome because of two things. The first is that the clerk of the court – usually a barrister who advises lay magistrates on the law – drops a heavy book on the floor at a crucial moment, ensuring that Mr Fang's more outrageous expressions are inaudible. The second is that the bookseller's strong sense of justice leads him to demand to give his evidence as a witness. It is possible to see the 'heavy book' as representing the actual learning of the law and the bookseller's courage to represent the public's idea of justice, these together being here only just sufficient to contain the presiding magistrate's one-man festival of judicial savagery.

Up to this point, there are no questions about Oliver's innocence, either in the workhouse or in the magistrates' court. So far, we have been concerned only with the iniquities of the systems in which little Oliver finds himself, first the system of poor relief and then that of summary jurisdiction. From now on, however, the question we are asked is somewhat different. The focus moves from exposing the faults in the system to examining Oliver's own moral resilience.

This development can perhaps best be seen in the context of Dickens' experience at the age of twelve, when his father John Dickens had been imprisoned for debt in the Marshalsea, the traumatic memory of which remained with Dickens for the rest of his life. Among his fellow employees in the blacking warehouse had been one Bob Fagin.

Forster in his biography records Dickens as saying:

> The blacking warehouse was the last house on the left-hand side of the way, at old Hungerford Stairs. It was a crazy, tumbledown old house, abutting of course on the river, and overrun with rats. Its wainscoted rooms, and its rotten floors and staircase, and the old grey rats swarming down in the cellars, and the sound of their squeaking and scuffling ... and the dirt and decay of the place, rise up visibly before me, as if I were there again. ... Two or three other boys were kept at similar duty downstairs on similar wages. One of them came up, in a ragged apron and a paper cap, on the first Monday morning, to show me the trick of using the string and tying the knot. His name was Bob Fagin; and I took the liberty of using his name, long afterwards, in Oliver Twist.

In beginning to write about Oliver, Dickens was not only aware of the New Poor Law legislation but also still painfully conscious of his own childhood experience. His time in Warren's blacking warehouse with Bob Fagin and Mealy Potatoes was twelve years in the past but remained with him sufficiently for Bumble to refer incidentally to a 'blackin' bottle'. In the crucial episode in chapter 18 where the Dodger invites Oliver to commit himself to Fagin's gang, Oliver is actually blacking Dodger's shoes.

Why did Dickens choose to apply the name of his young fellow-worker Bob Fagin to Fagin the essentially heartless and manipulative character presiding over the 'family' of young pickpockets near Field Lane, Saffron Hill? Bob Fagin, Mealy Potatoes and the others were not criminals. They were simply boys working for a living. Bob was friendly and protective towards young Charles, as Dickens relates. On one occasion when he felt unwell at work:

> I got better, and quite easy towards evening, but Bob (who was much bigger and older than I) did not like the idea of my going home alone, and took me under his protection.

Dickens nevertheless senses that there is some kind of loss or even danger in associating with these young men. The friendship Bob offered was probably genuine, but it deeply compromised him. As Dickens puts it in the 'fragment' of autobiography referred to earlier:

> No words can express the secret agony of my soul as I sunk into this companionship ... and felt my early hopes of growing up to be a learned and distinguished man crushed in my breast.

The danger Oliver himself risks from Fagin is of course far worse than the loss of a career as a learned man. Perhaps the financial insecurity of Dickens' own childhood led him to introduce Bob Fagin's name into Oliver's story because he saw the social position of Bob and of Mealy Potatoes as a precarious one – one in which the barrier between an honest life and criminality might be too thin and the pressures of physical need and questionable company too great to resist.

In October 1835, when Dickens was preparing the last of his Sketches by visiting Newgate Prison, he was struck by the 'villainous' appearance of a group of young boys:

> Villainous faces without any innocent or decent feeling, destined for the hulks or the gallows.

The locality through which Oliver passes as the Dodger takes him to Fagin's house is certainly the kind of place in which those very 'villainous' young boys Dickens saw in Newgate might have spent their formative years:

> A dirtier or more wretched place he had never seen. The street was very narrow and muddy, and the air was impregnated with filthy odours. There was a good many small shops; but their only stock in trade appeared to be heaps of children, who, even at that time of night, were crawling in and out at the doors, or screaming inside. ...Covered ways and yards ... disclosed little knots of houses where drunken men and women were positively wallowing in filth; and from several doorways great ill-looking fellows were cautiously emerging, bound, to all appearance, on no very well-disposed or harmless errands.

In his preface to the later edition of 1841 Dickens responds to public criticism that it was morally wrong to write about characters 'chosen from the most criminal and degraded of London's population'. He writes in response:

> I confess I have yet to learn that a lesson of the purest good cannot be drawn from the vilest evil.... I saw no reason when I wrote this book why the very dregs of life, so long as their speech did not offend the ear, should not serve the purpose of a moral, at least as well as its froth and cream. Nor did I doubt that there lay festering in St Giles as good materials towards the truth as any flaunting in St James's.

> In this spirit, when I wished to show in little Oliver the principle of Good surviving through every adverse circumstance and triumphing at last, and when I considered among what companions I should try him best, having regard to that kind of men into whose hands he would most naturally fall, I bethought myself of those who figure in these volumes. ...

> I have read of thieves by scores – seductive fellows (amiable for the most part), faultless in dress, plump in pocket, choice in horseflesh, bold in bearing, fortunate in gallantry, great at a song, a bottle, a pack

of cards or dice-box, and fit companions for the bravest. But I had never met (except in Hogarth), with the miserable reality. It appeared to me that to draw a knot of such associates in crime as really do exist; to paint them in all the deformity, in all their wretchedness, in all the squalid poverty of their lives; to show them as they really are, for ever skulking through the dirtiest paths of life, with the great, black, ghastly gallows closing up the prospect, turn them where they may; it appeared to me that to do this would be to attempt something which was greatly needed and which would be a service to society.

Unexpectedly, this passage leaves us with a question. What actually is the 'lesson of the purest good' that can be drawn from these scenes? It is perhaps less generous than we might think. It is not in fact about the redemption of the fallen. It is about whether an originally 'good' person such as Oliver, when placed in a bad environment, falls into crime or does not fall, despite temptations and pressures to do so. It perhaps parallels Dickens' own foreboding as to what an association with Bob Fagin might lead him to.

In his 1841 preface, Dickens declares that his book has two objects. The first is to dispel the illusion created by highwayman characters in literature, such as Macheath in the *Beggar's Opera*, that the criminal life can be the subject of romantic admiration, and to show instead that the criminal life is in reality always a wretched one, 'with the great, black, ghastly gallows closing up every prospect'. The second is to argue that someone of a truly moral character such as Oliver can and, it is to be hoped, *will* resist the attraction of the criminal life so that 'the principle of Good' could be seen to triumph at last.

The implication of this approach, however, is that a person by nature either is a criminal or is not. There are people of genuinely good moral character and there are others, such as the young boys 'destined for the gallows' that Dickens saw during his visit to Newgate in 1835. Of the 'good' people, some may fall and some may not, but only those of a good moral character can possibly survive the test of a criminal environment – others cannot, and all who do fall are destined for the gallows like the Newgate boys. If this were strictly true, of course, it would make forgiveness and schemes of reformation pointless.

Mr Brownlow's sending Oliver to return some books and come back with the money in chapter 14 becomes the experiment to test this theory. The resilience of Oliver's innocence has come to be examined. The chapter ends with Brownlow and Grimwig, with their two different opinions of Oliver's honesty, waiting with the watch on the table between them. Here Brownlow, apparently the more benign of the two judgelike figures waiting at the table for Oliver to return from the bookseller, is not actually merciful. He is merely optimistic that Oliver, morally innocent from the first, will be able to remain so, in which case there would be no need for mercy. His optimism is based simply on a memory of Oliver's mother and Oliver's reaction to her portrait.

Dickens might have seen his own position, if he had really become part of 'that companionship' of the warehouse boys, in the same way Mr Brownlow sees Oliver's: he, unlike his companions, had the capacity to remain good, but if he did not there would be no mercy or opportunity of redemption for him.

Of course, the preface of 1841 was written as part of a public argument rather than part of the creative process, and in any case it is not unusual to find Dickens holding two viewpoints at virtually the same time, a little like the entangled cubit of quantum physics. If, however, Dickens' original aim for the 'little knot of associates' was indeed 'to paint them in all their deformity ... in all their wretchedness ... forever skulking through the dirtiest paths of life, with the great gallows closing up the prospect,' this aim is only partly accomplished.

It is certainly true that all the characters live with the constant threat of imprisonment:

'Never mind where I come from young 'un. You'll find your way there soon enough, I'll bet a crown!'

says Tom Chitling to Oliver in chapter 18. The other boys laugh at this sally, but Fagin's manipulative power introduces darker notes, and the shadow of the gallows does indeed loom over them.

The strictly judgemental approach implied by Brownlow and Grimwig undergoes a considerable change as the characters come to life. The simplistic view gives way to a more complex picture. The same questions remain, but the answers are made more difficult by the vivid reality of the characters involved, whose fate in some cases becomes almost as important as Oliver's own. As the characters speak and interact, we are drawn into the drama of their lives in all aspects, comic and tragic, and led to a more comprehensive consideration of the moral and practical questions relating to criminality in London and the ability of the law to deal with it.

The Dodger is certainly the most memorable of these characters. On his first meeting with Oliver in Barnet we are reminded, when he puts his arms into his pockets 'as far as they would go', that he is wearing a coat that is far too big for him. Although he is only a boy, as Dickens had earlier described:

> He ... had about him all the airs and manners of a man. ... He had turned the cuffs back, halfway up his arm, to get his hands out of his sleeves: apparently with the ultimate view of thrusting them into the pockets of his corduroy trousers, for there he kept them. He was, altogether, as roistering and swaggering a young gentleman as ever stood four feet six, or something less, in his bluchers.

In the Dodger, in fact, we seem to have a juvenile prototype of the very kind of adult character – the dashing highwayman figure – that Dickens, in his later preface, declared that it was wrong to portray. As his character develops, he becomes undeniably attractive and brings into question the simplistic views Dickens professes in the 1841 preface.

It is by the Dodger that Oliver is 'introduced' to Fagin. Bestowing Bob Fagin's name on the leader and governor of the school for young criminals suggests the same ambiguous relationship that caused such anxiety to the young Dickens in Warren's warehouse. Fagin's sausages are better and tastier fare than the workhouse gruel but accepting them can lead to a fall in moral status even more damaging than workhouse hunger.

The 'knot of associates' into whose hands Oliver falls is seen as comparable to the 'companionship' into which Dickens himself had 'sunk' during his warehouse period. The warehouse companionship does not appear to have been an unkindly one, but Dickens speaks of it as causing him agony, seeming as it does to mark an irrecoverable lowering of status and an end to his ambition, almost in the same way that Fagin's house, though providing food and companionship, could lead to irredeemable criminality.

While Dickens sees Fagin's house as somehow comparable to his warehouse experience, his creative power and moral sensibility are unable to leave things there.

The first 'Fagin's kitchen' scene, before Oliver goes to Mr Fang's court and falls into Mr Brownlow's hands, is quite light-hearted on the surface. The 'little knot of associates' even at this point begins to untie itself as the individuals take on a life of their own. Oliver's innocence simply amuses the other boys and his introduction into the practice of thieving is a cheerful game. Despite Oliver's arrest, Nancy can raise a laugh when, in straw bonnet and white apron, carrying a house key and covered basket, she spontaneously acts the part of Oliver's anxious sister before going to the police office to find out his fate, so that even Sikes is moved, in his own way, to admiration:

> 'She's an honour to her sex,' said Mr Sikes, filling his glass and striking the table with his enormous fist. 'Here's her health, and wishing they was all like her!'

The sadness is nevertheless undeniable. When Nancy and Sikes recapture Oliver on his way back from the bookseller's, their journey over Smithfield and past Newgate Gaol is a gloomy one. Sikes recalls a night spent there when the noises of the Fair outside made the jail so silent that he wanted to beat his brains out against the iron plates of the door, and he dismisses the 'young chaps' now inside as being 'as good as dead'.

The scene in chapter 18 when Oliver is blacking the Dodger's boots is quite different, even poignant. Part of Fagin's plan to induce Oliver to commit himself to join the criminal way of life has been to keep him in isolation for many days, hoping that the experience of loneliness will lead him to welcome any company. On Oliver's release, he is asked in a companionable way to clean Dodger's boots, while the Dodger and Charley Bates continue to explain in amicable tones the advantages of their way of life. For the first time, Oliver engages the Dodger in conversation on almost equal terms:

> 'Go!' exclaimed the Dodger. 'Why, where's your spirit? Don't you take any pride in yourself? Would you go and be dependent on your friends?' ...
>
> 'You can leave your friends, though,' said Oliver, with a half-smile; 'and let them be punished for what you did'.

Oliver is of course recalling the pickpocketing incident which had led to his arrest.

The episode is a clear link to young Charles' blacking warehouse experience. To Dickens, it would seem that at this point Charley Bates and the Dodger are essentially the same kind of human beings as the real Bob Fagin and Mealy Potatoes. The scene itself conveys the same impression of ordinary humanity not entirely dispelled by the entrance of the manipulative Fagin praising the Dodger for teaching Oliver 'the catechism of his trade'.

We see Nancy's emotional nature and moral strength even more clearly in chapter 20 when she is sent to take Oliver to Bill Sikes' house. There, we see the wretchedness of her situation and her moral strength:

> 'Hush!' said the girl, stooping over him, and pointing to the door as she looked cautiously round. 'You can't help yourself. I have tried hard for you, but all to no purpose. You are hedged round and round'. ...
>
> 'I have saved you from being ill-used once, and will again, and I do now,' continued the girl aloud ... I have promised for your being quiet and silent; if you are not, you will only do harm to yourself and me too, and perhaps my death. See here! I have borne all this for you already, as true as God sees me show it.'

This could unravel into mere melodrama, but it doesn't. The picture that has been built up of Nancy as a real woman is too credible.

The Dodger himself has no misgivings about thieving as a way of life but in his own way he lives up to the romantic-heroic role exemplified by the eighteenth-century highwayman. He is never mean or unkind, is skilled and daring in his 'profession' and he leaves us on a high point, his memorable tour de force of self-justification and cultural table-turning – again wearing the coat too big for him – before the Magistrates' Court. Here the 'playfully ironical' style of discourse the Dodger used when he first met Oliver in chapter 8 is extended to an almost heroic scale. As a sustained piece of bravura it is worth quoting at length:

> It was indeed Mr Dawkins, who, shuffling into the office with his big coat sleeves tucked up as usual, his left hand in his pocket, and his hat in his right hand preceded the jailer, with a rolling gait altogether indescribable, and, being placed in the dock, requested in an audible voice to know what he was placed in that 'ere disgraceful sitivation for.
>
> 'Hold your tongue, will you?' rejoined the jailer.
>
> 'I'm an Englishman, ain't I?' rejoined the Dodger. 'Where are my priwileges?'
>
> 'You'l get your privileges soon enough,' retorted the jailer, 'and pepper with 'em.'

> 'We'll see wot the Secretary of State for the Home Affairs has got to say to the beaks, if I don't,' replied Mr Dawkins. 'Now then! Wot is this here business? I shall thank the madg'strates to dispose of this here little affair, and not to keep me while they read the paper, for I've got an appointment with a genelman in the City, and as I'm a man of my word and very punctual in business matters, he'll go away if I ain't there to my time, and then pr'aps there won't be an action for damages against them as kep me away. Oh no, certainly not!'

The Dodger asks the jailer the names of the magistrates, to much laughter round the court. When he is eventually found guilty of stealing a silver snuff box, he is asked if he has anything to say:

> 'No,' replied the Dodger, 'not here, for this ain't the shop for justice; besides which my attorney is breakfasting this morning with the Wice President of the House of Commons; but I shall have something to say elsewhere, and so will he, and so will a wery numerous and 'spectable circle of acquaintance, as'll make them beaks wish they'd never been born, or that they'd got their footmen to hand 'em up to their own hatpegs, 'afore they let 'em come out this morning to try it on upon me. I'll ...'
>
> 'There! He's fully committed!' interposed the clerk. 'Take him away.'
>
> 'Come on,' said the jailer.
>
> 'Oh ah! I'll come on,' replied the Dodger, brushing his hat with the palm of his hand. 'Ah! (to the Bench) it's no use your looking frightened; I won't show you no mercy, not a ha'porth of it. You'll pay for this, my fine fellers. I wouldn't be you for something! I wouldn't go free now, if you was to fall down on your knees and ask me. Here, carry me off to prison! Take me away!'

The Dodger has certainly committed crimes, but the argument he has used to persuade Oliver to join Fagin's gang in chapter 18 is probably his own genuine view:

'If you don't take pocket-handkechers and watches,' said the Dodger ... 'some other cove will; so that the coves that lose 'em will be all the worse ... and nobody half a ha'po'rth the better, except the chaps wot gets them – and you've as good a right to them as they have.'

The Dodger does not seek to do harm to anyone. He simply plays the cards life has dealt him with daring and skill, and his wit and courage give him a stature that his criminal surroundings cannot destroy.

Of the others in the 'little knot of associates', Charlie Bates is just a boy with a keen sense of the ludicrous. He will see the comic implications of almost anything. There is no feeling of cruelty in his reactions, simply a genuine enjoyment of the ironies of the situation. We finally see more of his nature in the scene in the Jacob's Island house: it is he who turns on the murderer Sikes and yells to the crowd to break down the door. The gullible Tom Chitling is almost too simple to be a criminal, regularly losing at cards to the more astute Dodger or 'Flash' Toby Crackit. Crackit himself is a serious thief but actually seems more interested in 'gentlemanly' manner and dress than in the proceeds of crime. After playing a boring game of cards with Chitling in chapter 39, Crackit exclaims:

'Damme, I'm as flat as a juryman; and I should have gone to sleep, as fast as Newgate, if I hadn't had the good nature to amuse this young-ster. Horrid dull, I'm blessed if I ain't!'

With these and other exclamations of the same kind, Mr Toby Crackit swept up his winnings, and crammed them nto his waistcoat pocket with a haughty air, as though such small pieces of silver were wholly beneath the consideration of a man of his figure; this done, he swag-gered out of the room with so much elegance and gentility, that Mr Chitling, bestowing numerous admiring glances on his legs and boots till they were out of sight, assured the company that he considered his acquaintance cheap at fifteen sixpenses an interview, and that he didn't value his losses the snap of his little finger.

It is Toby Crackit who, when Sikes threatened Oliver with a pistol during the robbery in chapter 22, dispels the crisis by knocking the pistol from Sikes' hand, saying he would give the boy a crack on the head if necessary.

These five, including Nancy, have long been engaged in criminal enterprises in various ways. What we now know of their characters and what their life-chances have been would make it impossible for us to dismiss them to retribution and punishment without considering a more merciful sentence and the possibility of reformation.

Dickens' portrayal of these people has taken us from the innocent-or-guilty analysis of Brownlow and Grimwig, where a legal decision would depend simply on whether someone was or was not entirely innocent, to a point where the legal system has the more difficult task of considering a range of measures to achieve the most humane and positive result in individual cases.

In framing the New Poor Law, the Benthamite approach had been to achieve the greatest 'amount' of good for the greatest number of people by looking at the consequences of certain legislative measures. The long-term consequences of a measure are the only determinant, and the humane sensibility which might govern our reaction to the particular case in front of us is disregarded. In passing the New Poor Law Bill, Parliament would appear to have been led to the conclusion that a greater number of people in society as a whole would be made happier if dependency was discouraged by confining the relatively much smaller number of the poor in workhouses on a minimum diet.

In the criminal law, such an approach would again favour the simple analysis, this time concerned not with the deserving or undeserving status of the poor but with the guilt or innocence of the accused. Social pressures and other mitigating factors would be given little or no consideration and severe sentences would be handed down to confine and deter socially undesirable individuals. Just as Dickens' sympathetic, generous instincts lead him to defy the logic of the consequentialists and expose the basic inhumanity of the treatment of Oliver and thousands of others in the workhouse, so here his portrayal of Nancy, the Dodger, Chitling and Crackit virtually demands that we look at their individual cases. We should regard them as living – two of them portrayed as intensely living – human beings and react and judge accordingly.

By the time that Oliver, after the robbery at Chertsey, finds himself seeking shelter in Mrs Maylie's house, we find that Oliver is judged in a way which has moved on considerably from that of Mr Brownlow and Mr Grimwig.

At first of course, Mrs Maylie, Dr Losberne and Rose Maylie herself don't know what to make of the boy which Mr Giles and Brittles claim to have captured. When in chapter 30 they view the boy as he 'stirred and smiled in his sleep' Mrs Maylie and Rose doubt that such a child, even if he had been involved, could ever have been the 'voluntary associate' of the robbers, but Dr Losberne points out that his innocent appearance does not guarantee he had not been fully involved in the crime. Rose then introduces a new approach:

> 'But even if he has been wicked,' pursued Rose, 'think how young he is; think that he may never have known a mother's love, or the comfort of a home; that ill-usage or the want of bread, may have driven him to herd with men who have forced him to guilt. Aunt, dear aunt, for mercy's sake, think of this, before you let them drag this sick child to a prison, which in any case must be the grave of all his chances of amendment'.

Rose, who takes the critical step away from Mr Brownlow's nominally fair but nevertheless judgemental approach with the words 'But even if he has been wicked...' is almost certainly modelled on Mary Hogarth, Dickens' young sister-in-law, who died suddenly at the age of seventeen and for whose tombstone he composed the words 'Young, beautiful and good, God in His mercy numbered her with his angels at the early age of seventeen'. Dickens felt her loss profoundly, idealising her memory, and in his eyes it is for someone of this unusual goodness to take this step.

Mrs Maylie replies:

> '...my days are drawing to a close; and may mercy be shown to me as I show it to others! What can I do to save him, sir?'

Once Mrs Maylie, who has actually suffered the robbery, has made her decision, Losberne briskly goes about implementing it, pressing Giles and Brittles into a state of confusion so that their stories are unconvincing when told to the constable. With the arrival in chapter 31 of the Bow Street Runners, sent for by Giles after the original alarm, things become more difficult.

Once again Dickens is recording a feature of the legal system which was on the point of disappearing. The Bow Street Runners, established by the magistrate and author Henry Fielding in 1748 and based at his house in Bow Street, were the precursors of the police force. Dickens describes their working methods in a slightly humorous tone but they are basically competent. When they hear a 'boy' mentioned, they want to know about him -'He didn't drop out of the clouds, did he, master?' They then proceed methodically: 'We had better inspect the premises first, and examine the servants arterwards,' and correctly conclude that the servants were not involved, that it was done by London criminals and that they had a boy with them.

Rose Maylie and Dr Losberne have to work hard to protect Oliver. Losberne browbeats and frightens Giles, who then is unable say that he identifies Oliver as the boy he encountered during the robbery, and in the end the case against Oliver is fatally weakened when the Doctor produces the other pistol of the pair used by Giles and shows that it is loaded only with gunpowder and a paper ball. Losberne had actually removed the lead ball, interfering with key evidence. He has taken what could be described as a humane risk, or an act of faith in Oliver while not necessarily believing him to be technically innocent – or as Rose Maylie had put it, 'even if he has been wicked'.

Of the 'knot of associates', three remain: Fagin, Sikes and the late-recruited Claypole. The law, which, as Losberne saw, would have been too clumsy to deal justly with Oliver, is able to deal with the first two of these, and in fact needs only to deal with one.

Fagin has little to redeem him. He is not as violent as Sikes but he does not need to be. He succeeds by manipulating others, as he announces to the landlord in melodramatic style at the glee concert in the Three Cripples after going there to inform Monks about the loss of Oliver:

> 'I say,' said the other, looking over the rails, and speaking in a hoarse whisper; 'what a time this would be for a sell! I've got Phil Barker here: so drunk, that a boy might take him.'
>
> 'Aha! But it's not Phil Barker's time.' said the Jew, looking up. 'Phil has something more to do, before we can afford to part with him; so go back to the company, my dear, and tell them to lead merry lives – while they last. Ha! ha! ha!'

There is something about his anxiousness over Oliver's loss, however, which may be more than just the need to prevent him 'peaching' against the gang, or his future value as an innocent-looking young thief. When he hears of his loss:

> The Jew stopped to hear no more; but uttering a loud yell and twining his hands in his hair, rushed from the room, and from the house.

It may be that Oliver represents a lost innocence for which Fagin has some deep longing. In his condemned cell, Fagin has a confused notion that Oliver can somehow save him:

> 'Say I've gone to sleep – they'll believe you. You can get me out, if you take me so'.

One almost feels that the intractably violent Sikes has the flames of Hell licking at his feet. 'Burn my body!' is his fairly frequent oath, as in chapter 22 when Oliver is unwilling to drink spirits before the robbery, and in chapter 39 when Nancy doses him with laudanum in order to visit

Rose by London Bridge. When Fagin puts his hand on his shoulder in chapter 44, Sikes declares it 'reminds' him of being nabbed by the devil. 'Hell's fire!' is Sikes' oath when he learns from Claypole in chapter 47 that Nancy had gone to meet Rose, and he becomes strangely involved in helping in a fire during his country wanderings after Nancy's murder:

> ...in every part of that great fire was he; but he bore a charmed life, and had neither scratch not bruise, not weariness nor thought, till morning dawned again.

Sikes eludes justice in the sense that he dies by accidentally hanging himself when trying to escape after being taken into custody at the Jacob's Island house.

The novel ends with a piece of what can be seen as 'home-made' justice. Following his investigations into Monks' life and background and Oliver's parentage, Brownlow has two strong men 'invite' Monks to his house. He then, in what is to become the familiar Dickens manner, keeps the legal system at arm's length while using its power to frighten Monks into giving information and confessing to his schemes against Oliver.

Brownlow is fortunate that Monks does not know about Nancy's death, as what Monks most fears are the disclosures that she would have made. When the information is assembled, Monks is required to sign a 'statement of truth' – a somewhat rambling story which is then produced at the denouement scene in chapter 51. Here, in the main hotel in Oliver's 'home town', Oliver's inheritance is restored to him and he finds that Rose is his sister. To complete the tale, the two Bumbles are produced and discredited as part of the general revelation, Mr Bumble famously announcing that if the law thinks his wife acts under his direction, 'the law is an ass'.

3.
NICHOLAS NICKLEBY

Squeers and the Power of the Law

1836 was probably the busiest year of Dickens' life. His 'day job' was still working as a Parliamentary reporter for the Morning Chronicle, but the success of the Sketches by Boz published that February had made him something of a literary celebrity.

The success of *Pickwick* following that of the *Sketches* meant that Dickens felt able to resign from the Morning Chronicle in early November 1836, and at the end of that month he accepted a proposal from Richard Bentley to edit a new magazine, *Bentley's Miscellany*, to which he would also contribute a monthly article of sixteen pages. He also undertook to write two three-volume novels for Bentley, one of which was tentatively named 'Gabriel Vardon, Locksmith of London'.

In the autumn of 1837 Dickens completed *Pickwick* and Chapman and Hall held a celebratory dinner for him that November. Despite this early success Dickens, now the sole earner in his new family, was keen to secure any chance of income – at least for the immediate future. Although he was still working on his monthly numbers of *Oliver Twist* for *Bentley's Miscellany* – he had reached chapters 18-19 featuring Fagin, Sikes and Nancy – Dickens accepted a proposal from Chapman and Hall to write for them another work, 'of the same extent and contents in point of quantity' as *Pickwick*, to be published by them in monthly numbers from March 1838.

The book his publishers had in mind was another humorous narrative in the *Pickwick* style. Dickens, though, was still concerned with the more serious theme that had emerged in *Oliver Twist*, the abuse of children. Stories were circulating about the conditions which children endured in various cheap Yorkshire schools, for which grandiloquent advertisements regularly appeared in newspapers. In October 1823, some fifteen years earlier, two civil law cases – *Jones v Shaw* and *Ockerby v Shaw* – had been brought against William Shaw, proprietor of Bowes Academy, after several boys at his school had gone blind.

The cases were heard before Mr Justice Park in the Court of Common Pleas at the Guildhall, London. The jury found against Shaw and awarded damages of £300 – a considerable sum – in each case, but the two cases, though widely reported in The Times and other papers, had had little effect. Shaw's school continued to operate, as did other similar Yorkshire schools, serving only to confirm Dickens' lack of faith in the law as an effectual remedy.

Nicholas Nickleby is probably the Dickens novel that most justifies Orwell's criticism that the only solution Dickens can propose for the injustices of our society is the chance kindness of individual people. In this novel the law is either threatening, ineffective or open to abuse and no other structural solutions emerge. What nevertheless remains undeniable is the power of the fiction itself to bring about a change in public feeling so great that it can lead to legislative action.

Dickens' first impulse in legal matters, in fiction as in real life, was to use the most direct approach possible. His fictional Pickwick, on receiving the writ in *Bardell v Pickwick*, visits the office of opposing solicitors Dodson and Fogg almost immediately. Mr Browning in *Oliver Twist*, hearing of Oliver's arrest, goes directly to Mr Fang's appalling court, politely offering his card to that intractable magistrate. Dickens' real-life reaction to the Shaw case was to investigate the matter in person. He obtained a letter of introduction to a solicitor in the neighbourhood,

Richard Barnes, and in January 1838 travelled up to Yorkshire with his illustrator, Hablot Browne, to obtain local material.

They did not stay long. Dickens in his diary recorded simply, 'Met Shaw'. In the local churchyard, he found the gravestone of a nineteen-year-old pupil from Bowes Academy who had died at the school. Dickens later said that this had given him the idea for the character of Smike, and it is Smike who continues to figure in the book long after Dotheboys Hall and Yorkshire have been left behind.

Dickens' directness of approach seemed to demand some kind of physical confrontation, followed by real-world public exposure. The aim of and impetus for *Nicholas Nickleby* was certainly the exposure of conditions in the Yorkshire schools, and to do this he created Nicholas – good-hearted and impetuous, with a gentlemanly background, strong moral feelings and no money – all the characteristics required to lead him to accept employment at Dotheboys Hall and confront Squeers.

Nicholas' uncle Ralph, the other powerful figure in the novel, had long had dealings with Squeers. In contrast to Nicholas' mild and unambitious father, Ralph Nickleby had no scruples about making money and, although thought of as 'a sort of lawyer', he certainly lends money at high interest. An indication of his other business activities is the magnificent account of the Public Meeting for the petitioning of Parliament in favour of the United Metropolitan Improved Hot Muffin and Crumpet, etc Company[1] described in chapter 2, which has little to do with the story.

On his brother's death, Ralph does the bare minimum for his sister-in-law and her two children, introducing Nicholas as a likely assistant to Squeers and apprenticing his sister Kate to a London milliner.

Nicholas' point of departure for Yorkshire is the Saracen's Head, Snow Hill, the coaching inn from which travellers to the north-east would depart. Significantly for Dickens, it lies between Smithfield Market and the Old Bailey, very close to Newgate Prison. Dickens describes its location:

...there, at the very core of London, in the heart of its business and animation, in the midst of a whirl of noise and motion, stemming the giant currents of life that flow ceaselessly on from different quarters, and meet beneath its walls, stands Newgate; and in that crowded street on which it frowns so darkly – within a few feet of its tottering houses – upon the very spot where vendors of soup and fish and damaged fruit are now plying their trades – scores of human beings ... four, six or eight strong men at a time, have been hurried violently and swiftly from the world, when the scene has been rendered frightful with the excess of human life; and when curious eyes have glared from casement and housetop, and wall, and pillar and when, in the mass of white and upturned faces, the dying wretch, in all his comprehensive look of agony, has met not one, not one, that bore the impress of pity or compassion.

Near to the jail, and by consequence near to Smithfield also ... is the coach-yard of the Saracen's Head Inn, its portal guarded by two Saracens' heads and shoulders ... there they are, frowning upon from each side of the gateway, and the inn itself, garnished with another Saracen's Head, frowns upon you from the top of the yard ... .

The baleful atmosphere of Newgate and the suffering and injustice contained within its walls extends to the Inn itself and casts its shadow over Nicholas at his starting out and the coach journey with Squeers and the new boys to Greta Bridge in Yorkshire, narrated with all its mishaps and stories, reflects the one Dickens himself travelled with his illustrator Hablot Browne at the end of January 1838, as does the description of Dotheboys Hall, with its bleak surrounding landscape and abused occupants.

The confrontation with Squeers comes within a couple of weeks. Mrs Squeers instantly dislikes Nicholas, and his evident sympathy for Smike leads that resentful lady to abuse and torment the boy with even greater severity than usual until Smike finally runs away during the night. The next day he is pursued, caught by Mrs Squeers and brought back, bound and in disgrace. Squeers himself now prepares to give

Smike a sensational beating, partly to make his fate an example to his wretched fellow pupils and partly to indulge his lust for revenge on the helpless boy:

> Squeers caught the boy firmly in his grip; one desperate cut had fallen on his body – he was wincing from the lash and uttering a scream of pain ...

Nicholas' way of preventing this abuse was by direct confrontation:

> – it was raised again and was about to fall when Nicholas Nickleby suddenly starting up, cried 'Stop!' in a voice that made the rafters ring.

The intensely emotional scene allows full scope for Dickens' inclination to melodrama. The enraged Squeers falls into the trap of attacking Nicholas physically:

> Squeers, in a violent outbreak of wrath ... struck a blow across his face with his instrument of torture, which raised up a bar of livid flesh as it was inflicted.

This of course allows Nicholas, acting in self-defence, to wrest the cane from Squeers' hand and beat him 'till he roared for mercy', indicating that he would not continue his attack on Nicholas. Early on the road back to London Nicholas meets the stalwart John Browdie, the fiancé of Fanny Squeers' friend Tilda, whom Nicholas had unwittingly offended at the tea party to which Fanny, temporarily enamoured of Nicholas, had invited him to meet her friend. Browdie, the embodiment of physical strength and good humour, is highly gratified to hear that Nicholas has "Beatten the schoolmaesther," and lends him money.

As Nicholas begins his journey to London, Greta Bridge and Dotheboys Hall fade into the background. Nicholas's magnificent defiance of Squeers seems in retrospect to have achieved little apart from the eventual escape of Smike. The 'school' continues in its routine barbarism, as did Shaw's real establishment despite the court cases brought against it. The reason it could continue becomes clear on Nicholas' first view of his pupils:

> But the pupils – the young noblemen! .... Pale and haggard faces, lank and bony figures, children with the countenances of old men, deformities with irons upon their limbs, boys of stunted growth, and others whose long legs would hardly bear their stooping bodies, all crowded on the view together; there were the bleared eye, the hare-lip, the crooked foot, and every ugliness of distortion thast told of unnatural aversion conceived by parents for their offspring, or of young lives which, from earliest dawn of infancy, had been one of horrible endurance of cruelty and neglect.

The pupils were simply unwanted children. Where there is a need, there is a commercial opportunity and a service to meet that need, in the form of the 'schools' remote from the capital, was not something which the legal system is able to regulate effectively. Nicholas' momentous defiance of Squeers bears practical fruit only in his subsequent nurture of and companionship with Smike. The only genuine remedy for the Dotheboys Hall scandal, it is implied, would be to provide the similar loving care of a parent or friend for each individual child, and in the book there is no foreseeable way of achieving that.

Even the rescue of Smike himself is not secure. In London, Nicholas and Smike make their way to the apartment of Ralph's clerk, Newman Noggs, and we are entertained by the humorous interludes with the Kenwigses and the Mantalinis. Fanny Squeers' letter to Ralph Nickleby, however, in which she complains that Nicholas attacked her father so violently that the schoolroom forms were 'steepled in his Goar', though hilarious in itself, reminds us that the Squeers are still active and malign. Although Fanny asks Ralph to 'let the thief and assassin go' – presumably because Squeers does not want to feature in another court case – this theme is not yet worked out.

Ralph, deeply frustrated and resentful of Nicholas' accusation that he has exposed Kate to the designs of Sir Mulberry Hawk, uses Fanny's letter to attempt – unsuccessfully – to discredit Nicholas in the eyes of his mother. Nicholas refuses to return Smike to Squeers and Ralph, to avenge himself on Nicholas, begins to encourage Squeers in his pursuit of his lost pupil-of-all-work.

With the first dramatic confrontations over, the novel broadens into a depiction of diverse scenes of English life, Kate's subsequent employment with the ludicrous Mrs Wititterly and Nicholas' unpromising journey with Smike to Portsmouth. His encounter with Vincent Crummles'stroupe of actors introduces an interlude of cheerfulness and actual success for Nicholas as an actor and dramatic author. It also contains its own parody on the theme of conflict resolution. One of the actors, Mr Lenville, feels that Nicholas's success is putting him in the shade and sends him by his second an elaborate challenge, not to a duel, but to have his nose pulled in the presence of the company. Nicholas's response is direct, in the Dickens manner – to meet him as appointed and, as he approached, to do the nose-pulling, knock him down.

The theme of duelling as a mode of settling disputes assumes a more serious and violent form when Nicholas feels compelled to take steps to challenge Sir Mulberry Hawk after hearing him make dishonourable reference to his sister. The baronet refuses to give his name and attempts to drive off in a cabriolet, applying his whip furiously to Nicholas. The cabriolet crashes and Sir Mulberry is seriously injured. Nicholas arranges for his mother and Kate to leave Ralph Nickleby's 'protection' and go back to Miss La Creevy's rooms.

Nicholas' fortunes improve when he meets Charles Cheeryble. While Dickens always insisted that certain Manchester merchants of exactly this generous disposition really existed, the Cheeryble brothers are examples of the rich, benevolent old men who, as Orwell argues, allow Dickens to resolve problems without disturbing the existing social order. They certainly do this as far as Nicholas is concerned.

Smike, however, is not so fortunate. In Chapter 38 when Smike is returning to Bow in the dusk after escorting Miss La Creevy home to her lodgings in the Strand, he is by chance seen by Squeers and his son and recaptured. Significantly, the incident is preceded by a glimpse of Newgate:

> At the foot of Ludgate Hill, he turned off a little out of the road to satisfy his curiosity by having a look at Newgate. After staring up at its sombre walls from the opposite side of the way with great care and dread for some minutes, he turned back again into the old track, and walked briskly through the City; stopping now and then to gaze in the window of some particularly attractive shop, then running on for a little way, then stopping again, and so on, as any other country lad might do.

The clocks strike three-quarters past eight and Smike hurries on, but then:

> ... felt himself violently brought to, with a jerk so sudden that he was obliged to cling to a lamp-post to save himself from falling. At the same moment a small boy clung tight round his leg, and a shrill cry of, 'Here he is, father – Hooray!' vibrated in his ears.

It is as if the grisly spirit of the law had somehow been awakened by Smike's brief visit to the precincts of the prison and had fallen upon him in the form of Master Wackford Squeers.

We get a similarly gloomy glimpse of Newgate in *Oliver Twist* when Sikes and Nancy are taking the recaptured Oliver back to Fagin in chapter 16. Smike is recaptured, just as Oliver had been. After he is seized by zealous young Wackford, Squeers himself, 'in a sort of rapturous trance' brushes aside the enquiries of a passing labourer by saying that Smike had 'joined in bloodthirsty attacks' and bundles the boy into a coach where he subjects him to a savage beating.

The Old Bailey theme is reiterated when Squeers accuses Smike of stealing the clothes he ran away in:

> Do you know I could hang you up outside of the Old Bailey, for making away with those articles of property?" said Squeers. "Do you know it's a hanging matter – and I ain't quite certain whether it ain't an anatomy

> one besides – to walk off with up'ards of the valley of five pounds from a dwelling house?

The 'anatomy' reference is to the practice of stealing or otherwise obtaining the bodies of executed criminals – the part-time occupation of Jerry Cruncher, the 'honest tradesman' in *A Tale of Two Cities* – and their subsequent use by the medical profession for dissection. This fate was regarded with particular horror as it meant that the body did not have a Christian burial.

The 'rapturous trance' induced in Squeers by Smike's recapture tells us that there is more to the Dotheboys Hall regime than simple neglect and commercial exploitation. Squeers is enraptured by the opportunity to re-establish his power over the boy and inflict pain upon him. This is the truly poisonous element in the establishment. Squeers' cruelty is intermittently mitigated by a basic profit-seeking pragmatism, but in his wife it is developed in its most acute form, extending even to Nicholas himself. In his earlier conversation with Ralph in London, Squeers had said he would like to be quits with Nicholas, but:

> I only wish Mrs Squeers could catch hold of him. Bless her heart! She'd murder him – she would, as soon as eat her dinner.

Smike is taken to Squeers' lodging in Mr Snawley's house on the edge of Somers Town, where he is locked in an upper room.

Squeers, as we learn in chapter 34, had come to London because of '…some bothering law case … connected with an action for what they call neglect of a boy', and had visited Ralph in the hope of persuading him to make some compensation because of the attack on him by Nicholas, who had been introduced to him by Ralph.

We now meet John Browdie and his new wife Tilda arriving in London on a honeymoon visit, accompanied by Tilda's bridesmaid Fanny Squeers. Mr Squeers meets them by chance at the Saracen's Head and relates how he and Wackford have recaptured Smike and have him secured at their lodging. The newly married couple are invited to tea with Squeers at Snawley's house the same evening, during which Browdie claims to feel ill and goes to 'rest' upstairs, where he releases Smike.

The following evening the Browdies and Nicholas again encounter Squeers and Fanny. Fanny is deeply offended to find Nicholas on good terms with her friend and Squeers rebukes Wackford for eating 'the food his enemies have left'. Browdie remarks that he would feed the whole school if he could, and Squeers then accuses him of releasing Smike.

Browdie openly admits that he had:

> 'Me!' returned John, in a loud tone. 'Yes, it wa' me, coom; wa'at o' that! It wa'me. Noo then.'
>
> 'You hear him say he did it, my child!' said Squeers, appealing to his daughter. 'You hear him say he did it'.
>
> 'Did it!' cried John. 'I'll tell 'ee more; hear this, too. If thou'd got another roonaway boy, I'd do it agean. If thou'd got twenty roonaway boys, I'd do it agean, I'd do it twenty times ower, and twenty more to thot; and I'll tell thee more,' said John, 'now my blood is oop, that thou'rt an old rascal...'

When Browdie refers to himself as an honest man, Squeers sneers. Browdie says he is honest in everything except sitting at the same table with such as Squeers. Squeers instantly calls on his daughter and son as witnesses to the 'scandal' and notes it down, saying it would be worth twenty pounds at the next assizes, even without the mention of honesty.

Browdie, in his frank admission that he had freed Smike, reflects Dickens' instinctive response to the law in its oppressive aspect. Browdie is an embodiment of human health, strength and good nature, and has taken personal delight in fooling Squeers and freeing the boy. His defiance of Squeers –

> Yes, it wa' me. Coom, wa'at o' that. It wa' me. Noo then,

is as powerful in its own way as Nicholas' more melodramatic protestations when he intervenes in the beating in Chapter 13. In its insistence on dealing with a 'legal' matter on the basis of the ordinary standards of kindness and civil behaviour is reminiscent of Pickwick and Brownlow. The direct approach is initially successful, as Smike is returned to his new 'family' with Mrs Nickleby, Nicholas and Kate in their cottage at Bow.

The threat has not receded, however. In Chapter 45, as the Nicklebys are entertaining Mr and Mrs Browdie one evening, John Browdie's rendition of a north-country song is interrupted by a violent knocking at the street door.

Ralph Nickleby is admitted. Nicholas protests that his presence is abhorrent and wishes him to retire. Browdie however has seen Squeers lingering in the passage and calls on him to show himself, which he does 'in a somewhat undignified and sneaking way', whereupon Browdie laughs heartily and even Kate is tempted to join him. The relief is only temporary. Ralph scorns to address Nicholas, speaks only to his mother and says that he has come to restore a son to his father. He then produces Snawley.

Ralph is now invoking the power of the law, using Squeers and his friend Snawley. Like a helpful lawyer taking his own client through his evidence, Ralph tells a story which apparently shows a clear set of connecting links between Smike's first appearance at Dotheboys Hall and his present situation. The story is supported at each point by documents which Ralph produces in their due order and Snawley identifies the boy before him as his son:

> 'You had a son by your first wife, Mr Snawley?'
>
> 'I had,' said that person, 'and there he stands'.
>
> 'We'll show that presently,' said Ralph. 'You and your wife were separated, and she had the boy to live with her, when he was a year old. You had a communication from her, when you had lived apart a year or two, that the boy was dead; and you believed it'.

'Of course I did!' returned Snawley, 'Oh the joy of.......'.

'Be rational, Sir, pray,' said Ralph. 'This is business, and transports interfere with it. The wife died a year and a half ago – not more – in some obscure place, where she was housekeeper to a family. Is that the case?'

'That's the case,' replied Snawley.

'Having written on her death-bed a letter or confession to you, about this very boy which, as it was not directed to you otherwise but by name, only reached you, and that by a circuitous course, a few days since?'

'Just so,' said Snawley. 'Correct in every particular, Sir.'

'And this confession,' resumed Ralph, 'is to the effect that his death was an invention of hers to wound you ... that the boy lived, but was of weak and imperfect intellect – that she sent him by a trusty hand to a cheap school in Yorkshire – that she had paid for his education for some years, and then, being poor and going a long way off, gradually deserted him, for which she prayed forgiveness?'

Snawley nodded his head, and wiped his eyes; the first slightly, the second violently.

Ralph then produces Snawley's certificates of marriage and of the boy's birth, and his wife's two letters and all other papers needed to support the account he had just given, and invites Nicholas and Browdie to examine them, which they do. Nicholas says that he fears the account is true. Browdie scratches his heads and says nothing.

Squeers asks whether 'Master Snawley' is to go with them, and Smike loudly protests that he won't go. Squeers then taunts Browdie, who scornfully responds. There is a struggle. Nicholas grasps Squeers by the collar, thrusts him out of the door and invites Ralph and Snawley to follow him.

They retreat, but not before Ralph had threatened to use the full power of the law against them in order to regain Smike:

> 'I never supposed that you would give him up tonight. Pride, obstinacy, reputation for fine feeling, were all against it. These must be brought down, Sir, lowered, crushed, as they shall be soon. The protracted and wearing anxiety and expense of the law in its most oppressive form, its torture from hour to hour, its weary days and sleepless nights – with these I'll prove you and break your haughty spirit, strong as you deem it now.'

Ralph has not just threatened to use the law's power abusively. He has given a perfectly clear textbook example of how it can be done.

Squeers, who, in the outside passage,

> ...was by this time wound up to a pitch of impotent malignity almost unprecedented.

was so inspired on hearing Ralph's threats that he returned to the parlour door and could not refrain from

> ... actually cutting some dozen capers with various wry faces and hideous grimaces, expressive of his triumphant confidence in the downfall and defeat of Nicholas.

In the next chapter Nicholas, fearing that Ralph will seek to discredit him with the Cheeryble brothers, tells Charles of Ralph's visit to Bow and his threats of legal action to restore Smike to his supposed father. Charles Cheeryble reassuringly replies that Ralph had visited them but 'came on a fruitless errand and went away with some wholesome truths in his ear besides'. He promises Nicholas and Smike his protection. The oppressive power of the law is challenged, and may perhaps be defeated, by the exercise of personal benevolence.

In the later parts of the book, as with *Oliver Twist*, the impetus of the original inspiration grows weaker. The narrative becomes contrived and melodramatic as Nicholas pursues the beautiful but mysterious Madeline Bray who, in a kind of pre-echo of Little Dorrit, cares for her spendthrift debtor father. Nicholas attempts to prevent Ralph from marrying Madeline off to the miserly moneylender, Arthur Gride, but she is freed in any case by the death of her father on the morning of the wedding. Ralph at the same time suffers a huge financial loss when a bank where he placed his money for a day fails.

Ralph's schemes are finally defeated in chapter 56, where young Frank Cheeryble and Newman Noggs jerk the machinery of the criminal law into action and secure the arrest of Squeers, who has been paid by Ralph to steal a will favouring Madeline. Squeers is taken before a magistrate and remanded in custody for a week. The news is then taken to Snawley who makes a full confession implicating Ralph and Squeers. The only indication we have of Squeers' subsequent fate is that Nicholas tells John Browdie in chapter 64 that

> '...after various shiftings and delays... he has been sentenced to be transported for seven years, for being in unlawful possession of a stolen will'.

He also says that Squeers is 'to suffer the consequences of a conspiracy'. 'Soomat in the Guy Faurx line?' asks Browdie.

Despite this brief intervention of the law, the main resolution of affairs is the 'homemade' justice performed by the Cheeryble brothers, who in chapter 60 produce the mysterious Brooker, an old associate of Ralph's, who knows and declares that Smike is in fact Ralph's son.

The book's central theme, of the iniquities of Dotheboys Hall, comes to an inconclusive end. Smike's early death was perhaps the inevitable result of his long-suffering. Following Squeers' conviction, the breaking-up of the school itself, although celebrated by the huge cheer called for by John Browdie, actually results in the pitiful scattering of the pupils in the fields and lanes around Greta Bridge:

> They were taken back, and some other stragglers were recovered, but by degrees they were claimed, or lost again.

It is in keeping with the spirit of the book that the only sustenance the boys come upon in their wanderings is provided by the generous but entirely random benevolence of John and Tilda Browdie.

4.
THE OLD CURIOSITY SHOP

A Scary Legal Dummy

By September 1839, Dickens had brought both *Oliver Twist* and *Nicholas Nickleby* to a conclusion, the event being celebrated with a splendid dinner at the Albion in Aldersgate Street. At this point, Dickens still seems to conceive his future work for Chapman and Hall as essentially having the same episodic structure as *Pickwick* rather than a developing and potentially thematic narrative.

Early in 1840, Dickens had therefore to give some practical shape to the vague idea for the new periodical he had 'sold' to Chapman and Hall six months earlier. His notion, as he confided to Forster, was of a certain old 'Master Humphrey whose house contained a 'quaint, queer-cased clock' in which 'Master Humphrey's friends' kept their papers. By March 1840, however, it was clear that Dickens would write every volume himself.

The first number appeared on 4th April 1840 and sold an impressive 70,000 copies. Early optimism soon evaporated unfortunately as sales fell when readers found that Dickens' pieces lacked the usual flair. The magazine was poorly reviewed and soon was selling only 50,000 copies – barely enough to break even.

This was certainly a crisis. Chapman and Hall had shown confidence in Dickens as an author, advancing the considerable sum of £3,000 to release him from his contract with his earlier publisher, Richard Bentley. If Dickens' reputation with his readership were to fade, his publishers would make a substantial loss and Dickens' personal financial position would become uncertain.

According to Dickens' friend and biographer John Forster, it was during a visit to Landor in Bath in February 1840 that Dickens first had the idea of a young and beautiful child who asks 'Master Humphrey' to help her find her way home at night in London. The idea of a child wandering London streets at night is certainly reminiscent of Dickens' defenceless girls and one might connect it with Dickens' recurring memories of his sister-in-law Mary Hogarth who had suddenly died, 'young, beautiful and good' as Dickens describes her, at the age of seventeen.

In the fourth number of *Master Humphrey's Clock*, Dickens begins to tell the tale of 'Master Humphrey's' night-time encounter with Little Nell in the streets of London, under the title of *The Old Curiosity Shop*:

> One night I had roamed into the City, and was walking slowly and in my usual way, musing upon a great many things, when I was arrested by an enquiry, the purpose of which did not reach me, but which seemed to be addressed to myself, and was preferred in a soft sweet voice that struck me very pleasantly. I turned around hastily and found at my elbow a pretty little girl, who begged to be directed to a certain street at a considerable distance and indeed in quite another quarter of town:
>
> 'It is a very long way from here,' I said, 'my child'.
>
> 'I know that, Sir', she replied timidly, 'I am afraid it is a very long way, for I came from there tonight'.
>
> 'Alone?' said I, in some surprise.
>
> 'Oh yes. I don't mind that, but I am a little bit frightened now, for I have lost my road...'
>
> I cannot describe how much I was impressed by this appeal, and the energy with which it was made, which brought a tear into the child's

clear eye, and made her slight figure tremble as she looked into my face.

The meeting of 'Master Humphrey' with the slight, innocent figure of Little Nell and her bravery and stoicism amid the perils of the London streets certainly touched on a deep concern and memory in Dickens and may well have empowered him as he wrote, literally, to save the Master Humphrey project and with it his reputation and career as an author.

In their 1979 biography[1], the Dickens scholars Norman and Jean MacKenzie gave this assessment of his ensuing novel *The Old Curiosity Shop*:

> The story which Dickens cobbled together in this emergency had little obvious merit. It was a weak and rambling tale about the ruin of a doting old gambler and his subsequent flight through the English countryside with his ailing and angelic grandchild, it was, indeed, a reversal of the plot of *Oliver Twist*, for Oliver rises to fortune while Little Nell declines to her fate. It read like a melodrama, complete with a villainous moneylender and other roles cast straight from the stage; it was padded out with comic turns and set pieces, it was mawkish, it moralised about the greed for gold, and it hinted crudely at lust and sexual cruelty. Dickens was hard put to put his stock parts into such characters as Dick Swiveller, the Marchioness, Mrs Jarley, Sally, and Sampson Brass and to furnish them with with patches of brilliant dialogue. In settling for a pubescent girl for his heroine, however, Dickens had carried over from *Oliver Twist* the secret of the success – the curiosity compelling, almost magical evocation of the bewilderment and fears of childhood; and as he described the confused changes of scene and mood in the odyssey of Little Nell the story became a child's half-remembered dream populated by such figures such as Punch and Judy men, freaks and waxworks. Once Dickens has translated his readers into that twilight world on the borders of memory and fairyland he held them there week after week, entranced by the struggle between the

monstrous Quilp, a bogeyman of restless destructiveness, and Little Nell, the spirit of goodness personified. Like Mary Hogarth, dying at the threshold of adult life, Little Nell became immortal, victorious over the terrors of night and the powers of evil.

Concern with the law and the effects of its operation does not pervade *The Old Curiosity Shop* as it pervades *Pickwick* and *Oliver Twist*. In *The Old Curiosity Shop*, Dickens does give us two fully drawn individual legal figures in Sampson Brass and his sister and co-practitioner Sally, and the role he gives to them seems to reflect his own interest in Brass as an example of a practising solicitor rather than their joint significance as a strand of the plot.

In choosing to place Brass' office in Bevis Marks, near St Mary Axe, on the extreme eastern edge of the City of London and almost two miles from the central lawyers' area around Chancery Lane, Dickens begins to suggest that this solicitor operates on a somewhat undistinguished fringe of the legal profession. The legal profession had historically centred itself around the Temple, the Strand and Chancery Lane and that remained so in Dickens' time. Pickwick's 'rascally' Dodson and Fogg have their office just over a mile east of Chancery Lane in Cornhill, and Bevis Marks is about a mile to the east of that. While Dodson and Fogg themselves are a partnership with several clerks, Brass is a sole practitioner and in fact is largely dependent on his sister Sally who, though not formally qualified, has a more vigorous grasp of the business than he.

We first see Sampson Brass in chapter 11 accompanying his client Quilp as he takes possession of Nell's grandfather's residence and shop – the 'Old Curiosity Shop' – when the grandfather cannot pay his debts. Dickens tells us this was done '…by virtue of certain legal powers to that effect, which few understand and none presumed to call in question', and Brass by his presence gives countenance to this dubious process. Dickens describes him thus:

> This Brass was an attorney of no good repute from Bevis Marks in the City of London; he was a tall, meagre man, with a nose like a wen, a protruding forehead, retreating eyes and hair of a very deep red. He wore a long black surtout reaching nearly to his ankles, short black trousers and cotton stockings of blueish grey. He had a ringing manner but a very harsh voice, and his blandest smiles were so extremely forbidding, that to have had his company under the least repulsive circumstances one would have wished him to be out of temper that he might only scowl.

Despite his harsh forbidding exterior, Brass seems to have little robustness of character, and it is here that we witness the first of his many humiliations at the hands of his client. Tobacco smoke apparently discomposes Brass so Quilp, simply to show his power, not only smokes vigorously himself and calls on his office boy to smoke, but requires Brass to smoke likewise:

> Quilp ... seeing that he was winking very much under the anguish of the pipe, that he sometimes shuddered when he happened to inhale its full flavour, and that he constantly fanned the smoke from him, was quite overjoyed and rubbed is hands with glee.

For his part:

> Brass ... as he was a creature of Mr Quilp's, and had a thousand reasons for conciliating his good opinion, ... tried to smile, and nodded with the best grace he could assume.

Dickens carefully sets this uninspiring legal figure against the joyfully anarchic, *Punch*-like Quilp. If the law's essential role is to confront and restrain the forces of anarchy we have a frighteningly unimpressive representative in Solomon Brass.

Quilp, perhaps unwilling to attract public calumny by evicting the Grandfather when he seems seriously ill, sleeps at the house and requires Brass to stay with him, locking the door to prevent the departure of the two other residents. Early in the next June morning Nell obtains the key from the sleeping Quilp and she and her Grandfather escape with a little money to embark on their journey to the country.

Later the same morning, as solicitor and client awake amid their makeshift bedding, Brass is described with ironic formality as 'of Bevis Marks in the City of London, Gentleman, one of her Majesty's attorneys of the Courts of the King's Bench and Common Pleas at Westminster and a solicitor of the High Court of Chancery'.

The two professions of attorney and solicitor therefore now appear before us in the single unappealing form of Sampson Brass.[2]

Though Brass is realised in great detail as an individual, he plays only a secondary part in the plot. The compelling nature of Little Nell has the central role in what is otherwise, in the view of Norman and Jean MacKenzie, 'a weak and rambling tale' in which Nell Trent's doting Grandfather foolishly tries to restore his broken fortunes by gambling and becomes indebted to the moneylender dwarf Quilp.

As we have seen, when Quilp realises he is unable to pay him he seizes his house and goods. Nell believes that the only way of breaking her Grandfather's compulsion to gamble is to flee the city of London and find refuge in some quiet country place. Quilp's reaction is furious anger and a determination to pursue them, though his motives appear confused.

The ensuing journey of Nell and her Grandfather into the country, usually on foot, sometimes on wagon or canal boat by the casual kindness of their drivers, their respite and employment with Mrs Jarley's travelling waxworks, their subsequent walk through Birmingham and the Black Country, spending a night under the protection of the keeper of the fire of the Furnace, and their eventual arrival at a village usually identified as Tong in Shropshire, with its view of the Welsh hills, are the most widely-remembered parts of the book, mainly because of their drama and the depiction of the purity and selflessness with which Nell sustains her gambling-addicted Grandfather.

The part played by Sampson Brass and his sister in carrying out Quilp's machinations provides the only comparable balancing weight to the journeyings of Nell and her Grandfather and their pursuit by Quilp, the only other focus of events – the career of Nell's loyal servant Kit in the service of the benevolent old Mr Garland – having the character of a somewhat anodyne fairy story.

In Sampson Brass and his sister, we have the first detailed depiction of lawyers at work since Pickwick's dealings with Dodson and Fogg in *The Pickwick Papers*. Although Pickwick fought valiantly with Dodson and Fogg and landed some telling blows, those sharp practitioners remained unashamed and essentially undefeated. It was as if Dickens' early feelings of frustration at the power of the law remained unresolved.

Some five years later, Dickens' anger remains but his indignation has given place to contempt. He seems now able to depict a lawyer who is not just without integrity but also in a strange way devoid of any personal substance. His name is monumentally ironic. Sampson Brass appears to move and act perfectly smoothly and maintains a flow of remarks but in fact has no inner strength and is systematically humiliated by his client.

We have already seen his humiliation when he was helping Quilp take possession of the Curiosity Shop in chapter 11. In chapter 33, we are acquainted with Brass's own residence and office in Bevis Marks. It is a small dark house:

> In the parlour of this little habitation, which is so close upon the footway that the passenger who takes the wall brushes the dim glass with his coat sleeve – much to its improvement, for it is very dirty in this parlour window. In the days of its occupation by Sampson Brass, there hung, all awry and slack, and discoloured by the sun, a curtain of faded green, so threadbare from long service as by no means to intercept the view of the little dark room but rather to afford a favourable medium through which to observe it accurately. There was not much to look at. A rickety table, with spare bundles of papers, yellow and ragged from long carriage in the pocket ostentatiously displayed upon its top, a couple of stools set face to face on opposite sides of this crazy piece of furniture; a treacherous old chair by the fireplace, whose withered

arms had hugged full many a client and helped to squeeze him dry; a second-hand wig box, used as a depository for blank writs and declarations and other small forms of law, once the sale contents of the head which belonged to the wig which belonged to the box, as they were now of the box itself; two or three common books of practice; a jar of ink, a pounce box, a stunted hearth-broom, a carpet trodden to shreds but still clinging with the tightness of desperation to its tacks; these, with the yellow wainscot of the walls, the smoke-discoloured ceiling, the dust and cobwebs, were the prominent decorations of the office of Mr Sampson Brass.

Even in his own office, Sampson Brass is not protected from his client's casually condescending treatment. One morning, after Sampson had broken off from his work to convince his sister of the advantages of tolerating and humouring Quilp, the top sash of the 'dim glass' described above is pulled down from the outside and Quilp himself looks down into the room:

'Is there anybody at home? Is there any of the Devil's ware here? Is Brass at a premium, eh?' says Quilp.

'Ha, ha, ha! Oh very good, Sir!' laughed the lawyer in affected ecstasy. 'Oh very good indeed! Quite eccentric! Dear me, what a humour he has!'

After addressing Sally in similar bold vein Quilp instructs Brass to open the door as he has the clerk here which he has arranged for him to employ, and Dick Swiveller appears. Quilp and Brass leave the office and Dick is left alone with Sally.

Sally ignores him and continues scratching away at her own work. Dick has accepted Quilp's offer to get employment for him partly because Fred Trent, who has Quilp's support in his plan for Nell, has urged him to do so, and partly because his aunt has stopped his allowance.

Dick takes off his coat, puts on a blue one with brass buttons he originally ordered for a boating expedition and has brought with him for 'office purposes', subsides onto Brass's stool and slowly begins to copy a document.

Quilp wants Brass to employ Dick Swiveller so that Dick can keep an eye on the Single Gentleman who might be engaged in a search for Nell and her Grandfather, and is currently lodging with Brass. Brass does not have the will or the means to resist him. When Sally taunted her brother for agreeing to employ Dick, Brass simply fluttered over the leaves in his bill-book in which the name of 'Daniel Quilp Esq' repeatedly appeared. Brass's practice is in such a feeble state that he is willing to endure frequent humiliation and even pay the wage of an unnecessary clerk in order to retain Quilp as a client.

In chapter 48, Quilp realises he has a further use for Brass. He has obtained from Dick the information that Kit and the single gentleman are in communication with each other, and that he and Kit's mother have followed that gentleman in his pursuit of Nell. Quilp's soliloquy of resentment ends:

> 'You are there, are you, my friend?' he repeated, greedily biting his nails. 'I am suspected and thrown aside, and Kit's the confidential agent, is he? I shall have to dispose of him, I fear'.

Quilp's resentment is stoked further by the fact that Kit subsequently outfaces him and rebukes him for trying to frighten his mother during the return journey to London after the single gentleman's unsuccessful search for Nell.

We are entertained with another example of Brass' subservience when Quilp returns home to find that his wife, having had no news of him for several days, believes him to be dead. As Quilp happily seizes on this opportunity for frightening and tyrannizing her with his reappearance, Brass deals with his own humiliation by pretending to admire Quilp's behaviour as an eccentric dramatic performance.

In chapter 51 we are given a magnificent depiction of Quilp in action. In pursuit of his plan to eliminate Kit, and incidentally to enjoy the sport of humiliating his legal advisor, Quilp invites Brass and his sister to tea at 'The Wilderness', a place strongly reminiscent of the summer house belonging to the riverside tavern to which he had invited Dick in chapter 21:

> ... the rugged wooden box, rotten and bare to see, which overhung the river's mud and threatened to slide down into it.

We have been told that it was a day of 'rain, mud, dirt, damp and fog':

> It was not precisely the kind of weather in which people usually take tea in summer-houses, far less in summer-houses in an advanced state of decay, and overlooking the slimy banks of a great river at low water. Nevertheless it was to this choice retreat that Mr Quilp ordered a cold collation to be prepared, and it was beneath its cracked and leaky roof that he in due course received Mr Sampson and his sister Sally.

Sampson and his sister meet with these adverse conditions in their different ways:

> 'You're fond of the beauties of nature,' said Quilp with a grin. 'Is this charming, Brass? Is it unusual, unsophisticated, primitive?'
>
> 'It's delightful indeed, Sir,' replied the lawyer.
>
> 'Cool?' said Quilp.
>
> 'N-not particularly so, I think, Sir,' rejoined Brass, with his teeth chattering in his head.
>
> 'Perhaps just a little damp and augue-ish?' said Quilp.
>
> 'Just damp enough to be cheerful, Sir.' rejoined Brass. 'Nothing more, Sir, nothing more.'

Quilp receives a somewhat more hard-headed response from Sally:

'And Sally?' said the delighted dwarf. 'Does she like it?'

'She'll like it better,' returned that strong-minded lady, 'When she has tea; so let's have it, and don't bother'.

Later Quilp explains that he wants Kit to be somehow 'put out of the way' as he is hindering his plans. Sampson Brass's method of putting Kit out of the way is to talk for some time about money missing from the office, then put a £5 note into the lining of Kit's hat, pursuing him when he leaves the office and leading the innocent Dick Swiveller to find the banknote there and calling a constable.

Kit, when accused, protests his innocence and wisely asks first to be taken to Witherden's where his master is. Brass, who has all along made a show of thinking well of Kit and wishing to treat him fairly, agrees. When Brass introduces himself at the notary's office his own lowly place in professional legal circles becomes apparent. Witherden refers him to his clerk and turns away. When Brass persists in speaking to Witherden and introducing his party he is asked 'in a decided tone' to state his business:

> 'Gentlemen,' says Brass, 'Gentlemen, I appeal to you – really gentlemen, consider, I beg of you. I am of the law. I am styled 'gentleman' by Act of Parliament. I maintain title by the annual payment of twelve pounds sterling for a certificate. I am not one of your players of music, stage actors, writers of books or painters of pictures who assume a station that the laws of their country does not recognise. I am none of your strollers or vagabonds, if one man brings an action against me, he must describe me as a gentleman, or his action is null and void. I appeal to you – is this quite respectful? Really gentlemen -'

Brass of course discredits his own protestation by saying that he has that title by annual payment for the certificate, implying that if he ceased to make the payments he would have no other claim to it.

Two trials follow this event, one the trial of Kit for theft of the £5 note, the other the trial of Brass himself after the Marchioness has come forward with her evidence of overhearing Sampson and Sally discussing their plot to incriminate the boy.

Kit's trial is the only one narrated at any length and, just as he had done in his account of Bardell v Pickwick, Dickens shows the barristers either using discreditable techniques to persuade a jury of the prisoner's guilt or failing to take an obvious step which would effectively challenge the prosecution. At Kit's trial the prosecuting barrister begins by telling the jury, 'as if he has something terrible to tell them', that Kit's barrister would attempt to discredit the testimony of the 'immaculate witnesses' he was about to call. Kit's own barrister fails his client badly when, after Dick accepts the prosecution's apparently damaging assertion that he had dined with Kit's brother the previous day, he omits to cross-examine Dick in order to show that this brother of Kit's was in fact a harmless infant.

Kit is inevitably found guilty and committed to prison. Hope comes when the 'Marchioness', Brass's small servant who has been befriended by Dick Swiveller and has nursed him in illness, confides that she had overheard Solomon and his sister Sally planning to incriminate Kit by putting a five-pound note in his hat and getting Dick to find it there.

The evidence of an illiterate 'runaway' servant would probably be given little weight against the evidence of her own master, a practising solicitor. Dickens therefore once again creates a scene of 'home-made' justice which relies on the possibility of legal sanctions but keeps the courts safely in the background.

Mr Witherden the notary, together with the single gentleman and Kit's employer Mr Garland, interview both Sally and Solomon. The scene is masterly in showing how Brass's own shortcomings of character lead him to incriminate himself by a full confession.

Their strategy is to send Sally Brass a letter asking her to meet a 'friend' who wishes to consult with her. She speedily arrives and is asked if she has advertised for a runaway servant. Witherden then relates how the servant in question has overheard Sally and Solomon plotting to incriminate Kit. Sally takes pinches of snuff at each stage of this revelation but remains 'wonderfully composed'. The notary promises her safety if she reveals the truth, as their real aim is to punish Quilp as the instigator of the affair.

Before she answers, however, Solomon himself appears, somewhat bruised and scratched after his last meeting with Quilp, speaking poetically of having 'feelings like other men' and describing himself as 'a falling house'. Despite Sally repeatedly telling him to 'Shut up!' he continues, finally expressing his anger and resentment against Quilp and saying that, as the truth has come out, 'if anyone is to split, I had better be that person and have advantage of it'. His spirited sister scorns his miserable attempt at self-preservation:

> 'I understand you. You feared that I would be beforehand with you. But do you think I would have been enticed to say a word? I'd have scorned it, if they had tried and tempted me for twenty years'.

Brass responds in his simpering manner that his sister would in fact have 'acted quite different' and would not have forgotten the maxim of 'Old Foxy', their father, whose maxim was 'suspect everyone'. He thus makes plain the one cynical notion that has governed his wretched career and which now, ironically and to the great satisfaction of Dickens' readers, will bring it to an ignominious conclusion.

Solomon does argue that he had been led to make his confession by promises of immunity or some form of favourable treatment but in fact, in his eagerness to be the first to give information about the crime, he had done so without any such promises being made. He is, however, allowed to serve a term of imprisonment in England rather than suffering deportation.

Dickens is pitiless in his depiction of Solomon Brass as a man without any redeeming qualities. Brass does not simply have faults; he is a shell within which there is a complete absence of virtues. As such, Dickens seems to relish in condemning him, together with his sister, to the ultimate degradation: after his release the pair are occasionally glimpsed emerging after dark from London's most notorious slum,

St Giles, to scavenge for 'refuse food or disregarded offal' in the more respectable streets where they would not dare to appear by day.

Of the two highly objectionable characters in the book, Brass is memorable for being both repulsive and empty. Quilp is actively cruel, but he does at least have the capacity for genuine enjoyment. He really relishes the success of his malicious acts. Brass has so little strength of character that he can only deal with his humiliations by pretending not to notice them, or by claiming that they are amusing and simpering passively at the hands of his tormentor.

Does Dickens seek to condemn the man, or to condemn the law which he practices and to some degree represents? 'I am of the law' protests Brass when he is rebuffed by the notary Witherden in Chapter 66. In fact he will do anything to scrape a living. The law can only be as it is practised, and Solomon Brass is among those who practise it. The actions he takes, when he is acting within the bounds of legal competence, are the law in action and they affect people for good or ill. From Witherden's reaction to him, we are led to assume that little good arises from Brass's legal business, whereas Witherden's practice itself appears to be one of honesty, competence and so far as the law allows, benevolence. Each forms part of that huge and complex social institution, the law, which Dickens is constantly exploring.

5.
BARNABY RUDGE

Prejudice, Populism and the Constitution

In May 1836, the 24-year-old Dickens signed a contract with the publisher John Macrone by which he would be paid £200 to write a novel to be called Gabriel Vardon, Locksmith of London. It was more than five years and three novels later, however, after *Oliver Twist*, *Nicholas Nickleby* and *The Old Curiosity Shop*, that Dickens produced 'Gabriel Varden', now bearing the title *Barnaby Rudge*.

Dickens began to write this novel of the Gordon Riots in October 1840 and finished it in November 1841. In July of that year with his wife Catherine he had made a Scottish tour, visiting Glencoe in the Scottish Highlands and Sir Walter Scott's old home of Abbotsford near Edinburgh, before returning to London to write the rioting scenes in the last third of the book.

The full title for Scott's 1814 novel on the Jacobite rising of 1745 was '*Waverley*, or *'tis sixty years since*,' and the book described the momentous events of the rising some sixty years before, which could still be recalled by some of his readers. Dickens, writing in 1841, set out to describe the Gordon Riots of June 1780, again just over sixty years before and again just within living memory.

Scott, in depicting the events leading to the 1745 rising, used a mixture of real and fictional characters whose various concerns and motives constituted the origins of the rebellion as Scott understood it. Dickens in *Barnaby Rudge* made much the same creative use of the events of the Gordon Riots, which stood at much the same historical distance from his own time, with the same interest in the political and constitutional ideas motivating the participants.

The eccentric Lord George Gordon, the chief instigator of the riots, sat in the Commons. On the introduction of a Parliamentary Bill to remove legal restrictions on Catholics entering the universities or certain professions, or inheriting property, he stirred up widespread public alarm by denouncing these perfectly justified and harmless proposals to his followers as evidence of:

> ... a confederacy among Popish powers to degrade and enslave England, establish an inquisition in London and turn the pens of Smithfield Market into stakes and cauldrons....and bygone bugbears which had lain quietly in their graves for centuries were raised again to haunt the ignorant and credulous.

Lord George had also become President of an organisation known as the Protestant Association and organised widespread protest against the Bill. The ensuing riots caused widespread destruction and hundreds of deaths over five days in June 1780.

Why write a three-volume novel about a locksmith? The answer is of course that while a locksmith has a fairly specialised occupation, the sign of the golden key which Gabriel hangs outside his shop will always possess symbolic significance. Locks and keys have power as images, just as they have the real power of giving access or imposing restraint. In the context of the chosen setting – the Gordon riots – the locksmith's trade sign indicates that from the book's first conception, Dickens, like Scott, was concerned about the origin of political forces within society, the possibility of breakdown of social order and the means by which the state might enforce or restore its authority.

The novel's plot is a typical Dickens tale, with a murder, a 'ghost' story, a weak-minded son with a wild affinity with nature and a devoted mother, two love stories and strife between fathers and sons.

The scene opens some thirteen miles north of London at the Maypole Inn, on the borders of Epping Forest. The Inn is described in great detail. The maypole itself, the sign of the inn, stood:

> ... about thirty feet in height, and as straight as any arrow that ever English yeoman drew.

while the structure to which it was attached was:

> ... an old building with more gable ends than a lazy man would care to count on a sunny day, huge zig-zag chimneys, out of which it seemed as though even smoke could not choose to come but in more than naturally fantastic shapes, imparted to it in the days of King Henry VIII, and there was legend, not only that Queen Elizabeth had slept there one night while upon a hunting excursion, to wit, in a certain oak panelled room with a deep bay window, but that next morning, while standing on a mounting block before the door with one foot in the stirrup, the virgin monarch had there and then boxed an unlucky page for some neglect of duty.

Should anyone question the legend John Willet, the landlord, points out the mounting block in question, still standing there to prove the truth of the story.

The building had been an impressive structure, formerly a great house. Though now showing signs of decay, it is nonetheless still capable of providing considerable comfort and sustenance and the bar with its twinkling bottles, huge cheeses and great fireplace is John Willet's pride. Willet himself is a ponderous figure whose chief satisfactions are to dominate the evening conversation with his cronies, to keep his son Joe in permanent subjection and constantly to disparage his only other helper, Hugh, a young man of basic appetites but huge strength and vitality.

The great age of the building, together with its references to English bowmen, to Henry VIII and the great Queen Elizabeth and to laziness and summer days suggests not only a timeless sense of English history but also an imaginative identification with England itself, and this naturally extends to include the landlord himself as characterising its mode of government. Willet is a man averse to or unaware of change, who ignores the 'new-fangled' stagecoaches that stop at this door and who wishes to keep his nineteen-year-old son in a childlike state of subordination.

The inn is part of the estate of Geoffrey Haredale, a Catholic gentleman living nearby at The Warren with his niece Emma. Geoffrey Haredale's elder brother Reuben had been murdered many years earlier by his steward, Rudge, who is in fact Barnaby's father. Rudge had also killed the gardener and then dressed the body in his own clothes and sunk it in a pond. His plan had worked. The recovery of the body wearing Rudge's clothes led people to believe that the gardener had killed Rudge and fled. Rudge himself first reappears in the neighbourhood as a 'ghost', frightening Solomon Daisy, one of Willet's cronies and later appearing in his real shape to his wife Mary, the carer of their simple-minded son Barnaby, terrifying her into silence.

John Willet's little kingdom of the Maypole is subject to two rebellions. In the first, a kind of prelude to the main action of the riots, John's son Joe, tired of his humiliating treatment, throws off his father's rule and goes off to seek his fortune elsewhere. Fourteen chapters later, as the riots are beginning, the inn is actually invaded and looted by the rioters themselves, led by Hugh the former ostler, who in an unusual instance of humanity saves John Willet from being hanged.

After the greater riots are over, the insurrection in the Maypole's regime is resolved when Joe, having lost an arm serving King and Country at the Battle of Savannah, the last victory of the English armies in the American wars, returns, marries Dolly Varden and takes over the inn with the acquiescence of his still-stupefied father.

These outcomes, taken together with Dickens' choice of the essentially pointless Gordon Riots as his subject, reflect the author's steady preference for Reform over Revolution. This disposition does not prevent him from considering, through the characters of Varden, Barnaby, Hugh, Dennis the hangman and Varden's apprentice Tappertit, difficult but important questions about the nature of our constitution and the tension at any time of change between populism and populist forces, legitimacy and justice.

It is on the road near the Maypole that John Willet, on his way to inform Mr Haredale of Solomon Daisy's story, encounters a party of three horsemen – in fact Lord George Gordon, his secretary Gashford and his servant John Grueby.

Lord George is uncontroversially depicted as a lonely, deluded figure. When we first see him during his stay at the Maypole in chapter 35:

> ... it was striking to observe his very large, bright eye, which betrayed a restlessness of thought and purpose, singularly at variance with the studded composure and sobriety of his mien, and with his quaint and sad apparel. It had nothing harsh or cruel in its expression: neither had his face which was thin and mild, and wore an air of melancholy; but it was suggestive of an air of undefinable uneasiness which infected those who looked upon him with a kind of pity for the man.

Most of the rioters had been stirred into action by Gordon's revival of the dim folk memory of a time of public burnings during the reign of the Catholic Queen Mary – 'Bloody Mary' to the rioters – and also the idea that the troubles of those times had been brought to an end by the accession of the protestant Queen Elizabeth, the very monarch who was believed by local people to have actually spent a night in the historic Maypole Inn depicted in such detail at the opening of the novel.

The riots inspired by Gordon are to a significant extent promoted and, in their early stages, managed by his secretary, Gashford. The historical characters of Gashford and Ned Dennis, the public hangman, together with four characters of the author's own creation – Vardon, Barnaby, Hugh the ostler at the Maypole and Varden's apprentice

Tappertit - play leading parts in the riots, Gabriel Varden himself being the most significant figure opposed to the rioters.

Barnaby himself seems to be motivated to join in these events by the same powerful but unarticulated love of freedom which leads him to ramble, as described in chapter 45, in the open country with the neighbourhood's dogs:

> With two or three of these, or sometimes with a full half dozen barking dogs at his heels, he would sally forth on a long expedition that would consume the day ... Barnanby's enjoyments were, to walk, and run, and leap, till he was tired, then to lie down in the long grass, or by the growing corn, or in the shade of some tall tree, looking upward at the light clouds as they floated over the blue surface of the sky, listening to the Lark as she poured out her brilliant song.

Hugh, the immensely strong man-of-all-work at the Maypole, had a gypsy mother who had been hanged at Newgate. His father is at this point unknown. He is regarded by John Willet as rather more animal than human, but emerges as the rioters' most vigorous and in some ways most capable leader. Hugh's motivation is partly resentment at his treatment by John Willet, partly a simple expression of animal spirits but also by a generalised wish to overturn what he feels is an oppressive society. When Hugh is being enrolled in the Protestant Association by Gashford in Chapter 38 he replies to Dennis' cry of 'No Popery, brother!' with 'No Property, brother!'. Gashford 'with his usual mildness' corrects him but Dennis replies 'It's all the same!'.

While the riot's declared aim is misconceived, the wider social injustice which feeds its anger is real. The description at the opening of the novel of the Maypole Inn, ruled over by its obstinate and selfish landlord invited comparison with the country-wide regime, although the inn's situation at a distance from London gives the earlier events there a somewhat removed, fable-like quality.

The riots gain momentum because they set in motion waves of poor people's indignation against a society that does not serve them well. For Hugh they are an opportunity to fight for what he believes is social justice, using the destructive methods which he feels are almost a celebration of his cause. His heroism and strange lightness of heart seem to elevate, even though they do not redeem, the barbarous scenes in the last stage of the riots, which for Dickens are the inevitable result of the power of the mob.

As a leader of the rioters, Hugh is unrelenting. In Chapter 60 when they decide to attack Newgate, Hugh declares:

> Not that jail alone...but every jail in London. They shall have no jails to put prisoners in. We'll burn them all down, make bonfires of them, every one!

Though Hugh spares John Willet's life in the earlier attack on the Maypole by distracting the rioters to a new purpose – burning The Warren – this is an isolated act of mercy or reflection and in later chapters it is Barnaby who tries unsuccessfully to restrain him from senseless acts of destruction.

Hugh is also manipulated by a representative of the very society he is attacking. John – later Sir John – Chester uses him to control his own son by sending him to waylay Dolly Varden and steal from her the letter which Emma Haredale was sending to his son Edmund with her bracelet as a pledge of faithfulness. Chester then intimates that he will have Hugh charged with the theft of the bracelet unless he does his further bidding.

Our awareness of oppressive elements in society is extended as the book progresses. Sir John Chester, admired as a master of the social graces, is revealed to be a ruthless parasite, insisting that his son Edmund should marry for money in order to support Sir John's gentlemanly existence. A 'country justice' treats Barnaby's mother as a vagrant during her journey to London and later at the Old Bailey tips the balance of the verdict in favour of Barnaby's hanging.

The locksmith Gabriel Vardon – the other significant figure in the events of the riot – is the maker of the lock on the front gates of

Newgate prison. In the exercise of his trade, the prison lock is part of his contribution to society. His character as a master-craftsman, employer, husband, father, householder, neighbour and friend is exemplary.

In Chapter 41, just as the first disturbances of Lord George Gordon's movement are beginning, we have a portrait of Varden at work in his shop:

> From the workshop of the Golden Key, there issued forth a tinkling sound, so merry and good humoured, that it suggested the idea of someone working blithely, and made quite pleasant music ... Tink, tink, tink – clear as a silver bell, and audible at every pause of the streets' harsher noises, as though it said, 'I don't care, nothing puts me out; I am resolved to be happy' Women scolded, children squalled, heavy carts went rumbling by ... still it struck again, no higher, no lower, no louder, no softer; not thrusting itself on people's notice a bit more for having been outdone by louder sounds – tink, tink, tink tink, tink.
>
> It was a perfect embodiment of the still, small voice[1], free from all cold, hoarseness, huskiness or unhealthiness of any kind; foot passengers slackened their pace and were disposed to linger near it, neighbours who got up that morning felt good humoured stealing upon them as they heard it ... mothers danced their babies to its ringing; still the same magical tink, tink, tink came from the workshop of the Golden Key.

We have a picture of Vardon himself:

> There he stood, working at his anvil, his face all radiant with exercise and gladness, his sleeves turned up, his wig pushed off his shining forehead – the easiest, freest, happiest man in all the world.

The description is certainly fulsome, but there is no trace of irony in it. It expresses what we find about Gabriel all through the book. We learn that he had loved and wished to marry Barnaby's mother when she was a young beautiful woman and that although his rival Rudge had won her, Gabriel, now married, remained a true friend and support in her supposed widowhood. We see him enduring with good humour the complaints of his fickle, somewhat perverse wife, rescuing and supporting his beloved daughter Dolly and giving his wayward apprentice Simon Tappertit numerous opportunities to redeem himself. He is respected by his neighbours, a good tradesman, good citizen and an all-round good egg.

His apprentice Simon is the least attractive of the rioters' leaders. He is initially a comic figure, whose resentment at imagined sleights, together with his expertise in the making of duplicate keys, lead to his taking the foremost role among the 'Prentice Knights, a band of discontented apprentices at whose nightly meetings Tappertit presides. In chapter 8 we see Simon entering a damp dirty cellar in the Barbican where he is greeted as 'Captain'. He descends a narrow flight of steps 'in gloomy majesty', issues various commands, is served with drink, and in due course one of his followers:

> ... going to a little cupboard, returned with a thigh-bone ... and placed the same in the hands of Mr Tappertit; who, receiving it as a sceptre and staff of authority, cocked his three corned hat fiercely on the top of his head, and mounted a large table, whereon a chair of state, cheerfully ornamented with a couple of skulls, was placed ready for his reception.

An applicant for admission to the 'Prentice Knights then enters, blindfolded. The blindfold is removed. Information about the applicant is then read out:

> 'Mark Gilbert. Age nineteen. Bound to Thomas Curzon, Golden Fleece, Aldgate. Loves Curzon's daughter. Cannot say that Curzon's daughter loves him. Should think it probable. Curzon pulled his ears last Tuesday week.'

> 'How!' Cried the Captain, starting.

> 'For looking at his daughter, please you,' said the novice.

'Write Curzon down. Denounced', said the Captain. 'Put a black cross against the name of Curzon'.

'So please you,' said the novice, 'that's not the worst – he calls his 'prentice 'idle dog' and stops his beer unless he works to his liking. He gives him Dutch cheese, too, eating Cheshire, Sir, himself: and Sundays out, only once a month!'

'This,' said Mr Tappertit gravely, 'is a flagrant case. Put two black crosses to the name of Curzon.'

'If the society,' said the novice, who was an ill-looking, one-sided shambling lad, with sunken eyes set close together in his head – 'If the society would burn his house down – for he's not insured – or beat him when he comes home from his club at night, or help me carry off his daughter, and marry her at the Fleet, whether she gives consent or no -'

Mr Tappertit waved his grisly truncheon as an admonition to him not to interrupt, and ordered three black crosses to the name of Curzon.

'Which means' he said in gracious explanation, 'vengeance, complete and terrible. 'Prentice, do you love the Constitution?'

To which the novice (being to that end instructed by his attendant sponsors) replied, 'I do.'

'The Church, the State, and everything established – except the masters?' quoth the Captain.

Again the novice replied 'I do.'

Having said it, he listened meekly to the Captain, who in an address prepared for such occasions, told him that under that same Constitution (which was kept in a strong box somewhere, but where exactly he could not find out, or he would have endeavoured to procure a copy of it) the 'Prentices had, in times gone by, had frequent holidays of right, broken people's heads by scores, defiled their masters, may even achieved some glorious murders in the streets, and in all which mobile aspirations they were now restrained, how degrading checks upon them were unquestionably attributable to the innovating spirit of the times, and how they united therefore to resist all change, except such change as would restore those good old English customs by which they would stand or fall. After illustrating the wisdom of going backward, by reference to that sagacious fish, the crab, and the not infrequent practice of the mule and the donkey, he described their general objects....binding him, at the bidding of his chief, to resist and obstruct the Lord Mayor, sword-bearer and chaplain, to despise the authority of the sheriffs and to hold the court of aldermen as nought, but not on any account, in case the fullness of time should bring a general rising of 'prentices, to damage or in any way disfigure Temple Bar, which was strictly constitutional and always to be approached with reverence.

This is of course the same Temple Bar which Dickens describes in chapter 1 of Bleak House as 'that leaden-headed old obstruction', and in Book 2 chapter 1 of *A Tale of Two Cities* as having a 'heavy shadow' and referring to the 'heads exposed on Temple Bar with an insensate brutality and ferocity worthy of Abyssinia or Ashantee'.

It is not until chapter 36 that we hear of Tappertit as the President of the United Bulldogs, formerly the 'Prentice Knights and in chapter 39 we find that their juvenile resentments and fantasies no longer seem ludicrous but have taken form as an actual social force: Tappertit and his followers are received 'with very flattering marks of distinction and respect' as they join the London rioters at the Boot Inn.

Dickens portrays the 'Prentices movement as significantly combining their demand for supposed rights and freedoms with fervent support for the established order. This has the same essential character as the Gordon Riots themselves, which in turn can be seen as a kind of distorted echo of the demands for constitutional reform that led to the English Civil War, when jurists such as Sir Edward Coke[2] and John Seldon argued that the Magna Carta and other documents enshrined ancient rights and freedoms of the English people that limited monarchical power. Such arguments had, and for understandable reasons still have, perhaps more persuasive power and force than their actual evidential foundations would admit, hence Dickens' reference to the 'Prentice Knights' constitution being 'kept in a box somewhere, but where exactly he could not find out'.

There is certainly irony in the fact that the leaders of the Gordon Riots were asserting not the power of the elected Parliament to restrain the monarch but, in the end, the rioters' own power to restrain that Parliament from enacting particular legislation.

Most of those in the first surging crowds may well have believed that they were simply presenting their petition and demonstrating outside the House to persuade the Members not to pass the Bill. That was certainly what Gashford pretends to believe when in chapter 50 he instructs Hugh and Dennis to do 'nothing' because Parliament has rejected the petition by 192 votes to 6 and therefore, according to ordinary law, 'the cause is lost'.

Hugh and Dennis, however, for very different reasons, certainly intend otherwise and Gashford implicitly encourages them to continue the rioting, which starts up again after a brief lull. The proceedings of Tappertit and his Apprentice Knights, ludicrous though they are, add a significant historical dimension to the narrative.

The ancient structure of the Maypole Inn is an eloquent reminder of the reign of the first Elizabeth and her Protestant settlement, while Dickens' description of the Apprentice Knights' proceedings suggests a confused memory of Parliament asserting its rights under Charles I. Both of these involved ill-defined but nevertheless important constitutional issues, and when Gashford encourages Hugh and Dennis to take a step beyond that of persuading Parliament by conventional means, Dickens opens the novel to a wider consideration of the riot's potential consequences.

Barnaby has a desire for freedom, spontaneity and communion with the natural world and longs to play a part in important affairs. Hugh certainly has the idea of a general overthrow of the existing powers in society – they shall have no jails and 'no property'. When John Chester asks if Hugh will invite him to dine when he is Lord Mayor of London, Hugh replies that there would be a different kind of Lord Mayor then. Dennis on the other hand believes that the purpose of the riot is to maintain the existing 'Protestant' society, as he sees it, something which he believes to be threatened by the proposed legislation.

We know that the riot is pointless and its consequences utterly destructive – the scenes in chapters 67 and 68 are almost as terrible as the Paris revolutionary scenes which Dickens describes in *A Tale of Two Cities*. Lord George, while too personally confused to be an actual demagogue, nevertheless has the effect of one, and the evils of demagoguery and mob violence are plain to see. In the context of such pointless destruction, it would be easy to dismiss without further thought the claim of the fetishistic hangman Ned Dennis that he is acting to preserve the country's constitution.

Dickens had already set the first overtly hostile manifestation of the riots in Westminster Hall which is, as well as being a place of public resort, the home of English Law from earliest times. It is here that Geoffrey Haredale happens to meet Sir John Chester talking with Gashford. We find that Haredale, Chester and Gashford had been schoolfellows at St Omer in France. Haredale is introduced to Lord George by Chester and civilly asks Lord George to 'refrain from these proceedings'. He also – quite accurately – describes Gashford as servile and a sycophant. When Gashford retorts, those nearby hear Haredale described as a 'Papist' and the crowd becomes hostile. Haredale is saved from this first outburst of the rioters' anger by Lord George's servant John Grueby who holds back the crowd and manoeuvres Haredale into a boat to safety by river.

There follows a sad depiction of two aspects of the riots – the weakness and indecision of the authorities and the rapid spread of fear among the citizens of London.

Large bodies of troops are placed on duty throughout London but are powerless to restrain the rioters because the civil authority has not authorised their action:

> All yesterday, and on this day likewise, the Commander-in-Chief endeavoured to rouse the magistrates to a sense of duty, and in particular the Lord Mayor, who was the faintest-hearted and most timid of them all ...

> ... the crowd, becoming speedily acquainted with the Lord Mayor's temper, did not fail to take advantage of it by boasting that even the civil authorities were opposed to the Papists.... These vaunts they took care to make within the hearing of the soldiers; and they were asked if they desired to fire upon countrymen, 'No, they would be damned if they did', and showing much honest simplicity and good nature. The feeling that the military were No Popery men, and for ripe for disobeying orders and joining the mob, soon became very prevalent in consequence.

In chapter 61 when the Catholic gentleman Geoffrey Haredale, having arrested the murderer Rudge, asks the villagers of Chigwell to help him take his prisoner into London '... not a man among them dared to help him by so much as the motion of a finger'. We are told that the drivers of public conveyances were afraid to carry passengers if they knew them to be Catholics, and people avoided recognising Catholic friends in the street. Haredale is told by a mild old Catholic priest that he doubted that he, Haredale, would find a magistrate brave enough to commit Rudge to prison on Haredale's complaint.

When Haredale eventually reaches the Mansion House, he finds an old gentleman asking – for the sixth time – for help as he has had threats to burn down his house. The porter is trying to shut the door, but Haredale sees the Lord Mayor – a dressing-gown-clad figure on the landing – who is told that Haredale's house has actually been burned. The old gentleman again asks for protection. He is told:

> '....you might have an alderman in your house, if you could get one to come.'

> 'What the devil's the use of an alderman?' Returned the choleric old gentleman.
>
> '....To awe the crowd, Sir' said the Lord Mayor.
>
> 'Oh, Lord ha' mercy!' whimpered the old gentleman, as he wiped his forehead in a state of ludicrous distress, 'to think of sending an alderman to awe a crowd....!'
>
> 'Then what,' returned the old gentleman, 'Am I to do? Am I a citizen of England? Am I to have the benefit of the laws? Am I to have any return for the King's taxes?'
>
> 'I don't know, I am sure,' said the Lord Mayor. 'What a pity you're a Catholic! Why couldn't you be Protestant, and then you wouldn't have got yourself into this mess? I am sure I don't know what's to be done. – There are great people at the bottom of these riots. – Oh dear me, what a thing it is to be a public character! You must look in again in the course of the day. Would a javelin-man do? – Or there's Philips, the Constable, – he's disengaged – he's not very old for a man at his time of life, except in his legs, and if you put him up at the window he'd look quite young by candle-light, and might frighten 'em very much – Oh dear! – Well – we'll see about it.'

This comic display of ineptitude becomes more sinister when Haredale, who still has Rudge with him as his prisoner, asks the magistrate to commit Rudge for trial:

> 'Oh dear me!' cried the Lord Mayor. 'God bless my soul – and body – Oh lar! – Well! – There are great people at the bottom of these riots, you know. – You really mustn't.'

When Haredale points out that every second's delay loosens the man's bloody hands again and leads to his escape, the Lord Mayor continues to prevaricate:

> 'Oh dear me!' cried the chief magistrate. 'These arn't business hours you know – I wonder at you – how ungentlemanly it is of you – you musn't – And I suppose you are a Catholic too?'
>
> 'I am,' said Haredale.
>
> 'God bless my soul, I believe people turn Catholic a 'purpose to vex and worrit me,' cried the Lord Mayor.'

Haredale eventually goes to Sir John Fielding, the magistrate who had established the Bow Street Runners, basing them at this own house in that street. Sir John unhesitatingly commits Rudge to Newgate prison, then newly built and believed to be immensely strong. Afterwards Haredale finds huge relief and reassurance in touching the stone walls of Newgate:

> With eager eyes and strained attention, Mr Haredale saw him (Rudge) chained, and locked and barred up in his cell. Nay, when he had left the jail, and stood in the free street, without, he felt the iron plates upon the doors, with his bare hands, and drew them over the stone wall, to assure himself himself that it was real; and to exult in its being so strong, and rough, and cold.

Haredale can thankfully put his hands on the walls of Newgate as a reassuring guarantee of safety and civil order, though we have a very different view of these walls elsewhere in Dickens. In *Nicholas Nickleby* for instance, they are the walls of the grim prison overlooking the place of public hangings close to the Saracen's head in chapter four, and they loom up as a threatening reminder to Smike of the law's power, just before he is seized by Squeers in chapter 38.

Tappertit's master, the fair-minded, tolerant Gabriel Vardon, has no sympathy with the rioters. Although he doesn't complain of the grotesque little Protestant Association collecting box kept by his wife, he indignantly tears up the No Popery leaflet, given to him by Tappertit, which purports to give protection from the mob.

The real trial of Vardon's fortitude takes place in Chapter 63 when he is forced by the rioters to go with them to Newgate prison to open the lock of the main gate which he himself has made.

When Varden defies the rioters by refusing and simply asks for the return of his daughter, Dennis, who is quite ready to hang Varden from the nearest lamp post, nevertheless declares that he is 'a very game old gentleman':

> 'I honour your principles,' says Dennis. 'They're mine exactly. In such sentiments as them...I'm ready to meet you or any man half-way. Have you a bit of cord anywhere handy? Don't put yourself out of the way if you haven't. A handkerchief will do.'

Is Dennis, in saying 'I honour your principles', simply honouring Varden's courage in his steadfast stand, or is he recognising something further that Varden represents? Whichever way it is read it is clear is that, in recognition of something he values and respects, Dennis is offering to 'work off' Varden in a skilful manner as part of a kind of grisly compact between Varden and himself.

In a dramatic scene in the next chapter, the Governor, Mr Ackerman, emerges on to the roof of his house and Gabriel calls to him, declaring that he had been brought by force to open the lock on the main gate but that he will refuse to do so. The Governor asks if there is any way he can help him. Gabriel replies:

'None, Mr Ackerman. You'll do your duty and I'll do mine,' replies Gabriel. He then turns to the mob, declaring that they could howl till they were hoarse, but he would refuse to undo the lock. Hugh in fact proposes a solution without violence – 'Let us have our friends, master, and you shall have your friend' and gets the rioters to cheer the proposal, but Gabriel will have nothing of it, calling on Ackerman to 'Keep 'em out, in King George's name'.

When Varden is brought up to the prison gate and refuses to dismantle the lock, Dennis suddenly and violently strikes him in the face. As they struggle together Dennis, articulating with difficulty, asks him:

> 'Is this all the return you make me, you ungrateful monster?'

Dickens puzzles us with this question and its accompanying violence, though things become clearer later.

In the following chapter, Dennis actually puts into practice the principles he claimed to uphold. When the rioters have finally broken into and set fire to the prison Dennis, instead of helping to free the prisoners, makes his way to the condemned cells and double locks the entrance to them, securing the prisoners inside. We are reminded that he had been 'bred and matured in the good old school, and had administered the good old laws on the good old plan', and now, ignoring the prisoners' cries to be released, he harangues them in the following terms:

> 'You've had the law,' he said, crossing his legs and elevating his eyebrows; 'laws have been made 'a purpose for you; a very handsome prison's a purpose for you, a parson's kept a' purpose for you; a constitutional officer's appointed a purpose for you; carts is maintained a purpose for you – and yet you're not contented! Will you hold that noise, you, Sir, in the furtherest?'

Dennis later refuses Hugh's request to release the four prisoners:

> 'Don't you know they're left for death on Thursday? Don't you respect the law – the constitution – nothing? Let the four men be.'

Dennis' concern extends even to the rights of suspect persons. In chapter 69, he protests at the shooting of a suspected looter – Stagg, the blind man – as he flees the scene:

> 'Look at this man. Do you call this constitutional? Do you see him shoot through and through instead of being worked off like a Briton? Damme, if I know which party to side with. You're as bad as the other. What's to

> become of the country of the military power's to go a-superceding the civilians in this way? Where's this poor feller's rights as a citizen, that he didn't have me in his last moments?'

While Dennis is protesting at the loss of Stagg's constitutional rights, the riots continue on their destructive course.

The old gentleman, who had earlier been asking the Lord Mayor for protection against rioters is Mr Langdale, a vintner, whom Joe Willets used to visit in London to pay for wines. In chapter 66 Haredale meets Langdale again on the fringes of the crowd accompanied by John Grueby, Lord George's old servant, now in Landale's service. He is taken for refuge to the vintner's house on Holborn Hill, while the rioting goes on through the night, with the burning of houses including that of Sir John Fielding and the great Judge Lord Mansfield, ruining his library:

> ... worst of all, because nothing could replace this loss, the great Law Library, on almost every page of which were notes in the Judge's own hand, of inestimable value – being the results of study and experience of his own life.

Haredale's earlier grateful touching of the rough walls of Newgate after Rudge is imprisoned there, the fortitude of the magistrate Sir John Fielding in committing him and Dickens' later lament for the rioters' burning of Lord Mansfield's library sound a simple but consistent note amid the turbulence of the rioting to remind us of the value of the rule of law.

The 'principles' of the public hangman, Dennis, on this matter are at the same time cruder and more complex. We learn something more of them in chapter 37 when he explains to Gashford his reasons for supporting Lord George's cause.

Dennis describes the work of Parliament in passing criminal statutes which, though severe, are mitigated by the use of the prerogative of mercy:

> 'George the Third steps in when they number very strong at the end of a session and says, 'These are too many for Dennis. Dennis shall have half for himself, and I'll have half for myself. Sometimes he throws me over one I don't expect.'

The one that Dennis didn't expect was the notable case of Mary Jones, a nineteen-year-old mother who was hanged simply for 'taking a piece of cloth off the counter of a shop in Ludgate Hill, and putting it down again when the shopman sees her'. Dennis doesn't 'expect' it – he thinks it an unjustified sentence – but his job is to carry out the sentence according to law – 'That being the law and practice of England is the glory of England'.

What we see Dennis so obsessively preserving during the destruction of Newgate is the right of the prisoners to be treated according to the law – something that, while spectacularly unappealing to those particular prisoners at that moment, is in legal terms of very great value. The right to 'due process' of a formal trial is a strong and indeed fundamental protection against the government's arbitrary use of power. The other matter on which Dennis protests – the ascendancy of the civil power over the military – is an equally vital element in any ordered, democratic society. And it certainly seems that that Dennis profoundly believes in these principles. After the taking of Newgate, Dennis could have continued with others in burning, stealing and drinking, but such things never occur to him. He goes straight to the condemned cells to harangue the prisoners there on the benefits of due process of law and constitutional propriety.

The only really effective basis for the principles which the hangman claims to uphold is the settled state of society in which the law can effectively operate. It is for this that Dennis looks back to the protestant religious settlement achieved in the 'glorious' – or at any rate comparatively benign – reign of Queen Elizabeth the First.

For the mass of the rioters, the picture no doubt seems simple: the supposed threat is an oppressive form of Catholicism and so the refuge and protection are seen to be Protestantism. They likewise look back to the reign of Queen Elizabeth, whose accession they believe ended the barbarous practices of 'Bloody' Mary and whose reign is recalled at the beginning of the story by the ancient structure of the Maypole Inn.

Dennis may shout 'No Popery!' with the loudest of the rioters but his concern is not really with religion at all but with what he sees as the law and the constitution. In Dennis' eyes it is the 'law and practice of England' – essentially the common law – that is being threatened if the country becomes subject to Catholic power:

> 'If these Papists gets into power, and begins to boil and roast instead of hang, what becomes of my work? If they touch my work, which is part of so many laws, what becomes of the laws in general, what becomes of the religion, what becomes of the country?'

Gashford himself is ostentatiously pious but for Dennis the religion is simply a badge of identity – he has actually been to church 'twice – counting the time I was baptised'. He is nevertheless firm in his conviction that -

> 'I mustn't have my Protestant work touched, nor this here Protestant state of things altered in no degree.'

While the locksmith and the hangman are each acting according to their principles, it seems that Varden in his refusal to open the lock of Newgate and Dennis in his insistence that the sentences of the Court must be duly carried out both in fact feel the same commitment to the constitutional foundation upon which the rule of the law depends.

This idea also hovers in the ambiguity with which Dennis, as we have seen, describes Varden as 'a very game old gentleman' and declares that he honours Varden's principles as they are exactly his own. Dickens leads us to ask how Varden's principles and those of Dennis can be the same, a conundrum to which the answer is actually quite simple. Varden believes that the proposed legislation does not threaten theconstitution but that the riot does, so the riot must be opposed. Dennis believed that the legislation does threaten the 'constitution so the riot must be supported.

Dennis recognises that Varden values the existing settled state of the country and respects him for that, but thinks he is wrong to believe that the legislation presents no threat, and so violently opposes him. He describes Varden as 'ungrateful' because Varden does not recognise the service Dennis is doing by rioting to uphold the existing regime.

While both men are, in their own ways, committed to preserving the settled state of things, or the ill-defined but nevertheless vital concept that Dennis refers to as the 'constitution', they are nevertheless very different people.

Varden is a good citizen, a man of integrity, a skilled master of his trade, generous, tolerant, upright and compassionate as a family man, courageous in defending what he believes to be right. Dennis is a very different creature, in appearance and manner almost studiously the opposite of Varden. He is described when we first meet him in chapter 37 as:

> ... a squat, thickset personage, with a low, retreating forehead, a coarse shock of hair, and eyes so small and near together, that his broken nose alone seemed to prevent their meeting and fusing together into one of the usual size. A dingy handkerchief twisted like a cord about his neck, left its great veins exposed to view, and they were swoln and starting, as though with gulping down strong passions, malice and ill-will. His dress was of threadbare velveteen ... discoloured with the soils of many a stale debauch, and reeking yet with pot-house odours.

We do see a slight improvement in his appearance when in chapter 69 Dennis gives away Hugh, Barnaby and his father to the military. His just-perceptibly smarter dress suggests a move towards resumption – in his own mind at least – of some kind of formal role:

> The front of the shed suddenly darkened, and Dennis stood before them. ... He was rather better dressed than usual: wearing the same suit of threadbare black, it is true, but having round his neck an

unwholesome-looking cravat of yellowish white, and on his hands, great leather gloves ... His shoes were newly greased, and ornamented with a pair of rusty iron buckles; the pack-thread at his knees had been renewed; and where he wanted buttons, he wore pins.

He declares that he's giving the three men up to the authorities because Hugh in particular opposed his detaining the prisoners in Newgate:

'You forced me to do it; you wouldn't respect the soundest constitootional principles, you know; you went and violated the wery framework of society'.

In chapter 70 we have what amounts to a reported soliloquy giving us Dennis's own thoughts. Having handed over Hugh, Barnaby and Barnaby's father to the military authorities, the hangman is walking through the streets of London reflecting on events and intending to solace himself with female society in the form of the captured Dolly Varden and Emma Haredale:

As he walked along the streets with his leather gloves clasped behind him, and his face indicative of cheerful thought and pleasant calculation, Mr Dennis might have been likened to a farmer ruminating among his crops, and enjoying by anticipation the bountiful gifts of Providence. Look where he would, some heap of ruins afforded him rich promise of a working off; the whole town appeared to have been ploughed, and sown, and nurtured by most genial weather; and a goodly harvest was at hand.

Having taken up arms and resorted to deeds of violence, with the great object of preserving the Old Bailey in all its purity, and the gallows in all its pristine usefulness and moral grandeur, it would perhaps be going too far to assert that Mr Dennis had ever distinctly contemplated and foreseen this happy state of things. He rather looked upon it as one of those beautiful dispensations which are inscrutably brought about for the behoof and advantage of good men.

> As to being taken up, himself, for a rioter, and punished with the rest, Mr Dennis dismissed that possibility as an idle chimera, arguing that the line of conduct he had adopted at Newgate, and the service he had rendered that day, would be more than a set-off against any evidence which might identify him as a member of the crowd ... and the common usefulness of his office, and the great demand for its functions, would certainly cause it to be winked at, and passed over. In a word, he had played his cards throughout, with great care; he had changed sides at the very nick of time; he had delivered up two of the most notorious rioters, and a distinguished felon to boot; he was quite at his ease.

In other words, while Dennis certainly has a fetishistic obsession with hanging people, the fact that the riots' outcome will give him many opportunities for gratifying such desires is merely an incidental benefit. His actual object in taking part in the riots was that of 'preserving the Old Bailey in all its purity, and the gallows in all its pristine usefulness'.

Dennis had changed sides, we may assume, to preserve himself when he saw that the military were prevailing against the rioters, who could now achieve nothing further. His only actions of note during the riot had been to detain the condemned prisoners in Newgate and to protest at the shooting of the blind Stagg as he fled from the soldiers, in both of which, he can argue, he was acting to maintain the 'constitution' as he saw it.

'Preserving the Old Bailey in all its purity and the gallows in all its pristine usefulness' are certainly words loaded with irony. Ideas of purity and pristine usefulness sit uneasily in any description of these harsh instruments of enforcement of the criminal law and even more uneasily with the inhuman gloating with which Dennis views the prospect of his future work.

But what do we say about the key to the lock of Newgate prison? We see no irony in Varden's courageous support of the criminal law by refusing to dismantle this equally vital element of the system of enforcement. Varden through the entire story lives out the virtuous life, Dennis in almost every way falls short of it. Yet while Varden courageously defends the way of life he himself exemplifies, he does not appear to consider its underlying principles, and perhaps does not need to. With profound Dickensian irony, it is left to the discreditable Dennis to articulate the principles of due process of law and civic control of the military that sustain the society Varden represents.

There is a further and more chilling irony in the fact that, in their respective crises, Varden reacts with courage and resolution while Dennis's mental world eventually disintegrates, leaving him with only desperation and fear.

What, if anything is Dicken's saying to us here about the principle of the rule of the law? Perhaps only that it has more than one aspect. While it is necessary to uphold justice and defend freedom, the rule of law inevitably involves suffering in particular cases. In describing the two contrasting human characters who in their very different ways defend and uphold it, Dickens is asking us to look at the essentially mixed and problematic nature of law as a social institution. Varden is as good a citizen as it is possible to be while still remaining credible as a human character, while Dennis's squalid nature is on the verge of the grotesque. The contrast between the virtuous, good-hearted Varden and the obsessive Dennis serves to emphasis the tension which, Dickens suggests, has inevitably to be contained within the legal system.

There can be a temptation to read the book a different way – to see the depiction of the flawed, degenerate Dennis as a means of discrediting the 'constitootional' principles he embraces. We ask ourselves whether this degraded and obsessive man's embrace of these principles casts a questioning shadow on the constitutional ideas themselves.

While Dickens certainly attacks the follies and abuses of the legal system of his time with great vigour, he never appears to embrace the profound pessimism that the above view would imply. Without the basic common law principles such as those Dennis points us to, harsh and difficult though they may be in their application, it is not easy to see how there could be any civilised system of law at all. Dickens does not bury his head in the sands of nihilism but chooses to look steadily at the legal system, warts and all, as a flawed but necessary human construct.

Dickens pairs together in a sort of balance Gabriel Varden, who acts out the virtuous civic life, with the degraded Ned Dennis, who articulates its constitutional essentials, and placing this narrative in its lightly sketched historical context of the Elizabethan settlement. In doing so the author allows himself to speculate that Varden's virtuous and compassionate civic life can be sustained only at a cost. What is the nature of that cost? Is it somehow represented by Dennis himself? Perhaps it is a recognition of the unavoidable grittiness of the legal system. Justice inevitably involves some harshness. It may be that we need to recognise this, both in those measures needed to foster a harmonious society of which the Elizabethan religious settlement was perhaps a pattern and also in the rigorous procedures which, as Dennis obsessively maintains, are necessary to uphold due process of law.

It may be from our admitting these necessities, Dickens seems to suggest, that a consensus can arise creating a certain sort of society – a society that is at once free and stable, tolerant and fair, one in which the common law can successfully operate as a source of authority above and independent of the government of the day, broadly, if not necessarily in the greatest detail, reflecting the values of the population as a whole.

It takes a genuinely creative writer to make Ned Dennis the only advocate of such an ideal. Dennis is as he is – as the creative processes of the author's mind made him. In part, he is one of Dickens' almost grotesque characters but in part, he is also a personification of the ideas, beliefs and emotions Dickens saw at play in the political situation of the time.

The tension arising from a state of internal contradiction is perhaps characteristic not only of Dickens but of many of the situations he describes. As Jeremy Tambling has observed:

> '... its singleness (ie of character) cannot, inherently, do justice to a divided subject. Dickens makes character a state of anxiety or desire, which divides it.'[3]

The contradictions embodied in Dennis' character are a reflection of the intractable nature of the subject Dickens wishes us to consider.

In fact, this is not the first time Dickens has a valuable constitutional principle articulated by an unattractive character in disreputable circumstances. In chapter 16 of Nicholas Nickleby, when Nicholas is looking for a job in London he follows up on an advertisement for the post of secretary to Mr Gregsbury, MP and seeks him out in Westminster. On the stairs he finds a deputation waiting to see the MP and is mistakenly admitted with them. Pugstyles, the leader of the deputation formally accuses Gregsbury of failing to vote in Parliament in accordance with various undertakings he had made to the during the election. Gregsbury replies with great politeness but as a response says simply, 'I deny everything'. Pugstyles then asks whether Gregsbury will resign his seat, at which Gregsbury presented a letter he had recently composed, copies of which he intended to send to the press.

In the letter, Gregsbury declares:

> I value that noble independence which is an Englishman's proudest boast and which I fondly have to bequeath to my children untarnished and unsullied. Actuated by no personal motives, but moved only by high and great constitutional considerations which I will not attempt to explain, for they are really beneath the comprehension of those who have not made themselves masters, as I have, of the intricate and arduous study of politics, I would rather keep my seat, and intend doing so.

As appears in his subsequent interview with Nicholas, Gregsbury is a lazy, ignorant MP who would pay his secretary a menial wage. However, the high and great constitutional considerations he refers to are in fact the principles first set out by Edmund Burke in this often-quoted speech to the electors of Bristol in 1774[4], where he said:

> Your representative owes you, not his industry only, but his judgement, and he betrays, instead of serving you, if he sacrifices it to your opinion. ...

> Parliament is not a congress of ambassadors from different and hostile interests ... but a deliberate assembly of one nation ... where not local prejudices ought to guide, but the general good, resulting from general reason of the whole. You choose a member indeed, but when you have chosen him, he is not a member for Bristol, he is a member of Parliament.

The exchange between Gregsbury and his constituent Mr Pugsley appears on the surface to be the kind of ironic writing Dickens commonly produces in situations of this kind, as when the Attorney General in Sydney Carton's trial at the Old Bailey produces certain incriminating lists which, he says, cannot be proved to be in the prisoner's handwriting and therefore are evidence to show how cunning the prisoner was in disguising it, or in the trial of Bardell v Pickwick when Sergeant Buzfuz describes Mr Pickwick's harmless notes to his landlady about chops and tomato sauce as being 'shallow artifices' used to disguise his real purpose of winning Mrs Bardell's affections.

The simple deceits and hypocrisies practised by the Attorney General and Sergeant Buzfuz show up the defects in the system. The irony in the Gregsbury – Pugsley exchange is operating differently. Here the principle on which this discredited political figure is relying is itself an essential element of democratic government. He may be false but the principle is not.

Perhaps Dickens is observing that even the most essential constitutional law does not operate in some ethereal medium but in the world of ordinary men and woman and so is inevitably, as Shakespeare puts it, 'subdued to what it works in, like the dyer's hand'[5], though unlike in the sonnet, where the dye always contaminates the dyer, here some lawyers also corrupt the law they work in. He would appear to be recognising that the institutions of the law, as well as being vital to society, are also essentially imperfect. It is always a complex picture. In the case of Mr Pugsley and his deputation, there is at least a partial remedy in that they are free to support another, perhaps more honest, candidate at the next election.

Gregsbury simply makes use of a constitutional principle to save himself the trouble of active political interventions, and for this reason we regard him as a hypocritical opportunist. This is a simple 'level one' kind of irony. With Vardon and, more importantly, with Dennis, both parties believe what they say. There is in fact no hypocrisy on the constitutional point, which leaves us in a more difficult position. The pairing of Vardon and Dennis, and the unspoken resolution of their differences by the reference back to the supposed benign stability of Elizabeth's reign suggests the value, and also the cost, of maintaining the status quo brought about by a kind of constitutional consensus.

The ancient and still commodious Maypole Inn, with its Elizabethan associations so leisurely described at the opening of the book, not only recalls for readers the settlement of Elizabeth's reign but also itself suffers a domestic upheaval which parallels the later rioting.

The domestic contention within the regime of the Maypole is between father and son. This introduces the parallel theme of the book – the tussle between fathers and sons, which leads us to consider the need for change and reform from an individual viewpoint as well as from the constitutional view outlined in the contention between Vardon and Dennis.

In *A Tale of Two Cities*, written some eighteen years after Barnaby Rudge, Dickens again links together the condition of a building, a regime and the relation between fathers and sons:

> Tellson's Bank by Temple Bar was an old-fashioned place.... It was very small, very dark, very ugly, very incommodious. It was an old-fashioned place, moreover, in the moral attribute that the partners in the House were proud of its smallness, proud of its darkness, proud of its ugliness, proud of its incommodiousness. They were even boastful of its eminence, in those particulars, and were fired by an express conviction that if it were less objectionable, it would be less respectable.... Any one of these partners would have disinherited his son on the question of rebuilding Tellson's. In this respect the House was very much on par with the Country; which did very often disinherit

> its sons for suggesting improvements in laws and customs that had long been highly objectionable, but were only the more respectable. (Book 1 Chapter 1)

Similarly, in *Barnaby Rudge* we find the long unchanged though now partly ruinous condition of a building – the Maypole Inn, with its links to the reign and the regime of Queen Elizabeth – and its current landlord's stubborn opposition to all change and his continuing subjection of his son Joe.

By chapter 30 Joe Willet at the Maypole finds his father becoming more despotic than ever:

> The more young Joe submitted, the more absolute old John became... conducting himself in his small way with as much high and mightiness as the most glorious tyrant that ever had his statue reared in the public ways....old John was impelled to these exercises of authority by the applause and admiration of his Maypole cronies, who...would shake their heads and say Mr Willet was a father of the good old English sort, that there were no new-fangled nations or modern ways with him... .

Significantly, John Willet was '...very anxious to flourish his supremacy before the eyes of Mr Chester', and it is this last flourish of his authority by John, who rebukes Joe for going out without leave to assist Chester to mount his horse, which leads to insurrection in the Maypole's little kingdom.

Joe's rebellion has a powerful impact as it takes place in the symbolic setting of the Maypole and presages the imminent Gordon riots. It is Edward Chester's rejection of his father John Chester, however, together with the revelation that Hugh is also John Chester's son by another mother who had been hanged at Newgate, that carries the theme into a wider consideration of contemporary society.

John Chester has the manners and studied charm of the perfect gentleman but is in fact a ruthless social parasite, long dependent on the money brought to him by his wife whom he regarded as of much lower standing than himself. His wife's father had actually been 'a great lawyer', whose chambers in the Temple now provided John Chester with living accommodation. His wife has died, her money is almost gone and the only means of his own support Chester can now see is to compel his son to marry an heiress whose wealth would ensure a living for himself.

We have seen the concerns of John Willet, Gabriel Vardon and Ned Dennis as representing various elements of law, government and society. Vardon exemplifies kind-heartedness, continuity, stability and loyalty to tried-and-tested institutions, Willet considers himself to stand for the settled state of things, transformed in his person into a kind of pugnacious inertia, while Dennis represents a fossilised form of the doctrine of due process of law.

John Chester apparently upright and charming but in fact ruthlessly selfish, seems to represent something less easy to identify, the relatively small part of society whose informal power and the ascendancy of manners and values can be said to constitute it as a dominant class. He perhaps embodies, though in a far more refined form, the 'Fine Old English Gentleman' described in Dickens' parody published anonymously in *The Examiner* in August 1841.

Edward rejects his father's attempts to marry him to a lady of sufficient wealth to enable his father to continue his polite existence, the corrupt basis of which has now been laid bare. He remains faithful to the comparatively poor Emma Haredale, the home of whose Catholic family has been burned by the rioters.

While Edward repudiates the pretensions of higher society, however, a second, wider social theme is introduced by Hugh, who we learn is John Chester's second, illegitimate son. During the early stages of the rioting, Hugh is shown to have some real ability in organisation and leadership, but the deprivations of his childhood have allowed deep flaws to develop in his character so that his strength and ability are drowned in excesses of drink and destruction.

Hugh becomes an example of what Dickens sees as the inevitable consequence of the follies and cruelties of society, which is that the results will in time rebound on those sections of society in whose name they were perpetrated.

A healing element is introduced by the emotionally more grounded Barnaby who, after meeting his father in the burning ruins of Newgate in chapter 38, is prompted by what Dickens imagines as 'vague hopes of duty and affection' and 'dim memories of children he had played with when a child himself, who had prattled of their fathers', to watch and tend his own father and lead him to safety in the country. On his return to London to find Stagg, he is horrified at the scenes of violence and cruelty, rescues the drunken Hugh and finds him a place to sleep. The next day Hugh, Barnaby and his father are given up to the authorities by Dennis.

At his execution Hugh praises Barnaby's goodness which, he says, is an example of what his own childhood experiences prevented him from ever achieving. Then 'like a savage prophet' he calls down the wrath of God on the gallows to which he is now the 'ripened fruit'. To his own father he leaves only a wish that he would die a violent and unmourned death.

In Joe Willet and his father we have, in the end, reconciliation and social renewal. Dennis, in his own uneasy way, speaks to us of the value of stability and the common law, and in Barnaby and his father, we eventually see the healing properties of human sympathy and harmony with nature. In the fate of Edward and Hugh Chester and their 'perfect gentleman' of a father, however, we find no reconciliation.

Edward rejects his father's schemes, Hugh's childhood shows the terrible cost of social abuse and deprivation and Sir John dies in the duel to which he had pointlessly challenged Geoffrey Haredale.

Hugh's mother had been determined to use Hugh as a means of revenge against Chester. As Gabriel relates to Sir John just before Hugh is hanged, she wished the boy to be brought up 'so that no arts might teach him to be gentle and forgiving' and then:

> ... trusted the God of their tribe to bring father and son together, and so revenge her through her child.

The theme of revenge for individual acts of abuse and social oppression seems to pre-echo the remorseless determination with which, in a *Tale of Two Cities*, Madame Defarge pursues the family of Evremonde:

> 'For other crimes as tyrants and oppressors, I have had this race a long time, doomed to destruction and extermination.....I was brought up among the fisherman of the sea-shore, and that peasant family so injured by the Evremonde brothers...is my family.'[6]

In Hugh's mother's long-burning project for revenge, we might detect – rather than the harmonious notes of the Elizabethan religious settlement – the faintest whiff of distant revolutionary France.

6.
AMERICAN NOTES AND MARTIN CHUZZLEWIT

A Law-Abiding Society?

Dickens finished *Barnaby Rudge* in 1841 and began his next full-scale novel, *Martin Chuzzlewit*, in 1843. In the intervening two and a half years he visited America, planning his visit during the autumn of 1841 and sailing to New York on the Britannia on 4th January 1842.

Six months were spent touring the USA and Canada, Dickens returning in June 1842 and beginning to write his *American Notes* as soon as he got back home. Scott's novels *Heart of Midlothian* and *Waverley* were not yet absent from his mind, as he compared one woman in a Boston asylum to Madge Wildfire and a preacher in the town to Balfour of Burley.

Three themes emerge in the *American Notes* – the manners of American civil society, particularly their commercial practices, the treatment of marginalised people – the poor, the disabled and offenders against the law, and in the southern states the institution of slavery.

Dickens and his wife received an enthusiastic welcome to the USA. In Boston the young men of that city gave them a grand dinner and in New York they were the guests of honour at a great 'Boz Ball' at the Park Theatre, which had been transformed into a ballroom with the walls covered in white muslin and decorated with large medallions representing Dickens' novels, and a portrait of Dickens surmounted by a laurel crown, gripped by an eagle. None of this is mentioned in the *American Notes*, however, Dickens preferring to describe at some length his visit to New York's notorious prison, The Tombs.

Dickens was impressed by the fact that the State of Massachusetts directly supported or assisted various institutions such as the Perkins Institution and Asylum for the Blind, the kind of institution which in England are supported only by private charities. He was particularly impressed by the enlightened and sensitive care given to Laura Bridgeman, who was deaf, blind and unable to speak, and also by a school for boys liable to fall into crime and a juvenile prison designed:

> ... to reclaim the youthful criminal by firm but kind and judicial treatment; to make his prison a place for purification and improvement, not of demoralisation and corruption.

In the courts of that place, Dickens notes, the lawyers wear ordinary clothes, not wigs or gowns, and they sit, rather than stand, to question witnesses. He takes a somewhat mixed view of this, saying that the absence of wigs and gowns might reduce the temptation of lawyers to use insolent bearing and language, but reflects also that 'some artificial barriers against the 'hail fellow, well met deportment of everyday life' might be of value in upholding the law in its necessary functioning. He observes that:

> ... no men know better than the judges of America that on the occasion of any great popular excitement the law is powerless, and cannot, for the moment, assert its own supremacy.

When viewing the Capitol building in Washington later in his tour Dickens again, this time rather strikingly, muses on Justice as a personified figure:

> In one of the ornamented portions of the building there is a figure of Justice; whereunto the Guide Book says, 'the artist at first contemplated

giving more of nudity, but he was warned that public sentiment in this country would not admit of it, and in his caution he has gone, perhaps, into the opposite extreme.' Poor Justice! She has been made to wear much stranger garments than those she pines in, in the Capitol. Let us hope that she has changed her dressmaker since they were fashioned, and that the public sentiment of the country did not cut out the clothes she hides her lovely figure in, just now.

In the New England town of Lowell, Dickens spoke with almost the same sympathetic admiration about the dress and demeanour of some young women workers in the woollen and cotton factories, as well as of their working conditions and accommodation:

> These girls, as I have said, were all well-dressed: and that phrase necessarily includes extreme cleanliness. They had serviceable bonnets, good warm cloaks, and were not above clogs and pattens ... They were healthy in appearance, many of them remarkably so, and had the manners and deportment of young women: not of degraded brutes of burden.

In the town of Hartford, which had a Puritan history and also a charter from Charles II, Dickens took his usual interest in the prison and the asylum, noting that, 'The Insane Asylum is admirably conducted, and so is the Institution for the Deaf and Dumb'. He notes later that, 'In this place, there is the best jail for untried offenders in the world'.

It was in this Asylum that he met a lady who might very well have served as the inspiration for Miss Flight in Bleak House:

> There was one very prim old lady, of smiling and very good-humoured appearance, who came sidling up to me, from the end of a long passage, and with a curtesy of inexpressible condescension, propounded this unaccountable enquiry:
>
> 'Does Pontefract still flourish, Sir, upon the soil of England?'
>
> 'He does, Ma'am', I rejoined.

'When you last saw him he was ...'

'Well, Ma'am, extremely well. He begged me to present his compliments. I never saw him looking better.'

At this the old lady was much delighted. After glancing at me for a moment, as if to make sure I was serious in my respectful air, she sidled back some paces; sidled forward again; made a sudden skip (at which I precipitately retreated a step or two); and said:

'I am an antediluvian, Sir.'

I thought the best thing to say was that I had suspected as much from the first. I therefore said so.

'It is a proud and extremely pleasant thing, Sir, to be an antediluvian,' said the old lady

'I should think it was, Ma'am,' I rejoined.

The old lady kissed her hand, gave another skip, smirked and sidled off down the gallery in the most extraordinary manner, and ambled gracefully into her own chamber.

Dickens' eventual view of the United States, however, was not so benign. What made the most impression was the predominance of an amoral, exploitative type of commercialism in which the power of money seemed untrammelled either by laws or by humane feeling of any kind.

One of the attractions of the USA had been that it presented itself as being free from the oppressive influence of an upper class which in *Barnaby Rudge* had been represented by such figures as Sir John Chester or in *Bleak House* by the Dedlocks and their circle. His disillusionment about America soon became apparent. As early as March 1842 he wrote to his friend Macready that, 'This is not the republic I came to see, ... this is not the republic of my imagination'.

The city of Washington, described as the City of Magnificent Distances, struck Dickens more as the City of Magnificent Intentions, with the Houses of Assembly being set among spacious avenues that began in nothing and led nowhere. Of the proceedings of the Assembly itself, he was damning in his opinion:

> Did I recognise, in this Assembly, a body of men who, by applying themselves in the new world to correct some of the falsehoods and vices of the old, purified the avenues of public life? ... I saw in them the wheels that move the meanest perversion of virtuous Political Machinery that the worst tools ever wrought ... Despicable trickery at elections, underhanded tampering with public officers, cowardly attacks upon opponents ... Here and there, were some drops of its blood and life, but they scarcely coloured the stream of desperate adventurers which set that way for profit and pay.

Dickens notes that this body, ostensibly dedicated to the cause of Liberty, had in the previous week formally tried and condemned one of its citizens simply for asserting that slavery was an infamous traffic. His comments on the slave state of Virginia were just as damning. On visiting Richmond, he observes:

> The soil is exhausted by the system of employing a vast amount of slave labour without strengthening the land. It is now little better than a sandy desert overgrown with trees ... In this district, as in all others where slavery sits brooding (I have often heard this admitted even by its warmest advocates) there is an air of ruin and decay abroad, which is inseparable from the system.

Charles and Catherine returned Virginia to Washington and then travelled south via Baltimore, Harrisburg and the Alleghany mountains to the industrial town of Pittsburgh, Pennsylvania. It was when arranging their passage by riverboat from there to Cincinnati that Dickens found himself dealing with the vagaries of the captain of *The Messenger*, the boat by which they proposed to travel:

> She had been advertised to start positively, every day for a fortnight or so, and had not gone yet, not did her captain seem to have any fixed intention on the subject. But this is the custom: for if the law were to bind down a free and independent citizen to keep his word with the public, what would become of the liberty of the subject? Besides, it is by way of trade.

Dickens makes the point that being able to rely on the public statements and undertakings of others is one of the essential elements of a society and that it is a proper function of the law is to support those who have placed reliance on such public undertakings.

The western part of their tour was from Cincinnati down the Ohio River to its junction with the Mississippi and thence to St Louis. It was at this point that Dickens saw an even more dispiriting landscape at Cairo, one in which he was to use in *Martin Chuzzlewit* as the setting for the 'city' of Eden:

> At length, upon the morning of the third day, we arrived at a spot so much more desolate than any we had yet beheld, that the forlornest places were, in comparison with it, full of interest. At the junction of the two rivers, on ground so flat and low and marshy that at certain seasons of the year it is inundated to the housetops, lies a breeding-place of fever, ague, and death; vaunted in England as a mine of Golden Hope, and speculated in, on the faith of monstrous representations, to many people's ruin. A dismal swamp, upon which the half-built houses rot away: cleared here and there for the space of a few yards and teeming, then, with rank unwholesome vegetation, in whose baleful shade the wretched wanderers who are tempted hither, droop, die and lay their bones... such is this dismal Cairo.

When his *American Notes* first appeared on 19th October 1842, the reaction of the American press was indignant, the *New York Herald* commenting that it was 'the production of a 'coarse, vulgar, impudent and superficial mind'.

He subsequently went on a holiday in Cornwall with Forster, Maclise and the artist Stanfield, walking and visiting tin mines, possibly with a view to finding out about working conditions there.

When moved either by indignation or the need for money, Dickens could write more than one book at a time. After reading a Report of the Children's Employment Commission sent to him by Dr Southwood Smith, Dickens began to write *A Christmas Carol*. The little book was an instant best-seller but brought Dickens less than £300, providing little relief from his money worries. Dickens was further angered by a particularly flagrant unauthorised version of the book, and took the offending publishers, Lee & Haddock, to court. He won, only to suffer a greater loss when the defendants declared themselves bankrupt and Dickens had to bear costs of £700.

The opening of *Martin Chuzzlewit*, with some uncharacteristically laborious jokes, portrays the Chuzzlewits as a long line of pretentious nonentities, ending with their current representative, the architect Pecksniff:

> Of his architectural doings, nothing was clearly known, except that he had never designed or built anything; but it was generally understood that his knowledge of the science was almost awful in its profundity.

As to his moral concerns:

> Some people likened him to a direction post, which is always telling the way to a place, and never goes there.

As a moralising hypocrite, Pecksniff is a great fictional creation, though he and his daughters figure rather strangely in an otherwise idealised landscape. The late sunlight of an autumn evening sheds glory on the little Wiltshire village 'in which its departed youth and freshness seemed to live again'. The declining sun temporarily brightens the running stream and the scanty patches of verdure, the vane on the church steeple gleams and the church windows reflect the evening sky as if the building were 'the hoarding-place of twenty summers, with all their ruddiness and warmth'. The ploughman and the village forge are in action still, but the end of day and the end of year are inevitably approaching and the wind is now banging the inn sign of the Blue Dragon public house so vigorously that before Christmas the dragon, 'reared clean out of its crazy frame'.

The description seems almost a lament, a threnody for a landscape and a rural society which Dickens feels might be passing, while in its midst Pecksniff – at least when the wind eventually lets him into his house – restores himself with the 'smoking dish of ham and eggs,' brought in by his younger daughter and served at a table laden with cream, sugar, tea, toast and ham.

The elegiac nature of the landscape setting affords no consolation for Pecksniff's injustice towards his pupils, such as John Westlock, who has received little of value for the premium of five hundred pounds paid for his pupillage. Even more outrageously, young Martin Chuzzlewit, grandson of the obsessively suspicious old Martin, is dismissed from the Chuzzlewit household for daring to fall in love with his grandfather's young companion Mary Graham.

The general themes of selfishness, and the obsessive suspicion of selfishness, are the ostensible concern of the opening chapters. Old Martin however, portrayed as a travelling recluse, seems suspicious of his own family to a degree so extreme as to be unconvincing, not only at this stage in the book but also in relation to his grand intention to deceive Pecksniff, revealed long afterwards in chapter 52. The Chuzzlewits' and Spottletoes' stupendous 'general council and conference held at Mr Pecksniff's house' in chapter 5 is successful as a celebration of recrimination and selfishness achieving almost pantomime form.

As an exponent of hypocrisy, Pecksniff himself is the master. Old Martin, Anthony Chuzzlewit, Jonas Chuzzlewit and to an extent Young Martin are selfish, but they are straightforwardly selfish and never pretend to be otherwise. Pecksniff combines selfishness with highly developed hypocrisy and thereby becomes the most spectacularly repulsive character in the novel. His two predominating characteristics invariably operate smoothly together, as we see when he and his daughters board the coach for their journey to London in chapter 8:

> When Mr Pecksniff and the two ladies got into the heavy coach at the end of the lane, they found it empty, which was a great comfort, particularly as the outside was quite full and the passengers looked very frosty. For as Mr Pecksniff justly observed – when he and his two daughters had burrowed their feet deep in the straw, wrapped themselves up to the chin and pulled up both windows – it is always satisfactory to feel, in keen weather, that other people are not as warm as you are. And this, he said, was quite natural, and a very beautiful arrangement; not confined to coaches, but extending itself into many social ramifications. 'For' (he observed), 'if everyone were warm and well-fed, we should lose the satisfaction of admiring the fortitude with which certain conditions of men bear cold and hunger. And if we were no better off than anybody else, what would become of the sense of gratitude; which,' said Mr Pecksniff with tears in his eyes, as he shook his fist at a beggar who wanted to get up behind, 'is one of the holiest feelings of our common nature'.

Young Martin has inherited a trace of this family disposition. In the course of his dealings with Tom Pinch, Mark Taplow and Mary Graham he gradually becomes aware of the value of other people's qualities and of his own responsibilities towards them.

In chapter 15 ('The burden whereof is *'Hail, Columbia!'*') Martin and Mark Tapley arrive in New York. Martin's relationship with Mark develops significantly during their travels in the United States. At the town of Watertoast the two reckon up their joint resources and it is clear that Mark's savings amount to considerably more than Martin's cash in hand. Martin says that he will contribute his cash and his professional expertise as an architect and that on this basis they can set up in business as equal partners under the name of Chuzzlewit and Tapley.

'We are no longer master and servant', he announces somewhat condescendingly, 'but friends and partners'. However he speaks, even now, 'in his old way, just as he might have spoken to Tom Pinch'.

Their plot of land at 'Eden' – the 'Cairo' of the American Notes – had been sold to them by a Mr Zephaniah Scadder as part of a well-planned city on the point of successful development, offering good opportunities to Martin as a professional architect. It is actually a disease-ridden swamp lying at the junction of the Ohio and Mississippi rivers, where a few poor settlers are making hopeless attempts at cultivation.

Martin despairs of their situation when they arrive but Mark insists they remain active and optimistic, claiming as usual to welcome adversity as an opportunity to rise above it and 'be jolly'. Martin falls ill and Mark fetches medicine from a neighbour and remains Mark's carer and cheerful companion. When Martin eventually recovers, Mark himself becomes ill and Martin takes the role of carer.

In this somewhat damp crucible, their relationship is changed further, as Mark is led critically to examine his own character:

'Eden was a hard school to learn so hard a lesson in, but there were teachers in the swamp and thicket, and the pestilential air, who had a searching method of their own.'

Martin made a 'solemn resolution' that 'selfishness was in his own breast, and must be rooted out.'

The large-scale fraud which Scadder has practised in issuing a false prospectus about his Eden settlement at Cairo is of course comparable to Tigg Montague's plan in England to set up the Anglo-Bengalee Disinterested Loan and Life Insurance Company with a paid-up capital, which the company secretary David Crimple describes in chapter 27 as 'A figure of two, with as many oughts in it as the printer can get into the same line'. Such practices are, however, regarded somewhat differently in the two countries.

While significant moral progress is taking place in Martin's relationship with Mark, we have, almost in parallel, the visit to the wretched cabin of the violent wanderer Hannibal Chollop:

> Mr Chollop was a man of a roving disposition; and, in any less advanced community might have been mistaken for a violent vagabond. But his fine qualities being appreciated in those regions where his lot was cast, and where he had many kindred spirits to consort with, he may be regarded as having been born under a fortunate star … Preferring … to dwell upon the outskirts of society, and in the more remote towns and cities, he was in the habit of emigrating from place to place, and establishing in each some business – usually a newspaper – which he presently sold; for the most part closing the bargain by challenging, stabbing, pistoling or gouging the new editor before he had quite taken possession of the property.

Chollop claims that he had 'shot a man down' in Illinois:

> 'I shot him down, sir,' pursued Chollop, 'for asserting in the Spartan Portico, a tri-weekly journal, that the ancient Athenians went a-head of the present Locofoco Ticket.'

The precise meaning of this controversial remark is something which, Chollop maintains, it is 'Europian not to know'. When, later in the conversation, Martin fails to display enough enthusiasm for the United States and her institutions, Chollop adopts a menacing tone, asserting:

> 'I have drawn upon A man and fired upon A man for less.'

Mr Chollop holds up the cynical rapacity of Zephaniah Scadder as an example of commendable business practice:

> 'Scadder is a smart man, sir? He is a rising man? He is a man who will come up'ards, right side up, Sir?'

Astoundingly, the impoverished Eden settler who has joined them actually expresses – as far as his enfeebled state will allow – complete agreement with Chollop.

When Captain Kedgick, the landlord of Martin's hotel in Watertoast, thought that Martin had left for Eden, he had confided to Mark the reason that the townspeople had made so much of Martin:

> 'Our people like ex-citement', said the Captain, whispering. 'He ain't like immigrants in general; and he excited 'em along o' this;' he winked and burst into a smothered laugh; 'along o' this. Scadder is a smart man and – and – nobody who goes to Eden ever comes back alive!'

The strange 'levee' that Captain Kedgick claims the townspeople are anxious for him to hold on Martin and Mark's departure suggests a deep communal element. The levee and the subsequent resentment and suspicion shown when they return alive might be compared to what might be imagined in to be the treatment accorded in ancient societies to those selected as sacrificial offerings to the gods – the divinities in this case being those of Fraud and Predatory Economics.

It appears that not only Scadder but pretty well the whole town knows that no one who goes to Eden comes back alive. Under English law at that time, if Scadder, knowing that there was a serious risk of death or serious bodily harm for anyone trying to settle in 'Cairo', nevertheless induces settlers to go there and a settler dies because of the conditions which created the risk, there would be strong grounds for a charge of murder. The case would be particularly strong where it could be shown that Scadder induced the settlers to go there by fraudulently misrepresenting the facts that created the risk.

In the case of *R. v Desmond* in 1868, the judge, Sir James Cockburn, the Lord Chief Justice of England, said:

> 'If a man did an act, more especially if it were an illegal act, although the immediate purpose might not be to take life, yet if it were such that life was necessarily endangered by it, – if a man did such an act, not with the purpose of taking life, but with the knowledge and belief that

life was likely to be sacrificed by it, that was not only murder by the law of England, but by the law of probably every other country.'[1]

The American citizens that Mark and Martin encounter on their way back to Watertoast seem entirely undisturbed by such considerations. On the boat deck, they meet the Honourable Elijah Pogram, a Member of Congress who praises Chollop as, 'a splendid example of our native raw material' and 'a true-born son of this free hemisphere!' Pogram then goes on to describe Martin's disapproval of the activities of Zephaniah Scadder and Hannibal Chollop as 'opposition to our Institutions'. Only the stalwart Mr Bevan, who saves Mark and Martin by sending the money for their journey back, sounds a note of humanity.

Back in England the themes of egotism, suspicion and hypocrisy work themselves out in the interaction of Old Martin, Young Martin, Pecksniff, Jonas and Pinch, with the figure of Jonas introducing a yet darker and deeper note of evil and the possibility that not all can be redeemed.

We are told in chapter 11 that the established firm of Anthony Chuzzlewit and Son, Manchester Warehousemen and so forth, had its premises in a very narrow street somewhere behind the Post Office, close to St Martin's Le Grand. Anthony Chuzzlewit had clearly made his money by hard business practices. When Jonas unfeelingly tells his father, on a cold spring day, not to sit close to the fire as it might burn his clothes into holes, Anthony observes, 'A good lad! ... A prudent lad!', and during the Pecksniffs' visit to Anthony Chuzzlewit's house in Chapter 11, when Jonas makes fun of the old clerk's inability to eat, Anthony:

> Chuckled covertly, as if he said in his sleeve, 'I taught him. I trained him. This is the heir of my upbringing. Sly, cunning and covetous, he'll not squander my money. I hoped for this; I worked for this; it has been the great end and aim of my life'.

Anthony's' cunning and covetousness is no match for the greater scale of cunning and deception practiced by the Anglo-Bengalee. While

Anthony Chuzzlewit is in many ways a Scrooge figure, his son appears to be beyond the redemption that Scrooge is allowed to achieve. Dickens is, however, here describing a social evil of a scope very different from the simple personal dispositions of griping employers or even of their more malignant sons. We now see a newly developing commercial environment which enables fraudulent businesses to materialise from virtually nothing.

We learn in chapter 26 that Tigg has joined with David Crimple, the pawnbroker's assistant whom Martin had dealt with when pawning his watch in chapter 13. Together they had intended, with the little money they had, to open an office and make a show, but then realised that:

> ... if we did it on a sufficiently large scale, we could furnish an office and make a show without any money at all.

In this way Montague Tigg, who appears in chapter four as a down-at-heel parasite attempting to borrow money to pay for his public-house lodgings, emerges in Chapter 27 with jet-black shining hair, clothes in the newest fashion, precious chains and jewels sparkling on his breast and his fingers clogged with brilliant rings as the Chairman of the Anglo-Bengalee Disinterested Loan and Life Assurance Company with, as we have seen, paid-up capital (as the Company Secretary puts it) 'of a figure of two and as many oughts after it as the printer can get into the same line'.

As Montague Tigg confides to Jonas in chapter 27:

> 'B wants a loan, say fifty or a hundred pounds, perhaps more; no matter. B proposes self and two securities. B is accepted. Two securities give a bond, B assures his own life for double the amount, and brings two friends' lives also, just to patronise the office ... ... B pays the highest lawful interest -'
>
> 'That ain't much,' interrupted Jonas.
>
> 'Right! quite right!' retorted Tigg. 'And hard it is upon the part of the law that it should be so confoundedly down upon us unfortunate victims;

> when it takes such amazingly good interest itself from all its clients. But charity begins at home, and justice begins next door. Well! The law being hard upon us, we're not exactly soft upon B; for besides charging B the regular interest we get B's premium, and B's friends' premiums, and we charge B for the bond and, whether we accept him or not, we charge him for 'enquiries' .... and we charge B a trifle for the secretary; and in short, my good fellow, we stick it into B, up hill and down dale, and make a devilish comfortable little property out of him. Ha, ha, ha!'

And as Tigg further explains:

> 'Then ... we grant annuities on the very lowest and most advantageous terms known on the money market: and the old ladies and gentlemen down in the country buy 'em. Ha,ha,ha!'
>
> 'But there's responsibility in that,' said Jonas, looking doubtful.
>
> 'I take it all myself,' said Tigg Montague. Here I am responsible for everything. The only responsible person in the establishment! Ha, ha, ha!' ...
>
> 'Whenever they should chance to fall in heavily, as you very justly observe they may, one of these days, then -' he finished the sentence in so low a whisper that only one disconnected word was audible, and that imperfectly. But it sounded like 'bolt'.

Paradoxically, the relationship between young Martin and Mark Tapley has been transformed in the swampy crucible of Cairo, Illinois, from one of master and servant to one of equality and mutual regard, a relationship that survives on their return to England. The relationship could only change, however, because of Martin's gradual recognition that Mark's indefatigable optimism and loyalty – together with Mr Bevan's kindness – has been the means of saving them both.

We know from Dickens' letters and from the savage attacks on some American institutions in the *American Notes* that Dickens was deeply disillusioned by his visit to the United States. He had seen it as a place relatively free from the corrupt and oppressive elements he knew all too well in England and admired the 'sprit of freedom' which, as the Americans claimed, prevailed in their country. What he actually found there is described in his *American Notes*. The American press' hostile reaction to the *Notes* following their publication in October 1842 would appear to have prompted the savage satire on American culture and business practices which begins in chapter 15 of Martin Chuzzlewit, begun in December of that year.

In England, the activities of the Anglo-Bengalee Insurance Company are, at least theoretically, within the law's hold and Jonah begins to fear that the law can also hold him to account for the murder – as he believes it to be – of his father and of Montague. Even English law, however, is so far powerless to prevent his appalling domestic abuse of Mercy described in chapter 28. With Scott's *Waverley* and his own *Barnaby Rudge* in the background, it seems that Dickens continues to consider how society can cope with antisocial behaviour in legal and even constitutional terms and so it is natural that he should consider how the newer and apparently freer society of America can deal with these problems.

It appears from his *Notes* that he concludes simply having a society that is 'free', in the sense that it is less bound by tradition and not subject to the influence of a monarch and landed aristocracy, offers no real remedy for humankind's rapacious and predatory instincts and in fact allows them further rein. Mark Tapley's later embrace of Mrs Lupin at the Dragon as 'kissing his country' indicates a view that while English society and constitution have many grievous faults, there exist within its social fabric elements which can operate to restrain the crude and predatory behaviour they have witnessed in the United States.

If Dickens has found American society more predatory and more corrupt than his own, to what extent does this experience change Dickens' view of English society? Dickens does not wish to write, and his readers do not wish to read, a book of social criticism or legal theory but his literary creativity is driven as much by moral concern as it is by the fertility of his imagination, and his narrative is frequently shaped by or reflective of social and legal institutions.

Dickens' own sensations on returning to England are not dissimilar from those of young Martin and Mark Tapley on their arrival in Liverpool, and as their story proceeds, we feel that Dickens has set himself to suggest what those intangible factors might be which create the sense of relief and reassurance experienced by both Martin – and Dickens himself – on their return to England.

The scene of Martin and Mark's arrival in England is lyrically described:

> Bright the scene was; fresh, and full of motion; airy, free and sparkling … The distant roar, that swelled up hoarsely from the busy streets, was music to their ears; the lines of people gazing from the wharves, were friends they held dear and the canopy of smoke that overhung the town was brighter and more beautiful than if the richest silks of Persia had been waving in the air.

The street noises were hoarse, but musical. The town was overcast with a canopy of smoke seeming brighter than the silks of Persia. The English scene, with all its faults, was beautiful to the travellers returning from America.

The sense of well-being continued after they disembarked, so that 'in a cheap tavern' they 'regaled upon a smoking steak and certain flowing mugs of beer.' When they looked through the window, 'Even the street was a fairy street, by being half-hidden in an atmosphere of steak and strong, stand-up English beer.' A closer look into this street, however, revealed the passing figure of Pecksniff, now hailed as the celebrated architect of the town's new Grammar School.

Pecksniff's fraudulent piety and selfishness have now expanded to an impressive scale. No longer confined to such trivial deceptions as can be practised in a Wiltshire village, he has become a celebrity and MPs and Mayors acknowledge his greatness. All this has been achieved by the simple expedient of taking Martin's design for a grammar school, adding a few inconsequential details, and submitting the plans as the product of his own master hand.

It is of course Mark who encourages Martin to view this piece of dishonesty with equanimity and to make a start on their journey to London. Despite all that Pecksniff can do the atmosphere of the book remains buoyant. In Salisbury, Tom Pinch has recently been dismissed by Pecksniff after he has overheard Mary Graham confiding to Tom that Pecksniff is forcing his sexual attentions on her, but Tom remains optimistic:

> He had his moments of depression and anxiety, and they were, with good reason, pretty numerous; but still, it was wonderfully pleasant to reflect that he was his own master, and could plan and scheme for himself.

The coach that Tom takes to London to see his sister and his friend John Westlock in chapter 36 is a brave, stylish vehicle:

> It was a charming evening. Mild and bright. And even with the weight upon his mind which arose out of the immensity and uncertainty of London, Tom could not resist the captivating sense of rapid motion through the pleasant air. The four greys skimmed along, as if they liked it quite as well as Tom did; the bugle was in as high spirits as the greys; the coachman chimed in sometimes with his voicer; the wheels hummed cheerfully in unison; the brass work on the harness was an orchestra of little bells; and thus, as they went clinking, jingling, rattling smoothly on, the whole concern ... was one great instrument of music.

The harmony and good feeling of the coach seem to extend to the countryside through which it passes:

> Yoho, past hedges, gates, and trees; past cottages and barns, and people going home from work. Yoho, past donkey-chaises ... Yoho, by churches dropped down by themselves in quiet nooks, with rustic burial grounds about them, where graves are green ... Yoho, past

streams in which cattle cool their feet ... past last year's stacks, cut, slice by slice, away ... Yoho, down the pebbly dip, and through the merry water-splash and up at a canter to the level road again. Yoho! Yoho!

Mrs Lupin from the Dragon had brought Tom's box up to the fingerpost to meet the coach on its way to London. Dickens wonders:

> Had she turned out magnificently as a hostess should, in her own chaise-cart ... and looking lovely?

She has, of course, and she has also handed up a splendid packet of provisions for Tom's journey, which Tom shared with the driver, who in his turn highly appreciated both the provisions and the person of their generous giver. The guard, meanwhile:

> ... sends the glad echoes of his bugle careering down the chimneys of the distant Pecksniff, as if the coach expressed its exultation in the rescue of Tom Pinch.

While the narrative alternates between the fortunes of Tom and his sister, the return of young Martin and Mark Tapley from America and the steadily darkening tale of Jonas Chuzzlewit, the episodes featuring Tom's coach ride and the arrival of Martin and Mark Tapley at the Dragon maintain a thread of optimism and good feeling, as if a kind of supportive benevolence was embodied in the landscape and the country of England itself.

When in chapter 43 the travellers from America finally return to the Dragon, Mark kisses his hostess many times and then asks for a final kiss, Mrs Lupin refuses:

> 'You've had plenty, I'm sure', said the hostess. 'Go along with your foreign manners!'

> 'That ain't foreign, bless you!' cried Mark. 'Native as oysters, that is! One more, because it's native! As a mark of respect for the land we live

in! This don't count as between you and me, you understand', said Mr Tapley, 'I ain't a-kissing you now, you'll observe. I have been among the patriots: I'm a-kissing my country'.

The streets of Liverpool and the landscape over which the Salisbury to London coach travels seem imbued with this supportive benevolence, but in its essence the spirit appears to be located in a particular place, the Dragon Inn, presided over by Mrs Lupin and stalwartly served until recent times by Mark Tapley.

When the scene moved to London, however, a second significant location appears.

Tom, on arrival in London, calls on his friend John Westlock in Furnival's Inn ('two storeys up'), rescues his sister Ruth from her position as governess with an overbearing brass-and-copper founder's family in Camberwell and visits Cherry and Merry Chuzzlewit at Todgers Boarding House.

At the start of chapter 38 Tom, in a London street, unknowingly brushes the sleeve of Mr Nadgett, whom we last saw in chapter 29 'in the darkest box of the coffee room' of the Bull Inn, Hertfordshire, where Lewsome, the man who had sold poison to Jonas, has been lying ill. Later in the chapter Lewsome is questioned by Montague and gives him damning evidence about Jonas' 'secret' which enables Montague essentially to blackmail Jonas into persuading Pecksniff to invest capital into their company.

The following chapter shows Tom and Ruth happily pursuing their domestic affairs, before John Westlock calls to tell Tom that an unknown person wishes to employ him 'as a kind of secretary or librarian'. Westlock takes Tom to see a Mr Fips, of Austin Friars, and Tom asks about the place of his employment. Mr Fips replies:

'Oh the place! The place is the Temple'.

Tom was delighted.

From this point on, references to the Temple provide a kind of leitmotif to the steadily darkening tale of Jonah and Montague's journey to Wiltshire, Jonah's murder of Montague and his eventual detection.

Mr Fips 'of Austin Friars' arranges to meet them 'At the Temple Gate, in Fleet Street,' and leads them 'through sundry lanes and courts to one more quiet and gloomy than the rest'. The door of the chambers 'yielded unwillingly' to reveal rooms where the dust lay thick:

> Dust was the only thing in the place that had any motion about it. When their conductor admitted the light freely, and lifting up the heavy window sash, let in the summer air, he showed the mouldering furniture, discoloured wainscoting and ceiling, rusty stove, and ashy hearth, all in their inert neglect.

Among the disordered furniture some thousands of books lay about the floor, which it was Tom's job to sort, catalogue, and arrange in order.

Despite the dust and disorder, Tom is very far from discouraged. As the next chapter opens, we are told that:

> There was a ghostly air about these uninhabited chambers in the Temple, and attending every circumstance of Tom's employment there, which had a strange charm in it. Every morning when he shut his door in Islington, he turned his face towards an atmosphere of unaccountable fascination, as surely as he turned it to the London smoke; and from that moment it thickened round him all day long, until the time arrived for going home again, and leaving it, like a motionless cloud, behind.

Early one morning on his way to work, accompanied by Ruth, Tom chances to witness Jonas' attempt to flee the country with his wife aboard the Antwerp packet boat. It is foiled by Montague who has been observing him. He asks Tom to give Jonas a letter which has the effect of making Jonas return to the quay and accompany Montague to their office in the City. By a wonderful coincidence, Mrs Gamp is taking the air on the wharf and Montague is treated to a sample of her uniquely freewheeling discourse before Jonah sullenly instructs him to take his wife home.

The journey that Jonah and Montague take in chapter 42 down to Wiltshire to persuade Pecksniff to contribute capital to the company is an ill-omened one. They set out on a 'hot, silent night' and as they leave London on the western road other travellers take shelter from the approaching storm:

> ...drivers watched the weather from the doors or open windows, or made merry within. Everywhere people were disposed to bear each other company rather than sit alone; so that groups of watchful faces seemed to be looking out upon the night and them from every house they passed.

It is as if human society is withdrawing itself from Jonas and Tigg Montague as they set out on their criminal enterprises – Montague intent on defrauding Pecksniff and Jonas intent on the murder of Montague.

After the storm-laden journey of Jonas and Montague to the Dragon, Young Martin's attempt at reconciliation with his grandfather, frustrated by Pecksniff, and Jonas and Montague's successful persuasion of Pecksniff to invest in their company, we return in chapter 45 to Ruth and Tom in London:

> There was a little plot between them, that Tom should always come out of the Temple by one way, and that was past the fountain. Coming through Fountain Court, he was just to glance down the steps leading into Garden Court, and to look once all round him; and if Ruth had come to meet him, there he would see her; not sauntering, you understand (on account of the clerks), but coming briskly up, with the best little laugh on her face that ever played in opposition to the fountain, and beat it all to nothing ... .

The surroundings of the Temple may be rather grim but, Dickens suggests in chapter 45, they may have enough life in them to respond to the cheerful spirit of Ruth as she passes through:

> Whether there was life enough left in the slow vegetation of Fountain Court for the smoky shrubs to have a consciousness of the brightest and purest-hearted little woman in the world, is a question for gardeners and those who are learned in the lives of plants. But, that it was a good thing for that same paved yard to have such a delicate little figure flitting through it; that it passed like a smile from the grimy old houses, and the worn flagstones, and left them darker and sterner than before; there is no sort of doubt. The Temple fountain might have leapt up twenty feet to greet the spring of hopeful maidenhood, that in her person stole on, sparkling, through the dry and dusty channels of the Law.

There is some strange figurative language used to describe the relationship both Tom and Ruth have with the Temple. Tom, on going to his work each morning, turns his face towards 'the London smoke' and at the same time turns towards the 'atmosphere of strange fascination', the 'ghostly air' which the Temple seems to hold for him. This atmosphere 'thickens all day long' – much like the London smoke – until he goes home, leaving the atmosphere of fascination behind 'like a motionless cloud'. There is a suggestion that though this atmosphere thickens, like the London smoke, which in general is a bad thing, it has some indefinable quality of its own, making it desirable and attractive to Tom.

In the same way, when Ruth passes through the Temple the shrubs may be smoky, the houses old and grimy and the paving stones worn, but Dickens suggests that the shrubs may have enough life to be conscious of her innocent and youthful spirit, and they and the fountain itself may respond to it. When Dickens says, 'it passed like a smile from the grimy old houses', the 'it' grammatically refers to the 'delicate little figure' of Ruth, but 'it' appears to pass from the face of the houses as she moves away, as if the houses of the Temple had themselves been smiling while she was near them.

Similarly, we are told the Temple fountain 'might' leap twenty feet – even though it actually didn't – to greet 'the spring of hopeful maidenhood' that 'in her person' stole on, sparkling, through the dry and dusty channels of the law'. Literally, it is the spring of hopeful maidenhood in the person of Ruth who steals on, sparkling, through the law's dry channels, but really we imagine that it is the fountain that is sparkling and running through channels, as this is an action more watery than human.

It is this kind of fertile ambiguity that leads us to feel there is a sympathetic connection between Ruth and Tom on one hand and the Temple on the other, in which both sides play an active part and suggest that the smoky, grimy, dry and dusty appearance of the Temple may conceal the possibility that there is something within that ancient institution that is capable of appealing to Tom and responding to the goodness in Ruth.

In much the same way, out in the country, the Dragon Inn and the landscape of Wiltshire are supportive of Tom when, during his 'Yoho' journey to London after being dismissed, the coach guard's bugle sends notes of cheerful defiance down Pecksniff's chimney and when Mrs Lupin drives out from the Dragon to present Tom with her sustaining packet of food and money for his journey.

The Temple fountain itself, after (perhaps) leaping twenty feet in the air to mark Ruth's passage through the Temple, continues sympathetically to support and celebrate the growing love between her and John Westlock.

Quite often, John Westlock happens by the merest coincidence to join them, and when Tom takes one of Ruth's arms and suggests that John take the other:

> Merrily the fountain leapt and danced, and merrily the smiling dimples twinkled and expanded even more, until they broke into a laugh against the basin's rim, and vanished.

John invites them to dine with him in his chambers in Furnival's Inn, where we know Dickens himself had had rooms both before and after his marriage. It was not an Inn of Court but an Inn of Chancery, a similarly ancient institution principally for the use of attorneys rather than barristers and at that time coming towards the end of its functioning life. For Dickens it was essentially part of the same world:

> There are snug chambers in those Inns where the bachelors live, and, for the desolate fellows they pretend to be, it is quite surprising how they get on. John was very pathetic on the subject of his dreary life … but he really seemed to make himself pretty comfortable. The rooms were the perfection of neatness and convenience at any rate…

They have a beautiful dinner. After Tom and Ruth leave, John begins a sketch of Ruth from memory – and:

> Busily the Temple fountain murmured in the moonlight.

There follow the darkest chapters in the book, with a particularly bizarre combination of comedy and wickedness as Jonas employs Mrs Gamp to keep old Mr Chuffey from telling what he believes he knows about his father's death.

After Jonas' dramatically unseen murder of Montague we find him:

> Still listening! To every sound. He had listened ever since, and it had not come yet. The exposure of the Assurance office; the flight of Crimple and Bellamy with the plunder, and among the rest, as he feared, with his own bill, which he had not found in the pocket of the murdered man, and which with Mr Pecksniff's money had probably been remitted to one or other of those trusty friends for safe deposit at the banker's; his immense losses, and the peril of still being called to account as a partner in the broken firm; all these things rose in his mind at one time and always, but he could not contemplate them. He was aware of their presence, and of the rage, discomfiture and despair they brought

along with them; but he thought ... of one thing only. When would they find the body in the wood?

Just as Jonas believes himself freed from his father's murder by Mr Chuffey's evidence, he is arrested for Montague's murder by Slyme, now a law officer, on the evidence of the watchful and persistent Nadgett.

It is quite likely that Jonas' elaborate precautions – the pretence of staying asleep in his own home on the relevant night, the disguise, the complicated routes taken to and from the place of the murder – would have foiled any ordinary attempt at detection with the resources available at the time. Jonas' downfall comes in fact not by the action of any law enforcement agency but by the singular persistence of Mr Nadgett, the man whom the Anglo-Bengalee had kept 'at a pound a week' to make enquiries about potential customers:

> It was no virtue or merit in Nadgett that he transacted all his Anglo-Bengalee business secretly and in the closest confidence, for he was born to be a secret. He was a short, dried-up, withered old man who seemed to have secreted his very blood; for nobody would have given him credit for possession of six ounces of it in his whole body. How he lived was a secret; where his lived was a secret; and even what he was, was a secret.

As so often in Dickens, it is one or more of the civilian characters who follows up the detection of the wrongdoer, obtaining the assistance of the police in making the final arrest, which reflects the organisation of policing at this time. Until the formation of the Metropolitan Police in 1829, the system was not so much policing by consent as policing on request. Historically it had always been for the victim of a crime to detect, pursue and apprehend the malefactor and bring him or her before a magistrate who would decide, on the evidence then offered, whether or not to commit the accused for trial, either at the Old Bailey or at the local Assizes where they were held.

Between 1829 and 1839 the Bow Street Runners operated alongside the new Metropolitan Police but were effectually merged with them by 1839, some five years before *Martin Chuzzlewit* was written. The part taken by Nadgett in detecting the crime and accusing Jonas reflects the fact the event took place in this period of transition. Nadgett accuses Jonas and relates the process of his detection but the officer – in the unlikely person of Slyme – now feel that they should be directing the proceedings and urge Nadgett to complete his story so that they can arrest and remove Jonas.

In one sense, Nadgett's pursuit of Jonas is simply something required in order to arrive at an emotionally satisfying ending to a commercial novel. In Dickens' hands, however, Nadgett becomes a more powerful figure than that. Nadgett's strange lack of identity and continual self-effacement never diminish the man in our eyes. His lack of personality gives him an impersonal force. The fact that he has no actual connection with Jonas or his father, and would receive no payment for revealing the crime, gives his persistence and watchfulness the status of an anonymous avenging power belonging to society as a whole. It is perhaps not surprising that he seems to Jonas to be 'another of the phantom forms of this terrific Truth'.

For the reader, as for Martin and Mark, the continued sense of reassurance and relief they felt on their return to England from America seems to be sustained by the action of Nadgett, as if it represents something through which a society can achieve justice by and of itself.

In the following chapter we are on happier ground. The general 'setting right' of the narrative takes place in the Temple, a location about which we have had intimations that somewhere beneath its worn and grim appearance there might exist at least the capacity to respond to and to sustain goodness. In preparation for the showdown with Pecksniff and the final revelation of all his hypocrisy, Old Martin enlists the help of Mark and Mrs Lupin from the Dragon Inn.

Old Martin asks Mark, Young Martin, Ruth and Tom Pinch, Mary Graham, Mrs Lupin and Pecksniff to meet him in Tom's working room. When Pecksniff arrives, he addresses Old Martin as 'my venerable friend' and abuses Young Martin and the others as swarming vermin. Old Martin dramatically reveals that he knows his true nature and strikes him down with his stick. He then recognises Young Martin as his grandson and blesses his projected marriage to Mary. The presence of Mark and Mrs Lupin brings something of the benevolent influence of the Dragon to be added to the atmosphere of the Temple to create a place where justice – in human if not in legal terms – can be administered.

The setting-right done, the leitmotif returns for the last time as chapter 53 begins:

> Brilliantly the Temple fountain sparkled in the sun.

7.
DAVID COPPERFIELD

An Unlikely Partnership

> 'Whether I shall turn out to be the hero of my own life, or whether that station will be held by anybody else, these pages must show.'

The opening chapters of *David Copperfield* certainly reflect some events in Dickens' early life. While the important early themes continue throughout the book other characters evolve as protagonists in their own right, of whose careers David becomes merely an observer.

Early in 1847 Charles Wentworth Dilke, who had been a friend of Charles' father John Dickens, had a conversation with John Forster. He described to Forster an occasion some 25 years before when he had been walking with John Dickens near the Strand in London and had seen the young Dickens working in the window of a building, fastening and labelling pots of blacking alongside another employee. The warehouse had been Warren's Blacking warehouse, where Charles had worked from the age of twelve for just over a year. The firm had at this point moved from the rat-infested premises by the river at Hungerford Stairs to Chandos Street just north of the Strand.

Dilke had recognised the boy as his friend's son and had tipped him half a crown. Charles had bowed in thanks, but in fact the incident had been excruciatingly embarrassing for him and probably for his father too, who soon afterwards was persuaded to take Charles from the warehouse and send him to school.

Dickens was a successful novelist of thirty-five before he learnt that his friend Forster had been told of this incident. It was then to him as if a curtain had suddenly been raised on a shameful experience of his childhood. Shortly afterwards he made a start in writing an autobiography and passed some pages dealing with this period – the 'autobiographical fragment' – to his biographer John Forster, who records the part dealing with his early warehouse experience in chapter two of his *Life of Dickens*.

It is this passage which we find repeated, in parts practically word for word, when David begins his work at Murdstone and Grinby's bottle warehouse in chapter 51 of *David Copperfield*, which he began to write in 1849:

> No words can express the secret agony of my soul as I sank into this companionship; compared these everyday associated with those of my happier childhood – not to say Traddles, Steerforth and the rest as well.

As we have seen, it seems that at the age of 36 Dickens still wished to relate something of his experiences at that period of his childhood, both as a 'little labouring hind' in Warren's blacking warehouse and also as a regular visitor to his father in a debtors' prison.

He had made use of this experience earlier in his writing career. In *The Pickwick Papers* the narrative of Mr Pickwick's experiences in the Fleet Prison was almost certainly inspired by the almost daily visits the twelve-year-old Charles made to his father in the Marshalsea, but the intervening thirteen years between *Pickwick* and *Copperfield* seem to have modified the effect of the memory.

When Dickens describes Mr Micawber's imprisonment for debt in the King's Bench Prison in chapter 11 of *Copperfield* he is certainly recalling his father's time in the Marshalsea. Now, however, Dickens is making somewhat different use of his early experience.

The Pickwick and the Micawber episodes both have strong elements of comedy mixed with the grim reality of prison life, but in the Pickwick episodes, despite their ironic humour, the bleak and pessimistic tone predominates. For Mr Pickwick there seems nothing, in the end, to redeem the cruel and largely pointless imprisonment in the Fleet Prison and the story of the Chancery Prisoner confined there until his death confirms the system's oppressive power. In *David Copperfield*, the ironies of the prison life are somewhat gentler. The drawing up of a petition about imprisonment for debt, though probably ineffectual, is a positive activity and Micawber himself actually applies for and gains his release under 'The Act' – at that time, the Insolvent Debtors Act of 1813. Just as significantly, Mr Micawber is later able to view both his past and his prospective imprisonment in the King's Bench Prison as an experience through which he can, in a sense, pay his debt to society and so recover his self-esteem.

Four characters from David's childhood and early youth continue to affect his life. Two are Traddles and Steerforth, schoolfellows from his Salem House days. The others are the Yarmouth figures of Mr Peggoty and Little Emily. Steerforth's seduction of Emily and Mr Peggoty's search for her is followed mostly at one remove. Traddles re-emerges as a focus of interest in chapter 25, when David sets up as an independent young man in London, and he plays a key part in that most dramatic episode, the exposure and downfall of Uriah Heep.

Heep shares with Sampson Brass in *The Old Curiosity Shop* and Vholes in *Bleak House*, the right to be regarded as one of Dickens' entirely repulsive legal characters. David first meets Uriah in chapter 15 when he is a pupil at Dr Strong's school in Canterbury, boarding at the house of Mr Wickfield, his aunt's solicitor.

While David is waiting for Mr Wickfield and his aunt he sees Uriah copying from a paper on a frame suspended above his desk:

It made me uncomfortable to observe that, every now and then, his sleepless eyes would come below the writing, like two red suns, and stealthily stare at me for I dare say a whole minute at a time, during which his pen went, or pretended to go, as cleverly as ever.

The next evening when David, seeing Uriah reading *Tidd's Practice*, says he supposes that Uriah is quite a great lawyer, the clerk makes his well-known profession of humility:

> 'Me, Master Copperfield?' said Uriah. 'Oh no. I'm a very 'umble person. ... I am well aware that I am the 'umblest person going,' said Uriah Heep, modestly, 'be the other where he may.' My mother is likewise a very 'umble person. We live in a numble abode...'

Uriah, who 'had a way of writhing when he wanted to express enthusiasm, which was very ugly', goes on to declare the excellence of Mr Wickfield and the sweetness of David's Aunt Trotwood, who in turn admires Agnes. When David agreed that everyone must admire Agnes, Uriah 'writhed himself quite off his stool in the excitement of his feelings' and then made preparations for going home.

The defeat of Uriah Heep's plans to take advantage of the weak Mr Wickfield, gain control of his employer's firm and secure Agnes, as his wife, and the story of David's marriage to Dora and later to Agnes form the principal narrative threads in the second half of the book. While the fortunes of David and Dora, and David and Agnes, have their own conventional energy, the more intense drama is the defeat of Uriah's schemes by Traddles and Micawber acting in concert with David, Aunt Trot and Mr Dick.

We have a sense of the strength and determination of Heep and his mother when David meets him in the street in Canterbury, and Uriah reminds him of his promise to take tea with them. Once the Heeps have got David into their 'umble abode' they proceed to examine him:

> Presently they began to talk about aunts, and I told them about mine, and about fathers and mothers, and I told them about mine; and then

> Mrs Heep began to talk about fathers-in-law, and I began to tell them about mine, but stopped, because my aunt had advised me to observe a silence on the subject. A tender young cork, however, would have no more chance against a pair of corkscrews, or a tender young tooth against a pair of dentists, or a shuttlecock against two battledores, than I did against Uriah and Mrs Heep.

The unexpected appearance of Mr Micawber passing the open street door prepares us for this beguiling man's further involvement.

At this point, Dickens decides to make use of his experience as a Doctors' Commons law reporter sharing a box with Tom Charlton, a relative of his aunt Charlton, and we are led into one of the odder byways of the legal system.

Mr Spenlow, the proctor dealing with Aunt Trotwood's will at the Doctors' Commons, has a vacancy for an articled clerk and Betsy Trotwood believes this might suit her nephew.

Dickens' familiarity with the place has been shown earlier, in chapter 10 of *The Pickwick Papers* when Mr Jingle goes there to obtain a marriage licence and asks Sam Weller the way:

> 'Do you know – what's a-name – Doctors' Commons?'
>
> 'Paul's church-yard, sir; low archway on the carriage side, bookseller's at one corner, hot-el on the other, and two porters in the middle as touts for licences.'
>
> 'Touts for licences?'
>
> 'Touts for licences,' replied Sam. 'Two coves in white aprons – touches their hats ven you walk in – 'Licence, Sir, Licence!' Queer sorts, them, and their mas'rs, too, Sir – Old Bailey Proctors – and no mistake.'
>
> 'What do they do?'
>
> 'Do! You, sir!'

It is through this same low archway that David walks towards his new career in chapter 23. Steerforth had described the Doctors' Commons during their journey from Yarmouth earlier in the chapter as a place:

> '... where they play all kinds of tricks with obsolete old monsters of Acts of Parliament ... a very pleasant and profitable little affair of private theatricals, presented to an uncommonly select audience.'

David now sees one of the Courts in action:

> ... a large dull room not unlike a chapel to my thinking, on the left hand. The upper part of the room was fenced off from the rest; and there, on the two sides of a raised platform of the horseshoe form, sitting on easy old fashioned dining-room chairs, were sundry gentlemen in red gowns and grey wigs, who I found to be the Doctors aforesaid. Blinking over a little desk like a pulpit-desk, in the curve of the horseshoe, was an old gentleman who, if I had seen him in an aviary, I should certainly have taken for an owl, but who I learned was the presiding judge. In the space within the horseshoe, lower than these, that is to say, about the level of the floor, were sundry other gentlemen of Mr Spenlow's rank, and dressed like him in black gowns with white fur upon them, sitting at a long green table. ... Altogether, I have never, on any occasion, made one at such a cosey, dosey, old-fashioned, time-forgotten sleepy-headed little family party in all my life.

Apart from their Admiralty work, the Doctors' Commons courts were ecclesiastical courts, the official sanction available to them being excommunication – exclusion from receiving the sacraments of the Church for a stated period. The sanction that people usually felt most keenly however was the award of costs against them, including the considerable cost of copying the vast quantities of evidence that seemed to be required. As David observes:

> 'We had an adjourned cause in the Consistory that day – about excommunicating a baker who had been objecting in a vestry to a paving rate

> – and as the evidence was just twice the length of *Robinson Crusoe*
> ... it was rather late in the day before we finished. However we got him excommunicated for six weeks and sentenced in no end of costs... .'

David's misgivings about the Doctors' Commons as an institution seem to be substantiated by the revelation, following Mr Spenlow's sudden death in chapter 38, that his affairs had not been what they seemed. Not only had he himself made no will, but also he had very much less property to dispose of than had been generally believed. The Commons would not have afforded David much of a career in fact, as after the establishment of secular courts for probate and divorce in 1857, some seven years after the book was written, they lost their monopoly of audience in those matters and lost their monopoly in Admiralty cases two years later. Work for the proctors and doctors faded away, and the Commons' library and buildings were sold in the early 1860s.

By chapter 24 David is established as an independent young man studying at the Doctors' Commons and living in a 'compact' set of chambers at the top of the Adelphi building in Buckingham Street, close to the Thames. The chapter brings together the two key figures of Traddles and Heep in a more dramatic narrative.

During a drunken evening with Steerforth at the theatre, David is recognised by Agnes, who asks him to call next day. She is staying at the house of Mr Waterbrook, a colleague of her father. Agnes explains that her father is now completely in Uriah's power and that she must avoid offending him.

Mrs Waterbrook asks David to dinner the next day, and there are several legal figures present. Among them are Uriah Heep himself and a man he recognises as an old friend from the past – Traddles, the boy who had saved David from being too badly humiliated by Mr Creakle's 'HE BITES' placard. David remembers him as being 'very honourable' and at the same time the 'merriest and most miserable of boys' who after his frequent canings comforted himself by drawing skeletons all over his slate. The grown-up Traddles is believed to be based on Dickens' great friend Thomas Talfourd, who became a distinguished barrister and subsequently a Sergeant at Law and who worked on legislation to improve copyright for authors.

David asks his host about his old friend:

> 'Traddles,' said Mr Waterbrook, 'is a young man reading for the bar. Yes. He is quite a good fellow – nobody's enemy but his own.'
>
> 'Is he his own enemy?' I asked.
>
> 'Well,' returned Mr Waterbrook, pursing his mouth and playing with his watchchain in a comfortable, prosperous sort of way, 'I should say he is one of those men who stand in their own light. Yes. I should say he would never, for example, be worth five hundred pound. Traddles was recommended to me by a professional friend. Yes. Oh yes. He has a kind of talent, for drawing briefs and stating a case in writing, quite plainly. I am able to throw something in Traddles' way, in the course of a year, something – for him considerable. Yes. Oh yes.'

That evening David manages to exchange addresses with Traddles and to introduce him to Agnes, while Uriah never ceases to hover near them. When they leave, David, aware of the need not to offend Uriah, invites him back to his rooms for coffee. Uriah eventually says it is too late to return to his hotel and David has to endure the intrusive intimacy of his presence in his rooms overnight.

The house in Camden Town where David later pays a visit to Traddles somehow reminds him of Mr Micawber, and the resemblance is not misleading. Micawber turns out to have rented the house somehow, is letting out rooms and so becomes Traddles' landlord.

David goes up to Traddles' room:

> It was at the front of the house, and extremely neat, though sparsely furnished. It was his only room, I saw; for there was a sofa-bedstead in it, and his blacking-brushes and blacking were among his books – on the top shelf, behind a dictionary. His table was covered with papers, and he was hard at work in an old coat. I looked at nothing, that I know

of, but I saw everything, even to the prospect of a church on his china inkstand.

David and his old friend happily reminisce about their days at Salem House – Mr Mell, Creakle, suppers in the dorm with David telling stories. As Mr Waterbrook said, Traddles was now reading for the Bar, in an unpretentious, economical way. He had entered himself as a law student, just as Dickens had done in the Middle Temple twenty years earlier, and like Dickens, Traddles had paid his £100 fee on entering. He had felt this expense to be a 'great pull', but had paid it and he now supported himself by doing such legal work as Mr Waterbrook and others could send him.

Micawber appears in due course and David's friendship with him is resumed. He invites Traddles and the Micawbers to dine with him in his rooms in Buckingham Street but when Mrs Crupp, who 'does' for David, becomes ill, Mr Micawber saves the situation by using the gridiron – normally only used for David's morning rasher – to cook the mutton before the fire.

The occasion becomes a kind of indoor picnic:

> Traddles cut the mutton into slices; Mr Micawber (who could do anything of this sort to perfection) covered them with pepper, mustard, salt and cayenne; I put them on the gridiron, turned them with a fork and took them off, under Mr Micawber's direction; and Mrs Micawber heated, and continually stirred some mushroom ketchup in a little saucepan. When we had slices enough done to begin upon, we fell-to, with our sleeves tucked up at the wrists, more slices spluttering on the fire, our attention being divided between the mutton on our plates and the mutton then preparing.

> With the novelty of this cookery, the excellence of it, the frequent starting up to look after it, the frequent sitting down to dispose of it as the crisp slices came off the gridiron hot and hot, the being so flushed with the fire, so amused ... we reduced the leg of mutton to the bone. Traddles laughed heartily, almost the whole time, as he ate and

worked. Indeed we all did, all at once; and I dare say there was never a greater success.

The joy and informality of their shared feast and happy interaction – informal but very effective – in a sense prefigures the informal but very effective way in which three of those people will later act together in chapter 52 in the exposure of Uriah.

The happy atmosphere is unexpectedly frozen by the appearance of Steerforth's servant Littimer inquiring about his master. Littimer is vague about Steerforth's activities but believes he might possibly be at Yarmouth. Amazingly, he then assumes a butler-like role in serving supper to the rest of the embarrassed company.

The effect is the collision of two worlds – the cold, formal world of Steerforth's almost aristocratic family imposing itself on the open friendliness and human warmth of David's guests – almost comparable to the effect of a wandering iceberg on the peaceful ecosystem of a tropical bay. The handle of the hastily concealed fork which sticks out of the bosom of Mr Micawber's coat 'almost as if he had stabbed himself' is at once comic and slightly sinister, suggesting the harm which the values of Steerforth's world might at some point inflict, or cause him to inflict, upon himself.

The companionship created by the joys of the impromptu mutton supper nevertheless continues. It even survives Micawber's failure to satisfy a bill of debt of 'twenty-three pounds, four shillings and fivepence-halfpenny' to which Traddles had put his name, together with another debt of 'eighteen, six, two'. Eight chapters later, when he is about to leave London and take up a job with Uriah Heep's firm in Canterbury, Micawber with great formality declares he is about to 'perform an act of justice' and presents Traddles with 'a document which accomplishes the desired object' – an IOU for the exact amount of the two debts.

David now takes advantage of a visit to see about the letting of his aunt's cottage in Dover to visit Agnes Wickfield in Canterbury. Uriah, now a partner in the firm is installed in Mr Wickfield's house and David finds him

> ...in possession of a new plaster-smelling office, built out into the garden; looking extraordinarily mean, in the midst of a quantity of books and papers.

Mr Micawber is working at Heep's old desk. He is 'dressed in a legal-looking suit of black, and loomed, burly and large, in that small office'. He makes it clear that he feels he is in a position of trust and confidence as far as the affairs of the firm were concerned, but David feels uneasy about his, 'as if his new duties were a misfit'.

Uriah's mother is also living in the house and keeps close watch on Agnes. The pair were 'like two great bats hanging over the house'. Uriah confides in David that he had been taught humbleness in a charity school, as indeed had his own parents, and David begins to understand the cause of the fierce resentment underlying all Uriah Heep's actions.

In one sense this is another of Dickens' warnings – poverty creates criminality, and cruelty and oppression can rebound upon society. Dickens' other product of a charity school was the self-centred, talentless young criminal Noah Claypole in *Oliver Twist*.

This single glimpse into Uriah's background allows us to see him as a living individual rather than a more generalised hate figure, though sympathy for him must be fleeting. As in the theatrical melodramas he so much enjoys, Dickens now works up our indignation against him to an even higher pitch with Heep's suggestion to Dr Strong that his wife Annie has an improper relationship with her cousin Charles Maldon, resulting in David's striking him on the cheek and Heep's unctuous 'forgiveness' of David. After the section about David's married life with his child-wife Dora in chapter 44, we anticipate Heep's exposure in chapter 51 with a certain keenness of expectation.

In chapter 49 David receives a gloomy letter from Mr Micawber asking to meet him in London. Micawber describes himself as a 'fallen tower' and suggests that, as his feet would naturally tend towards the

King's Bench Prison, they meet at the south wall of that institution. Traddles, too, has an anxious letter from Mrs Micawber describing her husband's disturbed condition and asking Traddles to meet him in London and reason with him.

They find Micawber standing before the wall of the debtors' prison, looking at the spikes on the top of the wall 'with a sentimental expression, as if they were the interlacing boughs of trees that had shaded him in his youth'. He had changed his black legal suit for his usual clothes, though he wore these 'with not quite the same air'.

The cause of his deep distress is eventually revealed. He has found that Uriah Heep is carrying out fraudulent actions and Uriah requires him at the least to acquiesce in them. He is faced with a dilemma. If he goes along with this, he is countenancing dishonesty. If he does not, he betrays his position of trust, loses his job and he and his family are reduced to penury. At last, 'puffing and sobbing, to that degree that he was like a man fighting with cold water,' he declares that he will expose Heep.

In almost Kantian terms, Micawber is a person of goodwill carrying out the categorical imperative of following the course of moral duty irrespective of any personal or other considerations[i].

In chapter 36, after he had failed to redeem a bill of exchange to which Traddles had put his name, Micawber had solemnly given Traddles a carefully calculated IOU for the same amount, observing that 'I am happy to recover my moral dignity, and to know that I can once more walk erect before my fellow man!' Micawber can do this because for him the promise of payment, however remote, is a real promise. He has acknowledged the debt and not defaulted on it. In his own eyes, he has thereby upheld the principles of honest dealing essential to the proper relationship between members of a society.

At the time, David humorously observed that 'I am persuaded not only that this was quite the same to Mr Micawber as paying the money, but that Traddles himself hardly knew the difference until he had had time to think about it'. Dickens often deals with sad situations by 'throwing a little humour over them', but on occasions, the veneer of humour also covers significant truths.

Micawber's honesty and courage in deciding to expose Heep's fraud allowed us to see his actions in something of a new light. His musings at the sight of the King's Bench Prison walls carry the matter a little further. If he is actually not able to pay the debt, then for him imprisonment in the debtors' prison is the only path open to him. He doesn't deny the debt, he acknowledges that he cannot pay and uncomplainingly accepts the consequence of imprisonment as his only way of paying his dues to society. By his imprisonment he has upheld the principle. Within the prison therefore, even while his children play their games in the shadows cast by the spikes on top of the wall, he can 'walk erect before his fellow man'.

In the case of a man of Micawber's integrity, this would seem to provide a justification for debtors' prison, though the moral kaleidoscope Dickens constructs for us will turn the equation in a somewhat different direction in *Little Dorrit*.

The 'explosion' in the affairs of Wickfield and Heep at which David assists, takes place in chapter 52.

David, Traddles, Aunt Trotwood and Mr Dick stay at a Canterbury hotel the previous night and by arrangement with Micawber call at Mr Wickfield's house the following morning. They find Micawber at his desk, the office ruler sticking from his waistcoat like the fork did during the last part of the mutton supper in David's rooms in chapter 28.

They are sonorously announced by Micawber. As they enter, ostensibly to see Agnes, Uriah:

> ... frowned to that degree that he almost closed his small eyes, while the hurried raising of his grisly hand to his chin betrayed some trepidation or surprise ... a moment later he was as fawning and as humble as ever.

Dickens has long prepared his readers for this scene, creating a character that inspires repulsion and fear in equal measure and who gains not only power over his weak employer but also more complete and intimate power over Agnes as her future husband.

What is significant is that there has been no formal legal process involved in what Mr Micawber, using the words of a former occasion, might have called 'an act of justice'. The forces operating to this end are mixed. The key actor is Mr Micawber himself who, beneath his outward cover of loquacity and financial ineptitude is a man of integrity and courage. The other actors are Traddles and Mr Dick. David, though the central character in the book, really does no more than observe the drama for us.

Agnes now enters the room and Traddles slips off unnoticed, returning with Mrs Heep. When Uriah tells him to go, Micawber says he chooses not to leave the room. At this unexpected defiance:

> Uriah's cheeks lost their colour, and an unwholesome paleness, still faintly tinged with red, overspread them. He looked at Mr Micawber with his whole face breathing short and quick in every feature.

When with a sickly smile, Uriah says he will have to 'get rid of' Micawber, Micawber launches undeterred into a dramatic denouncement of his employer:

> 'If there is a scoundrel on the face of the earth,' said Mr Micawber, breaking out with the utmost vehemence, 'with whom I have already talked too much, that scoundrel's name is HEEP!"

Uriah fell back, as if he had been struck or stung.

Dickens is enjoying himself. Uriah, faced with this resolute attack, accuses his opponents of conspiracy and threatens Aunt Trotwood, Agnes and Micawber with ruin or exposure by using against them the power he has acquired by working for the firm:

> 'I have got some of you under the harrow. Think twice before it goes over you.'

However, Heep doesn't know quite what to make of Traddles, who by the simple but effective legal device of obtaining a power of attorney from Mr Wickfield is able to act vigorously on his behalf when Micawber reveals the various frauds Uriah has committed against his former master.

Micawber, true to form, does this in a long grandiloquent letter which at first appears to consist of unsubstantiated claims. Uriah tries to snatch the letter and Micawber strikes him with a severe blow on the knuckles with the ruler which had been sticking out of his coat since the opening of the scene and which, unlike the fork handle which was a symbol of embarrassment during the mutton supper, has now become an effective weapon. Micawber continues reading the letter which becomes detailed and contains specific allegations, one of which is that Heep has forged Mr Wickfield's signature on a document authorising the withdrawal of 'twelve six fourteen, two and nine, ie £12,614. 2s 9d in old money and referring to a half-burnt pocketbook in which Heep had been practising Wickfield's signature. Micawber had also that morning removed the firm's books from the safe and placed them in the entirely legitimate hands of Traddles as Mr Wickfield's attorney.

The anguished Mrs Heep, meanwhile, now adds to Uriah's pains by calling on him to 'be 'umble and make terms', saying how she had said to the gentleman, 'when he told me upstairs that it had come to light, that I would answer for your being 'umble and making amends'.

Micawber continues with his litany of accusations, ending with the claim that Uriah had abused his power over Mr Wickfield to induce him to relinquish his share of the partnership and the ownership of the house in return for an annuity to be paid by Heep.

Uriah, faced with this formidable array of accusations and evidence finally appears to capitulate. He sits down by his mother and asks what they want him to do. Traddles says that first the deed of relinquishment must be handed over to him. Uriah interrupts:

'Suppose I haven't got it?'

'But you have,' said Traddles: 'therefore, you know, we won't suppose so.'

And I can't help avowing that this was the first occasion on which I really did justice to the clear head, and the plain, patient, practical good sense of my old schoolfellow.

Traddles continues, stating that Uriah must repay all the money he has fraudulently obtained 'down to the last farthing', and that all the books and papers of the Partnership must remain in their possession. When Uriah refuses to do this, Traddles simply asks David to 'go round to the Guildhall and bring a couple of officers', observing that:

> 'Though the law may be longer in righting us, and may not right us as completely as you can, there can be no doubt of its punishing you.'

Mrs Heep then breaks out into fresh tearful expostulation saying, 'It was all true,' and begging Uriah to do what was wanted. Seeing nothing else open to him Uriah tells his mother to fetch the deed in question and is himself confined in the custody of Traddles, and later of Mr Dick, until he has made restitution of his ill-gotten gains. Uriah then leaves the room muttering threats of revenge and resenting that the 'umbleness' he had been taught at his charity school did not after all serve him as well as he had been led to expect.

The scene is at once comic and dramatic – Micawber's letter begins with his usual ineffective grandiloquence; he performs mock-heroic fencing strokes with his ruler and Mrs Heep's tearful interventions provide a counterpoint to the accumulating allegations against her son.

Micawber's letter had produced accurate and damning facts. The ruler itself has struck a painful blow. Traddles' observations are few but telling and he has taken the decisive step of arming himself with Mr Wickfield's power of attorney, so he can act vigorously on his behalf. As a result of these measures, Heep is actually defeated and restitution is achieved – even Aunt Trotwood's lost investments are recovered.

The method of achieving Heep's downfall is significant. Importantly, there is no legal process. Heep is defeated by the collaboration of three carefully delineated characters – Mr Micawber, Traddles and Mr Dick.

On the face of it, these three are an unlikely combination. Micawber seems an improvident n'er-do-well, drifting with his ever-increasing family on the fringes of insolvency, Mr Dick, though respected and stalwartly supported by Aunt Trotwood, is a self-confessed simpleton and Traddles, though a member of the Inner Temple, is merely a law student maintaining himself by journeyman-work for other lawyers.

Micawber, though commercially inept, is not only scrupulously honest but brave enough to risk destitution in order to expose injustice. Mr Dick, who becomes Heep's custodian after his dramatic exposure is, despite the appearance of mental muddle, someone of deep moral perception and practical common sense.

These two would not have been able to defeat Heep alone. Nor would Traddles alone. Justice can only be achieved, Dickens is telling us, by certain factors working together. The honesty and courage hidden within Micawber and the simple directness and compassion of Mr Dick are clearly necessary, but they are not sufficient. They almost certainly would not have succeeded without the practical lawyerly skills of Tom Traddles 'of the Inner Temple', as Micawber is always pleased to describe him.

Micawber, Traddles and David have formed a strong companionable relationship in what was essentially a love-feast of the mutton supper in chapter 28. Here in chapter 52 we might even see the contrast between the joyful picnic atmosphere of the early stage of that occasion and the formal, slightly embarrassing part regulated by Littimer as comparable to the contrast between the informal but effective drama of Heep's exposure with the cooler and probably less effectual proceedings of the official alternative.

With regard to the first two of these three men, what makes them effective is simply their personal qualities, though of course such qualities, when possessed by numbers of people, become social forces. The third member of the trio, Traddles, whom we have seen as a 'very honourable' schoolboy rebuking Steerforth for humiliating Mr Mells, also brings another vital factor – access to the learning and traditions of the law, which here leads him to obtain and use his power of attorney and to contain and handle Uriah Heep's blustering threats to such good effect.

Traddles' virtues as a lawyer do not make him characteristic of the legal system as a whole. To Mr Waterbrooke he is essentially a minor, fringe figure, as we see in chapter 25. Traddles, he says, is 'quite a good fellow' and has a kind of talent for drawing briefs but will 'stand in his own light' and never be worth five hundred pounds.

Nevertheless, Traddles sees the law incontrovertibly as his own profession. In chapter 49 when David and Traddles were attempting to find the cause of Micawber's discomfiture, Traddles said he hoped he was not in low spirits because he had conceived a dislike for the law,

'... for I am a lawyer myself, you know.'

In the scene of final resolution in chapter 52 of *Martin Chuzzlewit* the necessary characters come together to achieve an 'act of justice' without formal legal proceedings but with what Dickens seems to see as the supportive symbolic presence of the Temple surroundings. In *David Copperfield* the proceedings are again informal but a member of the Inner Temple plays a key role, representing the law in its benign aspect.

While the formal functioning of the law may be clumsy, ineffectual and in some cases corrupt and oppressive, the law itself, as Dickens constantly reminds us, is an essential social institution. For it to function effectively two things are necessary, the first being the active participation of good people.

Dickens sees this intangible social factor, which supports and encourages people such as Mr Micawber to honour and perform their social obligations, as being an element of the law itself. It is different from the legal machinery currently set up to enforce it, but it cannot long exist without institutional support of some kind. The current legal system to some extent expresses and supports this social factor

– Traddles suggestion that David could 'go round to the Guildhall and bring a couple of officers' certainly has its effect on Uriah – but does so very imperfectly.

It is the absence of precisely this social factor that Dickens in *Martin Chuzzlewit* perceives among the inhabitants of the city of Watertoast who appear silently to collude in sending Martin and Mark Tapley to their virtually certain deaths in the nonexistent 'city' of Cairo. Dickens sees the same lawless indifference manifested in the more everyday context in the casual approach of the Mississippi steamboat captain to keeping to his publicly scheduled times of departure.

The second essential factor is the specialised learning of the law itself, here of course supplied by Traddles. Dickens' feelings in this instance reflect the famous observation of the seventeenth century legal commentator Sir Matthew Hale referred to earlier, that men are not born common lawyers.[2]

As noted earlier, one can see this second factor symbolically present in the resolution scene in *Martin Chuzzlewit* by its location of the Temple itself. In the early novel *Oliver Twist*, the presence in chapters 14 and 41 of Mr Grimwig anticipates this mode of legal reference. The aptly named Grimwig makes the harsh, judgemental assessment of Oliver in contrast to Brownlow's humane understanding. He had been 'bred to the law' but had left it, finding it a distasteful profession. When eventually presented with compelling evidence of Oliver's honesty, Grimwig:

> ...lifted up his head, and converting one of the hind legs of his chair into a pivot, described three distinct circles with the assistance of his stick and the table: sitting in it all the time.

Following Heep's exposure, Micawber is so joyful in being reunited with his wife that he declares he now welcomes poverty, homelessness and misery – prospects which David sees to be anything but welcome to the rest of the family. The situation is saved when Aunt Trotwood proposes to assist the Micawbers to emigrate to Australia, in company of the reunited Mr Peggotty and Emily. Micawber himself, true to form, makes comically impracticable preparations for life in Australia, but keeps entirely competent and exact accounts of the money advanced to him.

After the death of Dora, David goes with 'indisciplined heart' through his long solitary journey across Europe to come to terms with his grief. When he returns, the man whose career he – and we as readers – become interested in is that of Traddles.

On first landing in London on a wintry autumn evening, David sees 'more fog and mud in a minute' than he had seen in a year; fog and mud which seem somehow about to filter through from the ending of this book to the opening scene of the next – *Bleak House*.

David has heard that Traddles now has chambers in Gray's Inn. He goes to the Gray's Inn coffee house, which adjoins the Inn and in fact forms part of it, and asks the waiter where Mr Traddles chambers are. The waiter unhesitatingly says, 'Holborn Court, sir. Number two,' though he is unable to say anything of Mr Traddles' reputation. A more senior waiter, however, indicates that he has no knowledge of Traddles whatsoever.

As Dickens looks round the comfortable coffee house it seems to him to reflect the condition of the legal profession itself:

> As I followed the chief waiter with my eyes, I could not help thinking that the garden in which he (Traddles) had gradually blown to be the flower he was, was an arduous place to rise in. It had such a prescriptive, stiff-necked, long-established, solemn, elderly air. I glanced about the room, which had its sanded floor sanded, no doubt, in exactly the same manner as when the chief waiter was a boy – if he ever was a boy, which seemed improbable; and at the shining tables, where I saw myself reflected, in unruffled depths of old mahogany; and at the lamps, without a flaw in their trimming or cleaning; and at the comfortable green curtains, with their pure brass rods, snugly enclosing the boxes, and at the two large coal fires, brightly burning; and at the rows

of decanters, burly as with the consciousness of pipes of expensive old port-wine below...

When David calls on Traddles at his chambers 'up a crazy stair' in Holborn Court, there is a slight hesitation before he is admitted to where a breathless Traddles is sitting at a table. After their joyful greeting, Traddles calls his new wife Sophy from her place of concealment behind a window-curtain. They had been married on the strength of Traddles' growing reputation in the profession after he had delivered his argument on the case of *Doe Dem. Jipes v Wigzell*. David sees that Traddles and Sophy – together with Sophy's five sisters – are living in chambers which, as Traddles says, is quite unprofessional:

> We have put to sea in a cock-boat, but we are quite prepared to rough it.

Strictly speaking, it is irregular for Traddles to occupy his chambers with his family. It's a joyful household, full of fun and very skilfully making the most of the accommodation available. It is very different from the established legal world suggested by Dickens' view of the Gray's Inn coffee house with the unruffled depths of its shining mahogany tables, lamps without a flaw in their trimming and cleaning and comfortable green curtains.

After his experience of having his dinner in the Gray's Inn coffee house David had reflected that:

> ... both England, and the law, appeared to be very difficult to take by storm.

The impact of this concluding sentence is sudden and surprising, moving us from a calm review of the atmosphere of the Gray's Inn establishment to thoughts, literally, of taking not just the law but England itself 'by storm' – of revolution, in fact.

The obstacles which Dickens sees in his musings in the coffee room are in fact those faced by Traddles. Traddles himself, who had 'put to sea in a cock-boat' with his little family, living up a crazy stair in Gray's Inn and winning the approbation of his colleagues by the strength of his legal arguments, does not appear to be taking anything by storm. Yet Dickens suggests that a transformation of this scale might be the effect of the success at the Bar of Traddles and people like him.

The figure of Traddles is widely believed to have been modelled on Dickens' friend Thomas Noon Talfourd, a barrister who was for a time MP for Reading, who had pressed for copyright legislation and became a distinguished judge. By the end of the book, of course, Traddles has achieved success at the Bar.

At this point, Dickens has Traddles operating on the fringe of the profession but is gradually becoming recognised by it. David pursues his career as a writer and uses Traddles' chambers as an address. On one visit there Traddles, who confesses that he still sometimes draws skeletons, and recently left one – wearing a wig – on the ledge of a desk in one of the back rows of the King's Bench court, has received a letter from old Creakle, their schoolmaster, who is now a magistrate and invites Traddles to visit a model prison. Two of the 'model' prisoners are Heep and Littimer.

Our last picture of Traddles is of him working in his chambers – he has moved from Gray's Inn to the Temple, Dickens' own Inn of Court. He has:

> ... a busy aspect, and his hair (where he is not bald) made more rebellious than ever by constant friction with his lawyer's wig.

suggesting that, while he wears his wig just like any other lawyer, his character remains as of old and has not been smoothed down to the self-satisfied conformity of the Gray's Inn coffee room.

The two friends reminisce:

> 'But those were capital days, too, in Holborn Court! Were they not?'

> 'When she told you that you would be as judge? But it was not the talk of the town then!

'At all events,' says Traddles, 'If I ever am one -'

'Which, you know, you will be'.

'Well, my dear Copperfield, when I am one, I shall tell the story, as I said I would.'

They walk back to Traddles' house, which is one of the large houses that Traddles and Sophy had admired in their early days and in which there is now room for all Sophy's sisters, now married, and other relations too. Traddles, hospitable as ever, is clearly prospering and the prospect of a judgeship, that high honour of professional recognition, is a real one.

Lastly, we hear from the returned Mr Peggoty how the emigrants to Australia have prospered and how Mr Micawber has finally demonstrated the truth of his honest intentions by paying off, in many small remittances, every obligation he had incurred in England, even Traddles' bill of exchange, and is now a revered Magistrate in Port Middlebay.

The High Court of Chancery sitting in Lincoln's Inn Hall

8.
BLEAK HOUSE

A Troubled Dream of the Law

Dickens began writing *Bleak House* in the autumn of 1851. It had been an eventful year for him. Following the success of *David Copperfield*, he was relatively well off and he took a 45-year lease of Tavistock House, an eighteen-roomed dwelling in Tavistock Square, Bloomsbury. Sadder events of the year were the death of his father following a painful operation in March and the death of his baby daughter Dora in April.

In an article for his magazine *Household Words* towards the end of 1851 Dickens showed his continuing concern about the squalid and demoralising conditions of the London poor, particularly their children. In a speech to the Metropolitan Sanitary Association in May of that year Dickens, in an attempt to bring about decisive action, had warned that pestilence could be carried by winds from infamous slums such as the so-called Rookeries of St Giles to the fashionable quarters of London. In June, his friend Inspector Field of the recently established Metropolitan Police had taken him on a night visit to the St Giles area, around Denmark Street and Old Compton Street, described in Chapter 22 of the book and about twenty minutes' walk from Lincoln's Inn where the book opens.

In his earlier works, Dickens had been moved to write by awareness of a specific social abuse – in *Oliver Twist* the drastic effect of the 1832

New Poor Law, in *Nicholas Nickleby* the scandal of the cheap Yorkshire schools. In *Bleak House*, his concern is again with legal matters, this time focussed on a specific part of the law, the High Court of Chancery. As with earlier works, the scope of the book extends considerably beyond the initial subject of concern. This time it is on an even larger scale, though without losing the integrity of its original theme.

In the 1850s the inordinate delays and expense of the Court of Chancery had been regarded as a scandal for many years and they had been debated in The Times for several months before Dickens began to write *Bleak House*. The strength of his indignation at the injustices of its system shows powerfully in the great organ-tones of the book's opening chapter:

> London. Michaelmas term lately over and the Lord Chancellor sitting in Lincoln's Inn Hall...
>
> Fog everywhere. Fog up the river, where it flows among green aits and meadows, fog down the river, where it flows defiled among tiers of shipping ... Fog on the Essex Marshes, fog on the Kentish Heights. Fog creeping into the cabooses of collier-brigs; fog lying out on the yards, and covering in the rigging of great ships ...
>
> The raw afternoon is rawest, and the fog densest, and the muddy streets are muddiest, near that leaden-headed old obstruction ... Temple Bar. And hard by Temple Bar, in Lincoln's Inn Hall, in the very heart of the fog, sits the Lord High Chancellor in his High Court of Chancery.
>
> Never can there come fog too thick, never can there come mire and mud too deep, to assort with the groping and floundering condition which this High Court of Chancery, most pestilent of hoary sinners, holds this day, in the sight of heaven and earth.
>
> On such an afternoon, if ever, the Lord High Chancellor ought to be sitting here – as here he is – with a foggy glory round his head, softly fenced in with crimson cloth and curtains, addressed by a large

> advocate with great whiskers ... and an interminable brief, and outwardly directing his contemplation to the lantern in the roof, where he can see nothing but fog.

Towards the end of his previous book, when describing David Copperfield's return to England from his travels on the Continent, Dickens already seems to regard mud and fog as characteristic of England:

> I landed in London on a wintry autumn evening. It was dark and raining, and I saw more fog and mud in a minute than I had seen in a year.

In *Bleak House*, the fog and mud pervade the precincts of the Court of Chancery and of course provide a powerful metaphor for the condition of the Court and its procedures.

Dickens is here focussing on a particular part of the legal system. The Chancery Court of that time dealt mainly with wills and trusts, as its successor Chancery Division still does, applying a kind of law which had developed in a different way from the common law systems of civil and criminal law which featured in Dickens' earlier novels.

As Dickens faithfully depicts in *Bleak House*, the Chancery Court frequently sat during the legal vacation in the Hall of Lincoln's Inn, reflecting the fact that Lincoln's Inn was, and still is, the Inn of Court most closely associated with chancery practice.

The book's opening certainly had its effect on a solicitor of that time, one William Challenor. After reading the first monthly number in March 1852 he sent Dickens a copy of a pamphlet he had written a couple of years earlier, entitled *The Court Of Chancery: its Inherent Defects*. The pamphlet contains actual examples of injustice from Challenor's own experience, including the one which Dickens presents as that of Mr Gridley, the man from Shropshire, a Chancery suitor driven to despair and almost madness by the legal system which was supposed to serve him.

Gridley describes his own case in chapter 15. His father, a farmer, made a will. Mr Gridley was the executor. By the will, the farm and stock were left to his mother for life and on her death everything was to come to Mr Gridley except a legacy of £300 to go to his brother. At that point, Mr Gridley and some other relations raised the question of whether the brother had already had part of the value of this legacy in board, lodgings and other things. To settle this question the brother filed a bill in Chancery (the fatal step!). Gridley had to be a party to the case and seventeen other defendants, all relations, were added. The Master in Chancery then said he was not satisfied that Gridley was in fact his father's son, about which there was no dispute whatever, and this took two years to sort out before the case came to court. Then it was found there needed to be another defendant, so the whole case had to be begun again. The costs at that time were three times the actual legacy. They had to continue with the case, however, which ended only when the costs had increased to more than the value of the farm itself. When, after protesting in the court itself, he seems violent to his solicitor, Mr Gridley is put in prison.

It is something of an irony that although indifference to hardship, stubborn complacency and a desire to make money allowed the Chancery court to continue largely unreformed until Dickens' time, the system which produced these grotesquely unfair results had arisen through an early effort to improve access to justice.

From the thirteenth century, the common law courts operated a system of writs, issued by Royal authority, commanding individuals to come to court and justify specific actions they were alleged to have taken. The court was able to give relief in all cases which clearly fell within the provisions of an existing writ. The difficulty was of course that there is an almost infinite number of ways in which people can suffer a serious wrong, and the number of available writs was limited.

Subjects had the theoretical right to petition the King to use his residuary power to do justice in cases where the common law was unable to do so. Such cases were usually delegated to the Lord Chancellor of the day who kept the Great Seal of England, the essential means of authenticating documents and giving them the force of a royal command.

Chancellors were therefore free, where the common law could not provide a remedy, to inquire fully into the facts surrounding the claim and to make a judgement according to conscience. What subsequently became the Chancellor's Court was often referred to as a 'court of conscience'. By the early seventeenth century the then Chancellor, Lord Ellesmere, was able to explain the role of the Chancery Court by saying:

> Men's actions are so diverse and infinite that it is impossible to make a general law which may aptly meet with every particular and not fail in some circumstances. The office of the chancellor is to correct men's consciences for frauds, breaches of trust, wrongs, oppressions of whatever nature soever they may be, and to soften and mollify the extremity of the law.[1]

This power of the Chancery Court, coupled with the initial simplicity of its procedure, made the court extremely popular with litigants but the resulting increase in cases overloaded the system and exposed weaknesses in the court's functioning. Ironically, the attempt to bring simplicity and fairness into the law created, over the following two centuries, far more difficulties than it solved.

By the end of the eighteenth century the court, with the Chancellor as its single judge, did not have the capacity to deal with volume of work that had been created. Some reforms took place and Lord Eldon, Chancellor from 1801 to 1827, was regarded as having high judicial standards but as they were achieved only through slow and protracted proceedings the problems continued.

These seven centuries of development had created the institution which Dickens saw operating before him when he began to write *Bleak House* in 1851.

Within the fog-bound precincts of Lincoln's Inn and the surrounding streets, Dickens creates an other-worldly landscape. In chapter four, where Mr Kenge presents the youthful Ada and Richard, who are wards in the Jarndyce case, to the Lord Chancellor, we see the system operating at its best – the Chancellor has taken off his robes and questions the young people kindly and shrewdly before making the Order for them to live with John Jarndyce. Once outside the Chancellor's room, however, the atmosphere changes. They begin to feel 'like the children in the wood' and encounter Miss Flite, the genteel deluded victim of the chancery system, who may owe something of her origin to the 'very prim old lady of smiling and good-humoured appearance' whom Dickens met when visiting the mental asylum in Hartford, Connecticut, during his American tour, and who claimed to be 'an antediluvian' and unaccountably asked, 'Does Pontefract still flourish, Sir, upon the soil of England?'[2]

Miss Flite immediately recognises Ada and Richard as 'the wards in Jarndyce' and seems to have the quality of a fairy godmother by appearing to see into a future which remains unrevealed:

> It is a good omen for youth, hope and beauty when they find themselves in this place, and don't know what's to come of it.

For Miss Flite, the Great Seal of England, which, as we have seen, had been since early mediaeval times not only the symbol but the actual source of the Chancellor's authority and lay with the Mace on the table before him in court, had taken on a mystical significance:

> I expect a judgement. Shortly. On the day of Judgement. I have discovered that the sixth seal mentioned in the Revelations is the Great Seal. It has been open a long time! Pray accept my blessing.

In chapter 5 Esther, Ada and Richard go for a morning walk from their lodgings with Mrs Jellaby, but in the fog unexpectedly encounter Richard, who observes that they 'can't get out of Chancery'. They meet Miss Flite again, who takes them to her lodgings which are 'close by' and indeed seem to exist in Chancery's strange continuum:

> Slipping us out at a little side gate, the old lady stopped most unexpectedly in a narrow back street, part of some courts and lanes immediately outside the wall of the Inn, and said, 'This is my lodging. Pray walk up!'

Her lodgings are above the shop run by Krook, the drunken illiterate dealer in rags, bones and paper who claims to be the Chancellor's alter ego. Among the jumble of articles displayed are bottles of all sorts, including wine, ink and, significantly, blacking bottles, together with old legal documents and law books. The shop had:

> ... the air of being in a legal neighbourhood and of being, as it were, a dirty hanger-on and disowned relation of the law.

When Esther and John Jarndyce go to visit Miss Flight in chapter 14 Krook, who had been drinking as usual, declares, 'You know I am the Chancellor,' and suggests that it would be strange if he did not, as Chancellor, know something about Jarndyce and Jarndyce. He runs through the names of Miss Flite's caged birds which their owner does not care to utter:

> 'Hope, Joy, Youth, Peace, Rest, Life, Dust, Ashes, Waste, Want, Ruin, Despair, Madness, Death, Cunning, Folly, Words, Wigs, Rags, Sheepskin, Plunder, Precedent, Jargon, Gammon and Spinach,'

which he then somewhat confusedly describes as being all cooped up together by 'my noble and learned brother'.

By chapter 24 Richard, after tiring of medicine and the law, is trying the army as a profession. Before going to join his regiment at Holyhead he feels he must look in at the Chancery court where the Jarndyce case, through which he still believes he will inherit 'a fortune', is being considered. Esther, Ada and John Jarndyce realise that Richard is becoming ensnared by the delusory hope of success in the case and is beginning to mistrust his unfailingly upright guardian. Esther is sickened by the leisurely, ceremonious nature of proceedings which cause so much suffering and wretchedness:

'To see everything going so smoothly, and to think of the roughness of the suitors' lives and deaths; to see all that full dress and ceremony and to think of the waste, and want, and beggared misery it represented; to consider that, while the sickness of hope deferred was raging in so many hearts, this polite show went calmly on from day to day, and year to year, in good order and composure; to behold the Lord Chancellor, and the whole array of practitioners before him, looking at one another was a bitter jest, was held in universal horror, contempt and indignation ... '

Later, in chapter 34, Miss Flite describes its strange attraction:

'There's a dreadful attraction in the place ... But, my dear, I have been there many years, and I have noticed. It's the Mace and Seal upon the table.'

'What could they do, did she think?' I mildly asked her.

'Draw,' returned Miss Flite. 'Draw people on, my dear. Draw peace out of them. Sense out of them. Good looks out of them. Good qualities out of them. I have felt them even drawing my rest away in the night. Cold and glittering devils!'

Mr Pell, the Debtors' Relief Court attorney in *Pickwick Papers,* holds the Great Seal in almost the same superstitious awe. Relating a certainly imaginary occasion on which he dined with the Lord Chancellor he describes:

'The Great Seal on a dumb waiter at his right hand, and a man in a bag-wig and a suit of armour guarding the Mace with a drawn sword and silk stockings – which is perpetually done, gentlemen, night and day...'

The effect of Esther's factual description and rational sympathy alongside the semi-mystical tone created by Miss Flite and the drunken

Krook is extremely powerful, and continues throughout the book as other characters are introduced.

Despite his indignation at these enormities, Dickens cannot confine himself to simple condemnation. In *The Pickwick Papers* he had created Mr Pickwick as a kind of heroic innocent, in effect hurling himself at the legal system and bouncing off it again, remaining unhurt but also leaving the system unshaken, with Dodson and Fogg as brazen – and as unequivocally condemned – as ever. In *Bleak House* Dickens cannot propose easy solutions but seeks to widen the question by introducing the character of Harold Skimpole.

Skimpole appears at Bleak House in chapter 6 as a friend and to a great extent a dependant of John Jarndyce, who thinks of him as a charming child-adult. He had been trained as a doctor and had served a German prince, but as 'he had always been a mere child in point of weights and measures' he could never get the prescriptions right. Skimpole tells Esther that:

> ... He must confess to two of the oddest infirmities in the world; one was, that he had no idea of time; the other, that he had no idea of money. In consequence of which, he never kept an appointment, never could transact any business, and never knew the value of anything!

Though the young, clear-eyed Esther at first finds him enchanting, she soon 'feels confused when she tries to reconcile anything Skimpole says with what she believes about the duties and accountabilities of life'. Her misgivings are quickly confirmed when the maid appears, saying that Mr Skimpole's has been 'took' and Richard has asked her to come to his room. He is not in fact ill, as Esther first thinks. He has been arrested for debt, and the debt-collector from an establishment called 'Coavinses' was in the room with him. Skimpole's childlike innocence does not prevent him from realising that at that point he would be unwise to ask his friend John Jarndyce for more money, as he had asked him for similar help very recently. He now addresses Esther and Richard:

> I have an epicure-like feeling that I would prefer a novelty in help; that I would rather ... develop generosity on a new soil, and in a new form of flower.

With this he persuades Richard to give him ten pounds and Esther to part with what are in effect her life savings of just over fifteen pounds in order to pay off his debts and so avoid confinement in Coavinses as a preliminary to debtor's prison.

Skimpole plays a very minor part in *Bleak House*, but he is far from a minor character. He is a constant presence in the book, playing no significant part in the plot – Mr Vholes could no doubt have found some other way to gain Richard as a client – but he appears in eight chapters.

Skimpole next appears in chapter 15 during John Jarndyce and Esther's visit to Miss Flite in London. Skimpole had not been well and had consulted his doctor. He explains that, following the treatment, if he had had 'those bits of metal or thin paper to which mankind attached so much importance' he would have paid the doctor. As he had not had them, he had:

> ... substituted the will for the deed. Very well! If he really meant it – if his will was genuine and real: which it was – it appeared to him that it was the same as coin, and cancelled the obligation.

In chapter 36 of *David Copperfield* there a similar exchange between Mr Micawber and Tommy Traddles, where Micawber gives Traddles an IOU to replace a bill which he had been unable to honour:

> 'I beg to hand my friend Traddles my IOU for forty-one, ten, eleven and a half, and I am happy to recover my moral dignity and to know that I can once more walk erect before my fellow-man.'
>
> With this introduction (which greatly affected him), Mr Micawber placed his IOU in the hands of Traddles and wished him well in every relation of life. I am persuaded, not only was this quite the same to Mr

> Micawber as paying the money, but that Traddles himself hardly knew the difference until he had had time to think about it.

In economic terms the two cases are almost indistinguishable. In moral terms they are entirely different. Skimpole never keeps any account of money, or record of his debts. His 'will' to pay the money may be 'genuine and real' but it is essentially meaningless because it never engages with reality. Micawber on the other hand keeps scrupulous accounts and is entirely serious in his intention to repay, even though he is unlikely to be able to do so.

Skimpole happily goes on to give another example of his economic behaviour, when he fails to pay his butcher for spring lamb, explaining to him that he 'really did mean' to pay the money even if he did not pay it.

Jarndyce then moves the matter from a moral question to a specifically legal one. He asks whether the butcher had taken legal proceedings, which reminds Skimpole that Coavinses' debt-collector is in his house at that very moment. He is not the same debt collector as originally apprehended Skimpole, however. As Skimpole explains, the original man had 'been arrested by the Great Bailiff' and would 'never do violence to the sunshine any more'.

He then relates, while unconcernedly playing chords on the piano, that the debt-collector's children are left without either father or mother.

At this point Jarndyce clearly feels there is something wrong, not only in the children's fate but also in Skimpole's indifference to their fate and to the whole question of his indebtedness and the man employed to deal with it:

> 'I don't like this, Skimpole,' he said, thoughtfully.
>
> Mr Skimpole, who had quite forgotten the subject, looked up, surprised.
>
> 'The man was necessary,' pursued my guardian, walking backwards and forwards ... and rubbing his hair up from the back as if a high east wind had blown it into that form.

> 'If we make such men necessary by our own faults and follies, or by our want of worldly knowledge, or by our misfortunes, we must not revenge ourselves upon them. There was no harm in his trade. He maintained his children. One would like to know more about this.'

They enquire at Coavinses and a boy tells them the man's name, Neckett, and his address in Bell Yard, which still exists off Fleet Street, between Chancery Lane and the present Law Courts. They visit Neckett's children and find that their landlady, Mrs Blinder, has allowed them to stay in their lodgings despite the fact that Neckett was 'not liked in the Yard' because of his occupation.

> 'He was punctual and diligent,' observed Mrs Blinder, repeating the compliment made by the boy at Coavinses. 'He did what he had to, Sir,' said Mrs Blinder, unconsciously fixing Mr Skimpole with her eye, 'and it's something in this world even to do that.'

The ironically named Mrs Blinder cannot know anything of Skimpole's character but might be supposed to 'see' his moral shortcomings even though she is 'unconscious' of them.

Mr Skimpole continues to appear at various points in the book, each time telling the same story of financial irresponsibility. In chapter 18, on the way to Mr Boythorn's place in Lincolnshire with John Jarndyce, Ada and Esther, Skimpole 'explains' that his landlord had taken his furniture into possession but as it was only hired it didn't matter – how it is better for him to 'flit from rosewood to mahogany' rather than commit to owning any piece of furniture.

In chapter 43 John Jarndyce, Esther and Ada visit Skimpole at his home at the Polygon in London to ask him not to borrow any more money from Richard. The whole house is dilapidated but Skimpole's accommodation displays a particularly odd mixture of neglect and extravagance:

> It was dingy enough, and not at all clean, but furnished with an odd kind of shabby luxury, with a large footstool, a sofa, and plenty of cushions

> ... a piano, books, drawing materials, music ... a broken pane of glass in one of the dirty windows was papered and wafered over ... a little plate of hothouse nectarines on etc. the table, and another of grapes ...

The grapes, Skimpole explains, had been supplied by 'some amiable gardener' who, when told that it was not worth waiting for his money, had simply gone away.

Later in the chapter, Skimpole returns to his old theme. He had hired some armchairs and had worn them out. The owner, described by Skimpole's daughter as 'that bad man', objected to them being worn. 'I reasoned with him, and pointed out his mistake.'

Skimpole's part in the plot of *Bleak House* is very slight. He is involved when Jo is sheltering at Bleak House in chapter 31 and, when asked his advice as a medical man, recommends that they 'had better turn him out ...get rid of him', and actually persuades Jo to leave the house. It is also Skimpole who, as we learn in chapter 37, effectively seals Richard's fate by introducing him, for a payment of five pounds, to the predatory solicitor Vholes. Dickens could very easily have arranged these plot developments in other ways, and the actions tell us more about Skimpole than they function as steps in the narrative.

Skimpole's recurring appearance actually constitutes here, as so often in Dickens' work, the critical leitmotif which the author wishes to set against his withering condemnation of the Chancery Court. The perceptive Esther finds it difficult to reconcile anything Skimpole says or does with what she describes as 'the duties and accountabilities of life'. Skimpole, of course, has no sense of obligation whatsoever with regard to such duties or accountabilities. He is an irresponsible, self-absorbed parasite who damages anyone with whom he has contact and his recurring appearance in the novel raises the question of what sanctions society can have for dealing with people of this kind.

Skimpole is always seen through Esther's shrewd but sympathetic eyes and so presented to us nearly as objectively as possible. Just as something needs to be done about the iniquities of chancery, so something needs to be done about Skimpole. The reluctant accommodation which the good-hearted Mrs Blinder makes when she allows Neckett's children to stay, implicitly recognises the man's value to society. We know the legal system is inefficient and to a significant degree corrupt, but within it must lie the means of effectively enforcing accountability between citizens. The widely disliked but honest and diligent Neckett is the best means we appear to have of dealing with people who seek to evade their civil responsibilities.

While Skimpole and his conscience-free, parasitic ways shows the need for a legal system which supports and enforces the due performance of the 'duties and responsibilities of life', the actual legal practitioners in *Bleak House* give us little if any confidence in the system's ability to do so.

The most presentable lawyer is Mr Kenge of Carboy and Kenge, John Jarndyce's solicitors who have offices in Lincoln's Inn.

Mr Kenge, as his soubriquet of 'Conversation Kenge' suggests, is the civilised face of Chancery. He first appears on his visit to Esther at Miss Barbary's when she is about twelve, and he is clearly privy to the fact of Esther's parentage. Later, following Miss Barbary's death, Mr Kenge courteously accompanies Esther with Ada Summerson and Richard Carstone, the 'wards in Jarndyce' to see the Lord Chancellor in his chambers, where the order is made that Ada and Richard are to live with John Jarndyce at Bleak House with Esther as Ada's companion.

Kenge is astonished that Esther as a young woman has not heard of Jarndyce and Jarndyce. Dickens in the book's great opening might condemn the court as floundering in the fog and mud of its own procedures, but for Mr Kenge *Jarndyce v Jarndyce* is a source of professional pride:

> 'Not one of the greatest Chancery suits ever known? Not of Jarndyce and Jarndyce – the – a – in itself a monument of Chancery practice ... In which (I would say) every difficulty, every contingency, every masterly, every form of procedure known in that court, is represented

over and over again? It is a cause that could not exist outside a free country.'

The passage is ironic. Kenge is a chancery practitioner, and as we have seen earlier, there are some grounds for Kenge's pride in the system buried in the mud that surrounds it.

One of the greatest English lawyers, Sir William Blackstone, observed that *'In fictione juris semper est aequitas'* – 'In legal fiction there is always equity'.³ Some legal fictions, such as the Bill of Middlesex procedure, were developed simply to bring more cases within the jurisdiction of one court or another. Many others were devised to allow the law to deal with factual situations or relationships that had not arisen before. In the absence of legislative activity to create new law, the essential role of fictions was to allow the law to deal with such new situations in a way that avoided an 'arbitrary' decision.

Fictions were a form of legal argument that makes a link between existing law and the legal decision necessary to deal with a new situation in such a way that the decision cannot be said to be arbitrary. In this way, the legal system remains not only able to deal with new situations but also – at least in theory – coherent in its own legal reasoning and therefore a source of authority independent of the government of the day, thereby able to maintain the rule of law. In this sense, Mr Kenge is justified in claiming that the Jarndyce case 'could not exist outside a free country'.

Just as when Mr Gregsbury, the lazy, ignorant MP in *Nicholas Nickleby*, claims to be acting according to Edmund Burke's 1774 principles as a delegate and not a representative, and the seedy, obsessive hangman Dennis in *Barnaby Rudge* so stoutly maintains the principle of due process of law, Dickens is aware that many of the abuses he describes have survived only because they have, underneath all their bizarre and abusive development, the stubborn, flinty basis of some essential constitutional principle.

Because of the system's slow, expensive procedures and the greed and indifference of officials, these constitutional achievements have been of little help to Gridley, Miss Flite or the parties in Jarndyce. Mr Kenge, for all his civilised conversation, played his part in Esther's picture of the 'polite show' that 'went calmly on from day to day and year to year, in good order and composure' but was 'a bitter jest and was held in universal horror, contempt and indignation'.

Dickens writes on these matters with a distinctive and often astringent combination of satire and irony. Though he doesn't actually show the way to a solution of the problem he's describing, he does perhaps give some indication of where to start looking for one.

The most redoubtable of Dickens' chancery lawyers is Mr Tulkinghorn, whose very name faintly suggests a medieval hunt. He is a sustaining part of the order of aristocracy and landed gentry personified by Sir Leicester Dedlock and his country seat of Chesney Wold. He is 'reputed to have made good thrift out of aristocratic marriage settlements and aristocratic wills' and 'surrounded by a mysterious halo of family confidences'. He is:

> ... found sometimes, speechless but quite at home, at the corners of dinner-tables in great country houses, and near doors of drawing-rooms... where everybody knows him, and where half the Peerage stops to say, 'How do you do, Mr Tulkinghorn?' He receives these salutations with gravity, and buries them with the rest of his knowledge.

Conversation plays no part in Mr Tulkinghorn's method. He is dry and sparing in his utterances, observing others and waiting for them to reveal themselves. He chooses to regard the protests made by Mr Gridley as threatening to himself, and on that basis obtains a warrant for his arrest by the detective Bucket. His determined tracing of evidence of Lady Dedlock's affair with Captain Hawdon seems to be driven either by his instinct to protect the reputation of Sir Leicester, as he says it is, or a desire to exercise personal power, or both.

In chapter 42, after making clear to Lady Dedlock his intention to reveal her secret at a time of his own choosing, Tulkinghorn 'transfers himself' from the ancestral solidity of Chesney Wold to his London home, and:

> ... the manner of coming and going between the two places is impenetrable. He walks into Chesney Wold as if it were next door to his chambers, and returns to his chambers as if he had never been out of Lincoln's Inn Fields.

He shares this ability with Inspector Bucket, who appears to materialise in Tulkinghorn's chambers without Mr Snagsby understanding how he got in. These two figures pull together the various locations of the novel. In chapter 22 Bucket and Snagsby walk together from Snagsby's shop by Lincoln's Inn to the lodging of Jo the crossing sweeper in the squalor of Tom All-Alone's, a mere twenty minutes' walk away, near the present Denmark Street. The legal neighbourhood of Lincoln's Inn is the stepping-stone enabling Lady Dedlock, Tulkinghorn and Bucket to move across the huge void between the privileged inertia of Chesney Wold and the wretchedness of Tom All-Alone's in the London Rookeries.

While Tulkinghorn serves the aristocracy and is a familiar figure among them, he is not of them. He preserves a separate identity, which is a legal identity. When Sir Leicester's party lose in a Parliamentary Election, he informs Sir Leicester that 'You are beaten out of all reason', and Dickens observes that it he says 'you' and not 'we' because it was no part of Mr Tulkinghorn's policy to have political opinions. Like Scrooge, he is now solitary, his only real friend being long dead. His only real identification is with the law. His only real pleasure is the slow savouring of the port, which has been maturing for fifty years in his private cellar under the Fields lying between his own house and Lincoln's Inn - embedded as it were, like Tulkinghorn himself, in the physical landscape of legal London.

The pointing hand of a figure in the painted Roman scene on the ceiling of Tulkinghorn's chambers has through the book suggested that some significant event will occur on the spot beneath. It is there, in chapter 48, just after the death of Jo, that Tulkinghorn meets his violent death at the hand of Hortense, Lady Dedlock's passionate and resentful French maid. Tulkinghorn had paid Hortense to appear in the servant's bonnet, gown and veil Lady Dedlock had worn so that Jo could identify the lady to whom he had shown the grave of Captain Hawdon, Lady Dedlock's lover before her marriage to Sir Leicester.

In response to Hortense's later demand for more money or employment, Tulkinghorn presents a front which is as flinty and unyielding as the law he practises. He warns Hortense that if she comes to him again he will hand her over to the police who will carry her through the streets 'in an ignominious manner; strapped down on a board, my good wench'. He goes on:

> 'You were dismissed by your lady ... as the most implacable and unmanageable of women. Now turn over a new leaf, and take warning by what I say to you. For what I say, I mean; and what I threaten, I will do, mistress.'

Mr Tulkinghorn had effectively dealt with Mr Gridley by taking out a warrant for his arrest, executed by Mr Bucket.

Hortense, however, is not so easily manageable. She is in fact, as we have seen, implacable – 'a Frenchwoman of two-and-thirty, from somewhere in the southern country about Avignon and Marseilles', 'a large-eyed brown woman with black hair; who would be handsome, but for a certain feline mouth and a general uncomfortable tightness of face', who shoots Tulkinghorn dead under the pointing hand of the painted ceiling.

There is surely a whiff of revolutionary France about her – a suggestion that she has something in common with that other implacable Frenchwoman who will figure in *A Tale of Two Cities* – the dark-haired Madame Defarge, who was 'brought up among the fishermen of the seashore' and who in Paris walks the streets with a loaded pistol hidden in her clothing and:

> ... with the supple freedom of a woman who walked in her girlhood, barefoot and bare-legged, on the brown sea-sand.[4]

Just as Tulkinghorn, the impenetrable-faced legal agent of aristocratic families, meets his sudden end at the hand of the maid Hortense, so we see that Sir Leicester Dedlock and his extended network of Foodles and Doodles are losing support politically. We have another sign of social change in the son of Mrs Rouncewell, the Housekeeper at Chesney Wold. Mr Rouncewell is now a well-to-do manufacturer in 'the iron country' and speaks virtually as an equal to Sir Leicester about marrying Rosa, Lady Dedlock's personal maid.

Through Mr Tulkinghorn, the law is linked to the old landed political interest of the Dedlocks and to the social inertia which their family name so clearly reflects. The law itself, as portrayed in the Court of Chancery, is hidebound, usually ineffectual and often mercilessly destructive. As Dickens compels us to acknowledge, however, it is not enough simply to condemn the system. Certain essential elements of it are, as demonstrated by Skimpole, very necessary.

When John Jarndyce offers Trooper George the services of a lawyer after his arrest for the murder of Tulkinghorn, George refuses, saying that he does not 'like the breed' and prefers to rely for his defence on his own simple statement of the truth. His mother's friend Mrs Bagnet, however, is clear in her own mind that the 'simple truth' will not be sufficient:

> 'It won't do to have truth and justice on his side, he must have law and lawyers,' exclaims the old girl, apparently persuaded that the latter form a separate establishment, and have dissolved partnership with truth and justice for ever and a day.'

George is persuaded by his mother to have a lawyer. He doesn't need one in the end as Bucket's unusual talent and efficient police work identify the real killer. The facts of the case as they first appear form such a damning picture that without very competent advocacy George would likely have been convicted by a jury.

There is something of the same balancing pattern in the novel's portrayal of the aristocratic world, which itself can be seen to have certain redeeming features. Static and ineffectual as he is, there is nothing mean about Sir Leicester. He loves his wife and his response to the suggestion of her previous affair is to buy back the 'incriminating' letters and send Mr Bucket to search for her with a message of forgiveness. Trooper George, dispossessed of his shooting gallery, is persuaded by his mother to return to Chesney Wold, where Sir Leicester gratefully accepts his services as a nurse and companion. George has the opportunity of a position in his brother's new industrial firm in the north, but prefers to return to a respected place in the semi-feudal but somewhat gentler atmosphere of the Leicestershire estate.

Dickens identifies two further significant characters who follow their occupation within the world of Chancery. The most sinister is Mr Vholes.

Mr Vholes has an office in Symond's Inn, Chancery Lane, described in chapter 39 as:

> A little, pale, wall-eyed woe-begone inn, like a large dust-binn of two compartments and a sifter. It looked as if Symond were a sparing man in his day, and constructed his inn of old building materials, which took kindly to dry-rot and to dirt and all things decaying and dismal, and perpetuated Symond's memory with congenial shabbiness.

There is very little on record of Symond's Inn, but it is not a fictional entity, simply an obscure one.[5]

Vholes' natural environment seems to be darkness:

> Three feet of knotty-floored dark passage bring the client to Mr Vholes's jet black door, in an angle profoundly dark on the brightest midsummer morning.

When in chapter 45 Esther and her maid Rosa are walking in the garden at Bleak House, Esther sees:

> ... a long thin shadow going in which looked like Mr Vholes, and of course it is Vholes who has come to inform John Jarndyce that Richard has run out of funds, declaring 'his wish that everything should be openly carried on'.

By chapter 60 Esther feels, as she sees 'his long black figure reaching nearly to the ceiling of those low rooms' that there is 'something of a Vampire about him'. At this point Ada has married Richard and is sharing with him his wretched lodgings next to Vholes' office in Symond's Inn. Esther regularly calls on her and one day meets Miss Flite, who has come on a similar errand. Miss Flite describes Richard as, next to herself, the most constant suitor in court, who is beginning to amuse their little party. She says she intends to appoint him her executor, in place of Gridley.

Richard has now joined the little band of deluded suitors who haunt the court, but his fate is more tragic than theirs. Gridley remains essentially sane, despite his long years of desperation. Miss Flite, conscious of her own madness, retains an eccentric sense of proportion and genuinely cares for Gridley and Jo. Richard however seems to decay at his core.

Whereas Miss Flite and Gridley are ruined by the Chancery system, Richard seems to be Vholes's personal victim. While Vholes's speech is convincingly that of a bland lawyer, his predatory gestures and the blackness and shadows surrounding him suggest a destructive malevolence which is perhaps independent of the legal world, although it seems here to have an affinity with it.

Mr Kenge, by contrast, seems refreshingly human as he represents the system and articulates its defence. In chapter 65 Allan Woodcourt and Ada meet Kenge and Vholes in Westminster Hall on the very day when 'the whole estate is found to have been absorbed in costs' and that therefore, even though they have now found the authentic will, 'the suit lapses and melts away'.

Kenge, 'with excessive urbanity' chooses that moment to explain to the young doctor the unparalleled merits and virtues of the system:

> 'You are to reflect, Mr Woodcourt ... that this has been a great cause ... that this has been a complex cause. Jarndyce and Jarndyce has been termed, not inaptly, a Monument of Chancery practice.'
>
> 'And patience has sat upon it a long time,' said Allan.
>
> 'Very well indeed, sir,' returned Mr Kenge, with a certain condescending laugh that he had.

Kenge the lawyer contemplates the huge and complex legal structure in which he works and which he serves. Woodcourt the doctor immediately considers one of its victims:

> 'My dearest life,' whispered Allan, 'this will break Richard's heart.'

We find one other interesting occupant of the legal world. He is Kenge's clerk, Mr Guppy. We first meet him as a civil young clerk meeting Ada and Esther on their first arrival in London and escorting them to Kenge's office. In chapter 7 he calls, rather oddly, at Chesney Wold as a kind of tourist, saying that he and his colleague has been on legal business 'at a magistrates' court, ten miles off' and wished to see over the house as 'us London lawyers don't get out much'. He then rather unexpectedly reappears in chapter 9 when he is sent by Mr Kenge to Bleak House to speak to Laurence Boythorn who is staying with John Jarndyce.

Esther is asked to see that he is provided with lunch. She notices that he is:

> ... uncommonly smart. He had an entirely new suit of glossy clothes on, a shining hat, lilac-kid gloves, a neckerchief of a variety of colours, a large hot-house flower in his buttonhole, and a thick gold ring on his finger. Besides which, he quite scented the dining-room with bear's

grease and other perfumery. He looked at me with an attention that quite confused me.

The smart dress and attentive looks are soon explained. Mr Guppy has been smitten with love for Esther. After the business with Boythorn has been concluded, Guppy comes down to have lunch and after several false starts begins to set out for Esther his financial position:

'My present salary, Miss Summerson, is two pound a week. When I first had the happiness of looking upon you, it was one-fifteen, and has stood at that figure for a lengthened period. A rise of five has since taken place, and a further rise of five is guaranteed at the expiration of a term not exceeding twelve months from the present date.'

Mr Guppy goes on to say that his mother has a small annuity and is 'eminently calculated for a mother-in-law' and describes his own lodgings in Pentonville as 'lowly, but airy, open at the back and considered one of the 'ealthiest outlets.' He concludes:

'Miss Summerson! In the mildest language, I adore you. Would you be so kind as to allow me (as I may say) to file a declaration – to make you an offer!'

Esther remains composed and makes it clear that what he proposes is 'quite impossible' and 'entirely out of the question' but her words only partially achieve the desired result. For the rest of their stay in London she often encounters the sight of the despondent Guppy gazing soulfully towards her at a theatre or in the street.

Nine chapters later, after Lady Dedlock has seen Howdon's handwriting on a document, and Jo has been rejected as a witness at Hawdon's inquest, and Esther has met Lady Dedlock and Lady Dedlock has rewarded Jo for showing her Hawdon's grave, we meet Mr Guppy again in somewhat reanimated form.

He sees Jo being questioned by a constable about two half-crowns he has in his possession, hears him say he knows Mr Snagsby and that the money is what remains of his reward for showing Hawdon's grave to a lady. Guppy 'has an enquiring mind in matters of evidence'. He conducts a 'model' cross-examination of Jo in Snagsby's shop, is impressed by the way Jo sticks to his story and begins to suspect the existence of a link between Lady Dedlock and Captain Hawdon.

This is not the only significant action Guppy takes. During the inactive days of the long summer vacation, when 'the bar of England is scattered over the face of the earth', Guppy and his friend Smallweed, whose ambition 'is to become a Guppy', encounter a former clerk, Jobling. Jobling has recently been dismissed, or as his friends tactfully put it, has 'left the Inn'. Guppy stands them a memorable lunch, guided as to the menu by the experienced Smallweed, who advises, 'veal and ham and French beans – And don't you forget the stuffing, Polly!'

Jobling has been living among 'the market gardens down by Deptford', and his appetite:

> ' ... is so vigorous, that it suggests spare living for some little time back. He makes such a speedy end of his plate of veal and ham, bringing it to a close while his companions are midway in theirs, that Mr Guppy proposes another. "Thank you, Guppy," says Mr Jobling, 'I really don't know but what I will take another.'
>
> Another being brought, he falls to with great good will. Mr Guppy takes silent notice of him at intervals, until he is halfway through this second plate and stops to take an enjoying pull at his pint pot of half-and-half (also renewed), and stretches out his legs and rubs his hands. Beholding him in which glow of contentment, Mr Guppy says:
>
> 'You are a man again, Tony!'
>
> 'Well not quite, yet,' says Mr Jobling. 'Say, just born.'
>
> 'Will you take any other vegetables? Grass? Peas? Summer cabbage?
>
> 'Thank you, Guppy,' says Mr Jobling.'

The repast continues with orders for 'three marrow puddings', 'three Cheshires' and 'three small rums'. In the ensuing postprandial atmosphere, Guppy confides in Jobling that he and Smallweed have considered a way to improve his fortunes, which is to undertake law-writing for Snagsby. They also believe that suitable cheap lodging might be found above Krook's shop.

There is certainly some calculation in Guppy's luncheon arrangements. He has seen a way to install his friend Jobling where he might come upon the letters between Hawdon and the present Lady Dedlock, letters which Lady Dedlock might be anxious to possess. Finding the letters might place Mr Guppy in a favourable light with Esther as it would confirm a link between her and the Dedlock family, but also, and more importantly, would remove the threat of her mother's exposure.

But there is more than calculation in this genial luncheon. The generosity of provision and the atmosphere of friendship here are similar to that of the impromptu meal which David provides for Traddles and the Micawbers in his Adelphi rooms in chapter 28 of *David Copperfield* when, as we may remember, after the failing of more formal arrangements, Traddles cut the mutton into slices, Micawber covered them with salt, pepper, mustard and cayenne, David moved them on and off the griddle at Micawber's direction and Mrs Micawber prepared mushroom ketchup in a little saucepan. Everyone laughed continually and David believed there was never a greater success.

An element of self-interest had entered into the earlier occasion when Micawber persuaded Traddles to put his name to a bill as security for one of Micawber's debts. Just as with the Guppy luncheon, it never overshadowed the essentially generous, friendship-creating nature of the communal feast.

We next see Mr Guppy when Richard goes with Ada and Esther to see the Court of Chancery before he leaves for military duties in Ireland. Guppy, still smitten with love for Esther, gives her 'a forlorn bow'. He is far from forlorn, however, when five chapters later he is allowed an interview with Lady Dedlock. In a line of polite, cautious but factually decisive questioning he establishes that their conversation is in confidence, that Lady Dedlock has recently seen Esther Summerson, that Esther was brought up by Miss Barbary, that Miss Barbary is connected to her ladyship's family, that Esther's real name is Hawdon, that her ladyship has heard the name Hawdon before and that her ladyship would like to have the bundle of letters found in Hawdon's room. Guppy ends this quiet tour de force of interrogation by dismissing any suggestion of a financial motive – it would be quite sufficient for him if the outcome of these investigations were to make it more likely that Esther would look favourably on his own proposal to her.

Guppy's developing confidence suffers something of a setback in chapter 38 when Esther, now recovered from smallpox, calls on him at his home in order to ask him not to pursue his enquiries into her own family background. Mrs Guppy is full of maternal pride at her visit and Guppy himself smilingly attentive until Esther removes her veil, revealing her altered appearance. Her erstwhile suitor thereupon blushes, stammers, coughs and eventually, referring to Esther's earlier rejection of his proposal, requests her in legalistic form to 'admit' that she had declined his offer and further to 'admit' that his offer was finally terminated, though, he adds, it will be 'a retrospect entwined within friendship's bowers'.

Esther unhesitatingly gives the required assurances and proceeds to do what she came for – to ask Guppy not to investigate her background further. Esther comments:

> I must do Mr Guppy the further justice of saying that he looked more and more ashamed, and very earnest, when he replied with a burning face, 'Upon my word and honour, upon my life, upon my soul, Miss Summerson, as I am a living man, I'll act according to your wish!'

His heartfelt declarations run into legalistic form, reflecting the stressful mixture of heartfelt emotions and legal circumspection with which he has approached Esther, but Guppy keeps his word. In chapter 39 he visits Krook's old shop, now the property of the Smallweeds, and charges Weevle as a friend to bury the whole enquiry about Captain Hawdon in oblivion.

Guppy's romantic dream of marriage to the earlier beautiful version of Esther is at an end. Whatever we may think of that decision however, his abandonment of the investigation into Hawdon's background is without any element of self-interest. It is an act motivated purely by friendship and a wish to serve the former object of his romantic affections. Mr Guppy, when it comes down to it, is a man of honour.

He is also, despite all his awkward legal jargon, a pretty good lawyer. He realises that Jo the crossing sweeper is an excellent witness.

Jo was dismissed as a witness by the Coroner at the inquest on Hawdon in chapter 11:

> No father, no mother, no friends. Never been to school. What's home? Knows a broom's a broom, and knows it's wicked to tell a lie. Don't recollect who told him about the broom, or the lie, but knows both. Can't exactly say what'll be done to him arter he's dead if he tells a lie to the gentlemen here, but believes it will be something wery bad to punish him – and so he'll tell the truth.
>
> 'This won't do, gentlemen!' says the Coroner, with a melancholy shake of is head.
>
> 'Don't you think you can receive his evidence, sir?' asks an attentive Juryman.
>
> 'Out of the question,' says the Coroner. 'You have heard the boy'. 'Can't exactly say' won't do. you know. We can't have that in a Court of Justice, gentlemen. It's a terrible depravity.'

In dismissing Jo, however, the Coroner is depriving the inquest of an excellent witness.

When Mr Tulkinghorn, who had questioned Jo privately after the inquest, had gone with Bucket and Sangsby to Tom All-Alone's and brought Jo back to confront him with Hortense dressed in her gown, bonnet and veil, Jo clearly recognises 'the wale, the bonnet and the gownd' but also perceives that the wearer is not the same person who wore them when he last saw those articles of dress. He further notes that though the height is the same the voice is different and that figure's hand was not the same and the rings on it not the same as on the earlier occasion, when the hand was whiter and the rings sparkled. This is objective, accurate observation of the first order.

Guppy was not present on that occasion. However we know that in chapter 19 when Jo had been brought to Snagsby's shop by a constable, Guppy had taken Jo in hand as a witness:

> ... patting him into this shape, that shape and the other shape, like a butterman dealing with so much butter, and worrying him according to the best models.

Though we are told that the examination, like its models, elicited nothing, Guppy observes that, 'the boy sticks to it like cobbler's-wax, or there is something out of the common here that beats anything that came my way at Kenge and Carboy's.'

In chapter 29 when Guppy visits Lady Dedlock in her London house to ask whether Captain Hawdon's letters – should they be found – would be of interest to her, the most effective point in his questioning is when he mentions Jo's observation of the diamond rings on the fingers of the lady who had wished to see Hawdon's grave.

Guppy had not been present when Jo related this information to Mr Tulkinghorn in chapter 22. He can therefore only have gained it from his own examination of Jo in Snagsby's shop in chapter 19. Guppy, while he appears ludicrous in his heartfelt non-relationship with Esther, shows up really well in his professional capacity. Though merely a clerk – as yet without articles – he sees what the hidebound Coroner does not and ascertains the true value of Jo as a witness. He then reveals two essential lawyer's skills, first in extracting significant evidence by his questioning of Jo and then in then using that same evidence to great effect in his questioning of Lady Dedlock.

As we have seen with Mr Micawber, Dickens can depict hidden virtues in characters of unpromising appearance. Importantly, in the case of Micawber and Guppy the virtues are not only personal.

The legal system Dickens describes is made up of Acts of Parliament, recorded cases and the recognised procedures by which cases come before the courts, but it is administered, developed and moulded by the body of its practitioners – not only by judges but also by barristers and others.

Mr Tulkinghorn and Conversation Kenge certainly do not bode well for the future of this system. Dickens also creates Mr Guppy, the humble clerk who presides over the life-affirming lunch, transforming the destitute Jobling into 'a man again'. Though he appears in a foolish light when smitten with love for Esther, his proposal is perfectly straightforward and sincere. In legal terms, he is, in his inconspicuous way, impressive. Using Jo's evidence to good effect, he demonstrates that power of getting to 'the pith and marrow' of a case which Sydney Carton shows in *A Tale of Two Cities* and which Dickens describes as 'the most striking of an advocate's accomplishments'

In the slight figure of Mr Guppy Dickens permits us to see a glimmer of light within the mass of slow-moving lumber which at that time constituted the High Court of Chancery.

9.
LITTLE DORRIT

Recte Numerare[1]

In his Preface to the 1857 edition of *Little Dorrit*, Dickens tells us of three events which subsequently emerge as themes in the novel.

The state of the Civil Service had been a cause of public concern for some years, but the reforms proposed by the Northcote-Layard Report of 1854 had not so far been implemented. There were also deep misgivings about the Army High Command, whose arrogance and ineptitude during the Crimean War had moved Tennyson to write his poem *The Charge of the Light Brigade*. The heroism and sacrifice of the Brigade had been in vain because, as Tennyson said, 'someone had blundered'.

Of most immediate concern was the report of the Commission of Enquiry, headed by Sir John McNeil and Col Alexander Tulloch, who had visited the Crimea to investigate on the spot; their report to Parliament at the beginning of 1856 set out the clear failure of both civil and military authorities to provide appropriate equipment and medical care for the troops, as a result of which thousands more soldiers died of wounds and disease than died in battle. In March of that year Dickens was prompted to write an article in Household Words *Stores for 1st April* condemning the 'murderous muddle and mismanagement' of the authorities in Crimea.

The Palmerston government's response had been not to accept the damning report but to set up a further Board of Enquiry sitting at Chelsea Barracks which largely absolved the commanders involved, principally Lord Raglan and Lord Cardigan, and went so far as to contradict several of the findings of the earlier Commission of Enquiry. This was followed, to Dickens' disgust, by an article by Abraham Heyward in the August number of the *North British Review* which again attempted to argue that the adverse events, 'could be accounted for without imputing blame to any minister, civil or military officer or chief of department'.

The Report of the Chelsea Enquiry was widely regarded as a shameful whitewash, and it was this attempt by the establishment to avoid or deflect any blame for the disasters of the Crimea that appears to have raised Dickens' indignation to the pitch at which he began to write *Little Dorrit*.

The second significant public scandal followed the death of John Sadleir, an Irish MP and a founder of the Tipperary Bank, who had committed suicide on Hampstead Heath in February 1856. Sadleir had earlier caused controversy by accepting a post as a junior Lord of the Treasury in 1853, contrary to the policy of his Party, the Irish Independent Party. After his death, it became known that Sadleir had used the Tipperary Bank's funds for personal speculation in land and commodities and had then arranged for the Bank to issue a false prospectus in an attempt to attract funds to cover up his huge losses.

The failure of the Bank led to widespread bankruptcies and hardship, but the fact that Sadleir had been appointed a Lord of the Treasury caused an even more serious concern as it implied that the financial corruption was not simply that of an individual banker but had in some degree affected the political system itself.

The third theme arises not from public events but from Dickens' own recurring memory of those events some thirty years before: his father's imprisonment in the Marshalsea Prison and the young Charles's employment in Warren's Blacking warehouse during that time.

Some three days after Dickens finished *Little Dorrit* in May 1857 he visited the site of the then-defunct Marshalsea. In his Preface to the first edition, he tells us of this visit:

> Wandering, however, down a certain adjacent 'Angel Court, leading to Bermondsey,' I came to 'Marshalsea Place:' the houses in which I recognised, not only as the great block of the former prison, but as preserving the rooms that arose in my mind's eye when I became Little Dorrit's biographer.... Whoever goes into Marshalsea Place, turning out of Angel Court, leading to Bermondsey, will find his feet on the very paving stones of the extinct Marshalsea jail ... will look upon the rooms in which the debtors lived; will stand among the crowding ghosts of many miserable years.

This is a rather strange piece of writing. Modern readers might assume that Dickens here was publicly acknowledging facts about his early life. He indeed speaks of 'recognising' the great block of the prison and even points to a particular window where, he says, 'Little Dorrit' was born.

Dickens certainly wished to indicate to his readers how strongly the actual buildings of the Marshalsea prison inspired the narrative of the book, though from what he says elsewhere he seemed to have been reluctant to reveal the personal nature of the connection. The subject was, nevertheless, too important to be kept out of the novel.

Dickens' initial plans for the book had been focussed on the shortcomings of the government and the army in the Crimea, and the scandal following the suicide of the financier John Sadleir. The first title which appears in his working notes, 'Nobody's Fault', encapsulates the essence of the findings of the Chelsea Enquiry and Abraham Heywood's North British Review article defending those findings. Dickens goes on to use variations of this phrase in four of the book's early chapter headings.

For Dickens, these scandals were not simply the standard topics of a political satirist but symptoms of a deep national malaise. As he said of the public mood in April 1855 in a letter to Austen Layard, the political reformer:

> I believe the discontent to be so much the worse for smouldering, instead of blazing openly, that it is like the general mind of France before the breaking out of the first Revolution, and is in danger of being turned by any one of a thousand incidents: a bad harvest, the last strain too much of aristocratic insolence or incapacity, a defeat abroad – a mere chance at home – into such a devil of a conflagration as has never been beheld since.

Dickens goes on to lament the failure of the people to 'bestir themselves in the vigorous national manner', concluding that until they break out from 'this lethargy' 'I know of nothing that can be done beyond keeping their wrongs continually before them'.

During the writing of the first chapters of *Little Dorrit* thoughts on an apparently unrelated topic returned to his mind. For the February 1855 number of *Household Words* he had written an article entitled 'Gaslight Fairies', describing a young woman who earns a meagre living playing 'fairy' parts in theatrical productions and by this means supporting her drunken father and feckless brother.

The figure of the brave, unselfish 'Miss Fairy' was herself an archetype of a Dickens heroine in the line of Esther in *Bleak House* and Ruth Pinch in *Martin Chuzzlewit*. When linked to Dickens' memories of his own father in the Marshalsea, the figure seems to have inspired the creation of Little Dorrit and her dependent family in their debtors' prison setting. Indeed, Flora Finching addresses Little Dorrit as 'You industrious fairy' when she employs her as a seamstress in chapter 24. When Dickens became, in his own words, 'Little Dorrit's biographer', the role enabled him to expand the scope of the book from political polemic to a creative work dealing with the moral questions arising from the most formative experiences in his early life.

This is not the first time that Dickens has re-played his early experience of a debtors' prison. The first occurs, as we have seen, in Mr

Pickwick's adventures in the Fleet in chapters 41 and 42 of *The Pickwick Papers*.

The *Pickwick* prison scenes were not, however, the Marshalsea scenes that he referred to years later in his 'autobiographical fragment'. Perhaps wishing at that time to distance himself from such memories, Dickens set Pickwick's experiences in the Fleet Prison, relying for specific details of that prison on *Scenes and Stories by a Clergyman in Debt Written during his Confinement in the Debtors' Prisons*, a publication by a clergyman who had himself been imprisoned in the Fleet.

The entertaining narrative of Pickwick's earlier adventures continues in the prison episode but the those scenes give unavoidable glimpses into a very bleak and savage world. As well as the drinking and card playing, the dancing and the convivial opportunism of chancers such as Smangle and Mivins, we hear of the 'range of damp and gloomy stone vaults' where Mr Pickwick surmises that the debtors keep their coals but where people actually live, and where, according to the turnkey Mr Roker, they 'die down there, too, very often.'

At one point Mr Pickwick sums up his views of the prison:

> 'It strikes me, Sam,' said Mr Pickwick, leaning over the iron rail at the stair-head – 'It strikes me, Sam, that imprisonment for debt is scarcely any punishment at all.'
>
> 'Think not, sir?' inquired Mr Weller
>
> 'You see how these fellows drink, and smoke, and roar,' replied Mr Pickwick. 'It's quite impossible that they can mind it much.'
>
> 'Ah, that's just the wery thing, sir,' rejoined Sam, 'they don't mind it. It's a regular holiday to them – all porter and skittles. It's t' other vuns as gets done over vith this sort o' thing; them down-hearted fellers as can't svig avay at the beer, not play at skittles neither; them as would pay if they could, and gets low by being boxed-up.'

As the perceptive Sam sums it up:

'I'll tell you wot it is, sir; them as is always idlin' in public houses, it don't damage at all, and them as is alvays a-workin' wen they can, it damages too much.'

Weller then tells the tale of the 'little dirty-faced man in the brown coat' who seems to anticipate the outlook of Dr Haggage and William Dorrit. 'Number Twenty', as he was known, lived in the prison so long that the turnkey eventually allowed him out on trust to a nearby public house. When he returned late, the turnkey threatened to shut him out all together, whereupon 'the little man was seized with a wiolent fit of tremblin', and 'never vent outside the prison walls artervards!'

Dickens' amusing anecdotes almost invariably contain elements of painful reality. In describing the reluctance of 'Number 20' to face the outside world Sam Weller unerringly identifies the problem created by the protective nature of the debtors' prison, which we later see lying at the heart of *Little Dorrit*.

When Dickens made use of these memories a second time, in *David Copperfield*, he based his description of Mr Micawber's time in debtors prison on what he recollected of his father's Marshalsea imprisonment.

Mr Micawber, confined in the King's Bench debtors' prison, certainly does not view his residence there as an oppressive experience – for him it was in fact a sanctuary providing relief from pressing creditors. He describes it as a place:

> Where, for the first time in many revolving years the overwhelming pressure of pecuniary liabilities was not proclaimed from day to day, by importunate voices declining to vacate the passage; where there was no knocker on the door for any creditor to appeal to, where personal service of process was not required and detainers were merely lodged at the gate!

Mr Micawber nevertheless regards the imprisonment as a hard but nevertheless welcome process of redemption by which he could regain his status as a citizen and 'look his fellow-man in the face'. He eventually gains his freedom by applying to the Insolvent Debtors' Court. We should remember, however, that Mr Micawber is a somewhat unusual character. It is by no means clear, in view of what Dickens recorded in the autobiographical fragment, that his father regarded his period of imprisonment in the same light, or that his son believed he did. In the context of Dickens' own life it seems to have been seen as a period of disgrace rather than redemption.

Another twelve years on, in January 1855, the memories emerged for a third time when Dickens was about to begin *Little Dorrit*. In a letter to John Forster at the time he says that in re-reading *David Copperfield* he seems to see:

> Motes of new books in the dirty air, miseries of old growth threatening to close upon me. Why is it, as with poor David, a sense always comes crushing on me now, when I fall into low spirits, as one happiness I have missed in life ...

This time Dickens sets the scene in the Marshalsea itself. The prison does not figure in *Little Dorrit*'s early chapters. Dickens opens his novel under the blazing sun of far-away Marseilles, where we find the pantomime figure of Rigaud/Lagnier and his companion languishing in their prison cell. Rigaud, soon rightly or wrongly freed after a trial, joins a group of recently arrived travellers – Arthur Clennam, the Meagles family and Miss Wade – in the course of their journey to England. In chapter 6 the story moves to Clennam's mother's house in London, where Clennam meets Amy Dorrit employed as a seamstress, is interested in her and resolves to 'know more of her story'.

We are then transported to a scene at the gates of the Marshalsea several years earlier, where a 'very aimiable and helpless middle-aged gentleman' is about to enter the prison.

The parallels with John Dickens' imprisonment here are very close. The turnkey asks William Dorrit whether 'Missis and the littl'uns are coming to keep you company?', and they do, just as Mrs Dickens and her children moved in with John Dickens. The 'Address of Condolence', which the prisoners draw up after the death of Mrs Dorrit, recalls the petition which, according to the autobiographical fragment, John Dickens drew up in the Marshalsea and which was read aloud to the signatories.

This is how the same incident had earlier appeared repackaged in *David Copperfield*:

> I call to mind that Mr Micawber, about this time, composed a petition to the House of Commons, praying for an alteration in the law of imprisonment for debt ...
>
> ... There was a club in the prison, in which Mr Micawber, as a gentleman, was a great authority. Mr Micawber had stated his idea of this petition to the club, and the club had strongly approved of the same. Wherefore Mr Micawber (who was a thoroughly good-natured man, and as active a creature about everything but his own affairs as ever existed...) set to work at the petition, invented it, engrossed it on an immense sheet of paper, spread it out on a table, and appointed a time for all the club, and all within the walls if they chose, to come up to his room and sign it.

William Dorrit's affairs, unlike those of John Dickens and Wilkins Micawber, are too complicated to enable any application to be made under the Insolvent Debtors' Act. He remains in prison with his family and within 'five or six months' of his entering the Marshalsea, his wife gives birth to Amy. This event, with a drunken doctor, a fellow inmate, in attendance, is described in detail:

> The doctor was amazingly shabby, in a torn and darned rough-weather sea jacket, out at elbows and emminently short of buttons (he had in his time been the experienced surgeon carried by a passenger ship), the dirtiest white trousers conceived by mortal man, carpet slippers and no visible linen... It was a hot day and the prison rooms were baking between high walls.

The flies in the Marshalsea hover over the birth scene, almost as inauspicious guests:

> In the debtor's confined chamber Mrs Bangham, charwoman and messenger ... had volunteered her services as fly-catcher and general attendant. The walls and ceiling were blackened with flies. Mrs Bangham, expert in sudden device, with one hand fanned the patient with a cabbage leaf and with the other set traps of vinegar and sugar in gallipots ... 'The flies trouble you, don't they, my dear?' said Mrs Bangham, 'But p'raps they'll take your mind off it, and do you good. What with the buryin' ground, the grocers, the waggon-stables, and the paunch trade, the Marshalsea flies get very large ...'

The Marshalsea flies preside over more than one kind of decay. When Mr Dorrit expresses some regret that his child should be born in such a place, the doctor points out what are, to him, its virtues:

> A little more elbow-room is all we want here. We are quiet here. We don't get badgered here; there's no knocker here, sir, to be hammered at by creditors and bring a man's heart into his mouth. Nobody comes here to ask if a man's at home, and to say he'll stand on the doormat till he is. Nobody writes threatening letters about money to this place. It's freedom, sir, it's freedom!

Unlike Mr Micawber, however, the doctor does not use the relief afforded by the prison to re-establish himself in ordinary society but has decided to stay within its walls as a means of permanently evading his obligations. Mr Dorrit, in his own manner, eventually follows the same route. He at first finds a 'dull relief' in the prison, which soon develops into something more:

> He was under lock and key; but the lock and key which kept him in, kept numbers of his troubles out ... being what he was, he languidly slipped into this smooth descent, and never more took one step forward.

It is in this setting that Amy grows up, surrounded by the Marshalsea's particular atmosphere of inaction and waste:

> With no earthly friend to help her ... with no knowledge even of the common daily tone and habits of the common members of a free community who are not shut up in prisons: born and bred, in a social condition, false even with a reference to the falsest condition without the walls, drinking from infancy of a well whose waters had their own peculiar stain, their own unwholesome and unnatural taste, the Child of the Marshalsea began her womanly life.

What gives the Marshalsea waters 'their own peculiar stain' becomes clear as we see the steady demoralisation of William Dorrit. Unlike Micawber, who wished to keep exact account of his financial commitments so that he could walk erect before his fellow-man, William Dorrit and his son Tip, remaining within the Marshalsea's walls, have abandoned any sense of their financial obligations. Dorrit is fed and clothed decently because his daughter earns money as a seamstress, but he refuses to accept that she actually works to earn money, choosing to imagine that it somehow materialises in the air. Amy finds employment for Tip, but he never seriously attempts to earn his pay by working for it. He assumes, for the short time he remains employed, that it will simply come to him.

Under his facade of genteel abstraction, William Dorrit is cannily aware of the essentials of his existence. His income largely depends on a sentimental fantasy – the tribute due to him as 'Father of the Marshalsea' by his fellow inmates. When the delicate fabric of this position is threatened by Amy's refusal of Young John's proposal of marriage, his first thought is to beg Amy to overcome her profound reluctance and marry him.

In creating William Dorrit, Dickens is asking himself – and us – the two questions which have remained with him throughout his consideration of the legal system and which are never entirely resolved. The first question is whether it is morally right to distinguish between 'deserving' and the 'undeserving' when dealing with the poor, and secondly, if so, what practical measures can best put this into effect. In other words, is it possible to assist the poor without encouraging idleness and dependency among those who will simply take advantage of such assistance and make no or little attempt to earn their own living?

The question was first considered by Dickens in the context of the workhouse in which Oliver Twist found himself, and in which he so memorably 'asked for more'. This workhouse and its bleak, punitive regime had evolved through centuries of legislative measures by which society had attempted to deal with the 'problem' of the poor.

There had been punitive elements in much of the medieval legislation on this subject, and a Statute of Legal Settlement of Edward VI struck a remarkably Benthamite tone in warning against 'foolish mercy and pity'. The still operating, though much amended, Elizabethan Act For the Relief of the Poor of 1601 provided for poor rates to be collected by Churchwardens and Overseers of the Poor in each parish, to be spent on materials to provide work for the able-bodied poor, with any who refused such work to be placed in a 'House of Correction'. There was provision for the 'impotent' poor in almshouses and workhouses, together with outdoor relief in the form of food and fuel distributed at the discretion of the overseers. After 1723 a few parishes chose to adopt the provisions of Sir Edward Knatchbull's Act which made any relief conditional on residence in a poorhouse. Elsewhere, though the relief was usually meagre, the system was not predominantly coercive and was an essentially ad hoc regime of humane pragmatism.

During the eighteenth century, increasing pressure was put on the system by the movement of people to the cities and many, including the social reformer Jeremy Bentham, campaigned for a rationalisation of poor relief. In 1794 Bentham published a scheme of 'Pauper Management', in essence proposing that the principles of Knatchbull's Act should be implemented as a standardised national system. The publication of Thomas Malthus's famous *Essay on the Principles of Population*[2] some four years later greatly influenced public debate on the same matter, arguing that giving assistance to the poor increased the problem, as given easier conditions the poor would be likely to have more children, thereby increasing their number. This approach tended to support policies of draconian harshness where the poor were concerned, and at one point in his Essay Malthus goes as far as to observe that a man who is impoverished:

> '... has no business to be where he is. At Nature's mighty feast there is no cover (ie place at table) for him. She tells him to be gone.'

As we have seen earlier, the New Poor Law Act introduced by the Whig government in 1834 had been strongly influenced by Benthamite arguments, and the new Poor Law Commissioners were soon issuing sample dietary tables for use in workhouses, prescribing diets which were carefully calculated to provide the minimum necessary to sustain life.

Dickens, in creating Oliver, fiercely refutes the Benthamite principle of aiming for the greatest happiness for the greatest number on the grounds that the principle appeared inevitably to require deliberately inhumane treatment for those members of society who cannot or will not earn their own living. He continues to refute it in the 1850s when, in a *Household Words* article 'A Walk in the Workhouse', he considers the meagre, stultifying regime for adults to be abhorrent.

The question posed in *Little Dorrit* is, what of those who, though not in the absolute extreme of poverty and therefore not eligible for the workhouse, cannot or will not meet their financial obligations?

In *Bleak House*, Mr Neckett, the humble debt-collector who has been pursuing the financially irresponsible Harold Skimpole, himself dies leaving his children in poverty. John Jarndyce observes there that:

> 'The man (Neckett) was necessary ... if we make such men necessary by our faults and follies, or by our want of worldly knowledge, or by our misfortunes, we must not revenge ourselves upon them.'

The law punishes or constrains those who do not meet their social obligations, otherwise society cannot function. The sanctions of the law should therefore be of a kind which encourages people to honour their financial commitments. In *Little Dorrit,* Dickens shows us that the sanction of the law in cases of debt invariably does not do that. In many cases the Marshalsea fails to be such a deterrent and the social effects are not inconsiderable.

When Clennam accidentally has to spend the night in the prison, after being delayed by his first conversation with Little Dorrit, he is able to observe the scene at the gate the following morning:

> There was a string of people already straggling in, whom it was not difficult to identify as the nondescript messengers, go-betweens, and errand-bearers of the place. Some of them had been lounging in the rain until the gate should open; others, who had timed their arrival with greater nicety, were coming up now and passing in with damp whitely-brown paper bags from the grocers, loaves of bread, lumps of butter, eggs, milk and the like. The shabbiness of these attendants upon shabbiness, the poverty of these insolvent waiters upon insolvency, was a sight to see. Such threadbare coats and trousers, such fusty gowns and shawls, such squashed hats and bonnets, such boots and shoes, such umbrellas and walking-sticks, never were seen in a Rag Fair. All of them wore the cast-off clothes of other men and women; were made up of patches and pieces of other people's individuality, and had no sartorial existence of their own proper. Their walk was the walk of a race apart. They had a way of doggedly slinking round the corner, as if they were eternally going to the pawnbroker's. When they coughed, they coughed like people accustomed to be forgotten on doorsteps and in draughty passages, waiting for answers to letters in faded ink, which gave the recipients ... great mental disturbance and no satisfaction. As they eyed the stranger in passing, they eyed him with borrowing eyes, hungry, sharp, speculative as to his softness if they were accredited to him, and the likelihood of his standing something handsome.

The scene represents the worst fears of the Benthamites brought to life. Not only do those confined within the prison drink of the tainted waters, but also those who live nearby and supply its needs, so that the malaise seems to spread beyond the Marshalsea to the wider society, and the image of the damp whitey-brown paper bags disintegrating in the rain suggests a similar tendency in the character of the people carrying them. Those actually confined are able simply to continue with their way of life by this means – the very thing the strictest Bentham disciples wished to prevent. Their aim was to achieve the greatest good for the greatest number by creating such a harshly deterrent environment for those who fail to meet their obligations that scenes such as that depicted above would no longer have a place in public life.

Dickens' own despairing distaste of the 'insolvent waiters upon insolvency' might have brought him to an espousal of Benthamite ideas after all, had he not had the power to create Little Dorrit.

We see from her earliest days Amy Dorrit's personal immunity from the Marshalsea's contamination. Within her own sphere of activity she defeats its influence by a gentle persistence and diligence in all things, caring for the rest of her family, snatching an education for herself at an evening school and ensuring that her brother Tip and sister Fanny have some education too.

Amy Dorrit looks out keenly for whatever opportunities present themselves. She persuades a milliner-inmate to teach her the skills of sewing, gets an insolvent dancing master to teach his arts to Fanny and persuades Bob, the turnkey, to recommend Tip as a potential clerk to the professional gentlemen who at various times pass through the Marshalsea lodge and by this means obtains employment for him in the office of an attorney in Clifford's Inn.

Tip and Fanny respond to the Marshalsea environment in different ways. Tip never makes any effort to make his way in any of the jobs his sister found for him, and soon was, in his own words, 'taken off the volunteer list', ie he incurs a debt he can't pay and thus soon becomes a prisoner rather than a resident:

> Wherever he went, this foredoomed Tip appeared to take the prison with him, and to set them up in such a trade or calling; and to prowl about within their narrow limits in the old slip-shod, purposeless, down-at-heel way; until the real immoveable Marshalsea walls asserted their fascination over him, and brought him back.

When Clennam spends his accidental night in the prison, after delaying to talk to Amy, it is Tip who appears and shows him round the prison in an almost proprietorial way:

> ... the long-initiated Tip, with an awful enjoyment of the Snuggery's resources, pointed out the kitchen fire maintained by common subscription of collegians, the boiler supported in like manner, and other premises generally tending to the deduction that the way to be healthy, wealthy and wise was to come to the Marshalsea.

We see more of the qualities of Little Dorrit through the eyes of Arthur Clennam, that example of ordinary decency brought up on repressively strict principles and now strangely unmotivated in the society in which he finds himself. In chapter 14 Amy Dorrit calls on Arthur at his lodgings to thank him for paying Tip's debt and thus releasing him from the Marshalsea. As Clennam has done this anonymously, she cannot acknowledge his kindness directly and Clennam is moved as much by her care in maintaining the pretence of anonymity as by the depth of her gratitude.

When Amy finally leaves, she and her poor servant and companion Maggie find they are too late to gain admission to the Marshalsea and have to spend the night in the London streets. In this perilous place, Amy's goodness seems to protect her: 'more than once some voice from among a knot of brawling or prowling figures in their path called out to the rest, 'let the woman and the child go by!' and a prostitute sent to prey upon children warns her to go home.

Clennam later meets Little Dorrit taking the air for a few moments on the Iron Bridge over the Thames, and their conversation draws them together. Amy feels it unfair that she is able to enjoy the open air while her father remains confined, and Clennam argues that she does good by bringing the freshness and spirit of outdoors into the prison with her. When Amy then asks whether she could do good to Clennam in this way if he were confined, he heartily affirms that she would. Maggie then appears with begging letters written to Clennam from Mr Dorrit and Tip. This greatly distresses Amy, who has asked them not to beg from him. Amy then declares she must go back because she, 'is afraid to leave any of them. When I am gone, they pervert – but they don't mean it – even Maggie'. She must go '*home*' to the prison and that it is 'better for me to stay there, much better, much more dutiful, much happier'.

Amy's devotion to her father and brother is unconditional. It leads her to return to be with them both in the prison, even though she knows they are in a sense unredeemable. Clennam, however, distinguishes between the more and the less deserving of the two beggars, making a distinction between the father, whose age might argue for more sympathetic treatment, and the callow undeserving Tip, whose request he rejects. He cannot bring himself to adopt Little Dorrit's moral position, but he begins to love the quality which takes her there.

Amy's loving care of her prison-tainted family provides part of the answer to the conundrum Dickens faces when considering legal sanctions and penal institutions. The 'Crown of Thorns' image in chapter 31 where, as Little Dorrit accompanies Mrs Clennam to deal with Rigaud, 'great shoots of light streamed among the early stars, like signs of the later blessed covenant of peace and hope', indicates Dickens' idea of its true nature. The answer of unconditional love creates a moral imperative, whether seen in a Christian context or otherwise, even though in purely worldly terms it is both outrageously costly and largely ineffectual.

We are left asking whether it can be right that Little Dorrit should be condemned to lead the life she leads. Amy's marriage to Clennam at the end of the book provides a resolution in her case but such a resolution cannot be an inevitable one.

In works such as *Bleak House* and *David Copperfield*, the question of social obligations focussed largely on individual transactions – Harold Skimpole's butcher's bill or Uriah Heep's fraudulent entries in the books of Wickfield & Heep – and their implications for society as a whole. *Little Dorrit* puts the question from the other viewpoint. It considers the effect of the mores of society as a whole upon the individuals within it.

As Mr Pancks puts it in his conversation with Clennam in chapter 13:

> 'Keep me always at it, and I'll keep you always at it, you keep somebody else always at it. There you have the Whole Duty of Man in a commercial country'.

We are moving from a consideration of individual transactions to focussing on society as a whole – in this case 'a commercial country', although Pancks even at this stage may only be paying lip service to the prevailing mores – in fact he has worked hard, and at some cost to himself, to benefit Amy by establishing her father's entitlement to his fortune.

Amy's sister, Fanny Dorrit, shows another way of surviving in this world. Fanny is unique in the book. Self-interested but not entirely unkind, with a strong will, good looks and a way with words, she is an attractive cork who will float and bob on the turbulent water when the future financial crash wrecks the lives of thousands. Determined to 'go into society', she takes advantage of her dancing lessons, is engaged at a small theatre and there attracts the attention of Edmund Sparkler, the son, by a previous marriage, of Mrs Merdle, so carrying the story from the seedy hand-to-mouth world of the Marshalsea to the home of that great banker and financier Mr Merdle in Harley Street, Cavendish Square.

The original impetus of the book was to attack the incompetence and complacency of the civil and military authorities which had led to disaster and death in the Crimea, personified here as the Barnacles and the Stiltstalkings, those extensive families of minor nobility and gentry who maintain themselves by securing public appointments and seats in Parliament. Their power, and their effect on society, is exercised through the Circumlocution Office, which they dominate. As we learn in chapter 10:

> No public business of any kind could possibly be done at any time without the acquiescence of the Circumlocution Office. Its finger was in the largest public pie and in the smallest public tart. It was equally impossible to do the plainest right and to undo the plainest wrong without the express authority of the Circumlocution Office. ... This glorious establishment had been early in the field, when the one sublime principle involving the difficult art of governing a country was first revealed to statesmen. ... Whatever was required to be done, the Circumlocution Office was beforehand with all public departments in the art of perceiving – HOW NOT TO DO IT.

The scope of Dickens' attack is now far wider than the conduct of the Crimean War. Arthur Clennam and Daniel Doyce meet on the steps of the Circumlocution Office, one attempting to unravel the complexity of Mr Dorrit's debts and the other seeking government support to develop his invention, both fellow-victims of the Office's opaque and almost – but not quite – circular procedures.

The essential aim of the Office is disarmingly admitted in chapter 28 by sprightly and good-natured Ferdinand, brightest and best of the Barnacles, who visits Clennam when he is imprisoned in the Marshalsea following the fall of Merdle's empire and the failure of Doyce's business:

> It is there with the express intention that everything shall be left alone. That's what it means. That's what it's for.

The Barnacles aim to ensure that nothing changes. They wish simply to maintain the stable society over which they have such a profitable grip. Their attitude extends far beyond the field of public administration. Mrs Gowan, mother of Henry Gowan who marries Minnie Meagles, is a paid-up member of the Barnacle clan, her husband having served in British Embassies abroad. Her son Henry has only a 'small independence' and Mrs Gowan expects his father-in-law, the unassuming retired banker Mr Meagles, to pay his debts:

> 'You must remember that my poor fellow has always been accustomed to expectations. They may have been realised or they may not have been realised....'
>
> 'Let us say, then, that they have not been realised,' observed Mr Meagles.
>
> The Dowager for a moment gave him an angry look, but tossed it off with her head and her fan, and pursued the tenor of her way in her former manner.

When Mrs Gowan finds she cannot win the argument she simply tries to humiliate Meagles:

> 'It is vain ... for people to attempt to get on together who have such extremely different antecedents; who are jumbled against one another in this accidental, matrimonial sort of way.'

Up to this point, the society which Dickens describes has three basic elements – firstly, the Barnacles and others who benefit from and seek to perpetuate the status quo; and secondly, most of the rest of the population, including the Plornishes, who are not well served by the existing system but can't work our exactly what's wrong with it.

The third small, struggling element is made up of those such as Daniel Doyce, supported by Clennam and Meagles, who work on improvements for the benefit of society but are frustrated in their aims. Doyce is essentially a practical workman and an engineer of talent while Meagles was a banker of integrity who kept a set of scales – for actually weighing the coins – and a scoop as a reminder of his banking career and who could assess financial projects with 'arithmetical solidity'. Doyce and Meagles even working together, can make little headway in England.

So much for the Barnacles and their apparently unshakable hegemony. Into this society the arrival of the great financier Mr Merdle introduces a new and powerful factor. In striking contrast to the caution and 'arithmetical solidity' of Mr Meagles' banking principles, Mr Merdle's talent is for far more speculative ventures, admiringly if vaguely described by a representative of the Bar as 'instances of a comprehensive grasp, associated with luck and boldness'.

The Barnacles and their allies, arrogantly protective of their own rank and privilege, are not natural supporters of men such as Mr Merdle. Merdle's speculative capitalism demands innovation, something which the Barnacle-led Circumlocution Office operates steadfastly to discourage and frustrate.

However, the life-changing amounts of money which Merdle's investments offer now entice not only the conventional pillars of society – the Treasury, the Bar, the Bishops, as well as those MPs and holders of public appointments which constitute the Barnacle clan – but also, eventually, practical men of integrity such as Clennam, Pancks and Doyce, to make large speculative investments:

> The famous name of Merdle became, every day, more famous in the land. Nobody knew that the Merdle of such high renown had ever done any good to anyone, alive or dead, or to any earthly thing .. All people knew (or thought they knew) that he had made himself immensely rich, and for that reason alone prostrated themselves before him.

Far from enjoying his success, however, Merdle himself is so uneasy that he appears to be a prisoner of the system of which he is apparently in control. At his own dinners, he experiences:

> ... constant difficulty with his coat-cuffs, almost as if they were handcuffs.

At a 'Barnacle' dinner he

> ... looked far more like a man in possession of his house under a distraint than a commercial colossus bestriding his own hearthrug.

Merdle's financial successes continue nevertheless.

As Dickens originally planned, the narrative of the book is divided into two sections – 'Poverty' and 'Riches' and certainly the narrative divides decisively between the time before William Dorrit is discovered to be the heir to a fortune in chapter 35 of Book the First and the time after that discovery. Thematically however the critical turning point of the book is the decision of Lord Tite Barnacle in to appoint Mr Merdle's stepson Edmund Sparkler to be one of the Lords of the Treasury in chapter 12 of Book the Second, reflecting the appointment of the late notorious John Sadleir to the same post by Lord Aberdeen's government in 1852.

Up to this point the Barnacles' steadfast purpose of ensuring that 'everything is left alone', while it was wasteful of the public purse and frustrated genuine enterprise in the form of people like Daniel Doyce, did nevertheless have a certain social usefulness in restraining the most irresponsible forms of financial speculation. Society was unfair but stable and Mr Casby (who, we are reminded, is the town agent for Lord Tite Barnacle) could continue to 'screw' his rents from Bleeding Heart Yard. In such a society Benthamite ideas could find acceptance – those with a safe, comfortable living could afford to condemn as 'improvident' those such as Mr Plornish who in financially precarious circumstances dared, once a year, to take his family for a day out to Hampstead in a van.

The Barnacles' appointment of Merdle's son to a post near the top of government however introduced a fundamental change. It was a public signal that these two hitherto opposing powers had now embraced each other. The government now publicly supported Merdle, so thoughts of caution and restraint could be set aside.

The result is to create a force which will sweep all the conventional landmarks of the financial world away, as described in chapter 13 of Book Two:

> As a vast fire will fill the air to a great distance with its roar, so the sacred flame which the mighty Barnacles had fanned caused the air to resound more and more with the name of Merdle.

But the fire is a contagious disease, and its progress becomes an epidemic:

> ... the contagion, when it had once made head, will spare no pursuit or condition, but will lay hold on people in the soundest health, and become firmly established in the most unlikely constitutions ... .

Even the cautious and practical Pancks takes the contagion. Having 'gone into it' and made his calculations, he believes that Merdle's investments are 'safe and genuine'. He invests his money and encourages Clennam to invest the capital left in his care by Doyce in the same way, in order to compensate Doyce for his years of toil and give him 'the chances of the time'.

The desire to invest has certainly reached Blandois' old companion Cavaletto, now earning a living with the Plornishes in Bleeding Heart Yard, and the Plornishes themselves share in the wonderment. They have ventured to open a small shop, painted on the outside to suggest an idealised notion of rural England, presenting:

> ... the exterior of a thatched cottage; the artist having introduced (in as effective manner as he found compatible with their highly disproportioned dimensions) the rear door and window. The modest sunflower and hollyhock were depicted as flourishing with great luxuriance on this rustic dwelling, while the quantity of dense smoke issuing forth from the chimney indicated good cheer within.

Ironically, while speculative investment is all the rage, the economic micro-entity of the shop set up for the Plornishes by Clennam is, perhaps prophetically, failing because she has given too much credit to her neighbours:

> ... if the Bleeding Hearts had but paid, the undertaking would have been a complete success; whereas, by reason of their exclusively confining themselves to owing, the profits ... had yet to appear on the books.

When the crisis comes to a head, Merdle quietly calls on his stepson and his new wife Fanny and borrows a penknife which he uses to commit suicide in a public bath nearby, leaving a letter for his physician. The letter was produced at the inquest:

> The inquest was over, the letter was made public, the Bank was broken, the other model structures had taken fire and turned to smoke. The admired piratical ship had blown up, in the midst of a vast fleet of ships of all rates, and boats of all sizes; and on the deep was nothing but ruin: nothing but burning hulls, bursting magazines, great guns self-exploded tearing friends and neighbours to pieces, drowning men clinging to unseaworthy spars and going down every minute, spent swimmers floating dead, and sharks.

The financial wreckage involves the whole society. Before the crash we had seen Merdle continually hampered by his own cuffs, as if they were handcuffs, and feeling like a man occupying his house under distraint by the bailiffs. Even the entirely innocent 'Young John' Chivery, when he helps Clennam into his room at the Marshalsea, turns his right wrist in a socket made of his left thumb and forefinger, and 'turning it backwards and forwards, for it was rather tight'. The inescapable force of the speculative project has caught up and confined all manner of men and women in a prison of their own making.

During their protected confinement in the Marshalsea Tip and his father had partaken of the tainted water peculiar to that situation, which by eroding their sense of financial responsibility had created the mental prison from which neither Tip nor, spectacularly, William Dorrit in Rome, could escape.

Now, even in the apparently free and open society outside the walls of the Marshalsea, the investment schemes promoted by Merdle create such a storm of speculative investment that even the most prudent citizens yield to its unrealistic promises and are imprisoned in its grip.

The Benthamite debate now becomes pointless, as the distinction between the prudent citizen and the irresponsible debtor – in essence that between the deserving and the undeserving poor – loses its meaning. This is not because financial irresponsibility has become acceptable, far from it, but because all of us in fact are flawed. The crash has shown that even the most apparently economically virtuous of us can be seduced by the promise of money to be had without effort. In normal times some would have had the luck or the insulating comfortable circumstances to survive while others did not. The implosion of Merdle's speculative schemes shows us all to be the same under the skin.

Dickens' instinctive generosity and compassion is always at odds with his equally instinctive dread of the moral degeneracy which any length of stay in a debtor's prison can engender. The unfolding of the *Little Dorrit* narrative shows us the way out of the Benthamite trap.

Part of the answer can be found in understanding the frailty of every human being as revealed by the failure of the Merdle empire. In that context, the unconditional devotion of Amy in her care of her family can be seen as an example which is capable of more general application. While, like Clennam himself, we may not be fully able to follow Amy, we can admire her example and follow it in spirit and in action as far as our worldly condition allows.

The other part of the answer of course lies in realising that acts of self-sacrifice and devotion do not make financial irresponsibility acceptable. Despite his daughter's faithful care, William Dorrit's folly still gives rise to his daughter's tears and distress.

The sense of financial responsibility that is missing in Dorit and in his son is essentially a willingness to keep proper accounts and recognise our obligations in relation to them. As Mr Micawber has shown us, if you are prepared conscientiously to keep account of your indebtedness and to discharge it when and where possible, you may hold up your head in society and look people in the eye. Such a sense of responsibility in its members is, Dickens would argue, as important to the proper functioning of society as the money itself. In the last analysis, it is the money's basis.

The firm of Doyce and Clennam, nurtured and sustained by that prudent banker of the scales and scoop, Mr Meagles, is a forceful embodiment of such principles. Under the Barnacle hegemony Daniel Doyce could prosper only outside the country but, following the collapse of Merdle's schemes, the return of Doyce and his firm, a little like the return of Malcolm at the head of English forces in *Macbeth*, brings healing and hope from abroad.

Before Doyce left England we saw something of the character of this firm as a practical enterprise, respecting its employees and using innovation for genuine social benefit. As Doyce had departed:

> The workmen were at the gate to see him off, and were mightily proud of him. 'Good luck to you, Mr Doyce!', said one of their number. 'Wherever you go, they'll find they've got a man as knows his tools and as his tools knows, a man as is willing and a man as is able, and if that's not a man, where is a man!' This oration from a gruff volunteer in the background was received with three loud cheers; and the speaker became a distinguished character for ever afterwards.

Doyce, returning at the head of the revived firm, is able to invite Clennam to his old place in this enterprise, thus enabling Arthur and Little Dorrit to embark on their married life, and the general feeling of a new dispensation is expressed when Mr Pancks casts off his allegiance to Mr Casby, denouncing him in front of his Bleeding Heard Yard tenants and 'spectacularly cutting off his flowing grey locks and exposing him as a bare-polled, goggle-eyed, big-headed lumbering personage.'

10.
A TALE OF TWO CITIES

The Lion and the Jackal

A Tale of Two Cities appeared in 1859, and in writing it Dickens was strongly influenced by Thomas Carlisle's *The French Revolution* published in 1837. The revolution in France itself of course figures in the *Tale* far more powerfully than any character in the book.

As the title plainly tells us, it is a novel about comparisons. Paris and London, England and France, are to be compared, the one with the other:

> There was a king with a large jaw and a queen with a plain face on the throne of England, there was a king with a large jaw and a queen with a fair face on the throne of France. In both countries it was as clear as crystal to the lords of the state preserves of the loaves and fishes, that things in general were settled for ever.
>
> France, less favoured on the whole as to matters spiritual than her sister of the shield and trident, rolled with exceeding smoothness downhill, making paper money and spending it. ... She entertained herself, besides, with such humane achievements as sentencing a youth to have his hands cut off, his tongue torn out with pincers and his body burned alive, because he had not kneeled down in the rain to

do honour to a dirty procession of monks which passed within his view at a distance of some fifty or sixty yards.

In England, there was scarcely an amount of order and protection to justify much national boasting. Daring robberies by armed men took place in the capital itself every night ... musketeers went into St Giles to search for contraband goods, and the mob fired on the musketeers, and the musketeers fired on the mob, and nobody thought these occurrences much out of the common way ... The hangman, ever busy and ever useless, was in constant requisition ... today taking the life of an atrocious murderer, and tomorrow of a wretched pilferer who had robbed a farmer's boy of sixpence.

The 'national boasting' referred to is of course the boasting that we English might be tempted to make, and actually did make, about the superiority of the laws and constitution of England to those of France, Dickens quickly proceeding to show how little grounds we have for any such self-congratulation, and how many and significant are the similarities between the two countries.

Dickens frequently describes the failings of London in terms which remind us of *Bleak House*. The scene in chapter 2 of the Dover Mail floundering through fog and mud is reminiscent of the fog and mud in the opening scene of *Bleak House* written some seven years earlier:

> ...steaming mist in all the hollows made its way through the air in ripples that visibly followed and overspread one another, as waves of an unwholesome sea might do.

Tellson's Bank, for which Mr Jarvis Lorry has worked for some forty years, is described in Book II chapter I as 'an old-fashioned place', and its partners were:

> ... proud of its smallness, proud of its darkness, proud of its ugliness, proud of its incommodiousness ... and of the partners would have disinherited his son on the question of rebuilding Tellson's. In this respect

the house was much on par with the country: which did very often disinherit its sons for suggesting improvements in law and customs.

The bank is situated close to Temple Bar, that same 'leaden-headed old obstruction' as is described in *Bleak House*. The windows of Tellson's are '... under a shower-bath of mud from Fleet Street made dingier by their own iron bars proper, and the heavy shadow of Temple Bar' and refers to the heads exposed there with 'insensate brutality and ferocity'.

It is from this same Tellson's, and from England, that Jarvis Lorry emerges on his mission of mercy, to bring to freedom someone who has been imprisoned, in effect buried, in the Bastille for eighteen years.

As we move to France in chapter 5, Dickens sounds a sad litany, a condemnation of the state of things, again reminiscent of the opening of *Bleak House*, except that what he sees is not fog, but something much worse, hunger:

> It was prevalent everywhere. Hunger was pushed out of the tall houses, in the wretched clothing that hung upon poles and lines: Hunger was patched into them with straw and rag and wood and paper; hunger was repeated in every small modicum of firewood that the man sawed off; Hunger started down from the smokeless chimneys and stared up from the filthy street that had no offal, among its refuse, of anything to eat. Hunger was the inscription on the baker's shelves, written in every small loaf of his scanty stock of bad bread, in every sausage-shop, in every dead-dog preparation that was offered for sale.

Dr Manette, reduced to an almost speechless shadow by the oppression of the Bastille, is saved and brought back to ordinary active life in England by the courage of Jarvis Lorry and the courage and love of his daughter. It is as if the tide of the book withdraws a little, preparatory to pushing on further in later scenes.

Back in England, the drama moves to a trial at the Old Bailey.

The trial, attended by Mr Lorry and Jerry Cruncher, is that of Charles Darnay, a Frenchman living in England, and of course it foreshadows his trial as Everemond before the revolutionary tribunal in Paris.

In London the court at the Old Bailey, like the Paris tribunal, is crowded with people, many of them relishing the sensational aspect of a treason trial and thereto sustaining themselves with ale and mutton pies. It is also a place of dread:

> Above the prisoner's head there was a mirror, to throw light down upon him. Crowds of the wicked and the wretched had been reflected in it, and had passed from its surface and the earth's together. Haunted in the most ghastly manner that abominable place would have been, if the glass could ever have rendered back its reflections, as the ocean is one day to give up its dead.

It is, though, a place that functions. The Attorney General's opening address to the court is full of indignant moralising and false logic: incriminating lists, for instance, are not actually in the prisoner's handwriting, but the Attorney General argues that this is 'all the better for the prosecution' as it shows the prisoner had been 'artful in his precautions'.

When the prisoner's defending barrister rises to question the prosecution's witness John Barsad, he is able to ask a series of penetrating questions. These either discredit the prisoner or are questions he is unable to answer. Another barrister, Sydney Carton, then on request dramatically takes off his own wig, revealing a striking resemblance to the man whom the four prosecution witnesses have identified as the man they have seen on other occasions. Mr Stryver asks the witnesses if they are still confident of their identification, and of course they are not. After hearing the penetrating questions, the negative or doubtful answers and the dramatic challenge to the identification evidence, the jury acquit the prisoner.

We later learn more, in Chapter five of Book II, of the relationship between Mr Stryver, Darnay's defending barrister, and the figure who removed his wig at the trial, Sydney Carton:

> It had once been noted at the bar, that while Mr Stryver was a glib man, and an unscrupulous, and a ready, he had not that faculty of extracting the essence from a heap of statements, which is among the most striking of an advocate's accomplishments. But a remarkable improvement came upon him as to this. The more business he got, the more his power seemed to grow at getting at its pith and marrow: and however late he sat carousing with Sydney Carton, he always had his points at his fingers' ends in the morning.

The improvement in Mr Stryver's abilities is explained when we see Stryver (described as the Lion) and Carton (described as the Jackal) working together in chambers late into the night. Great amounts of drink are consumed, but whereas the Lion, Stryver, is seen 'flirting with some lighter document' the Jackal, Carton, with knitted brows and intent face, is deep in the task and clearly does the essential brainwork in the case.

In status he remains the Jackal, however, seeming to have no ambition. As his friend Stryver says, he summons no energy and purpose.

As we have said, *A Tale of Two Cities* is a book of comparisons. In book II the thunderstorm that breaks over Dr Manette's garden in London presages the coming storm in Paris. The power of the London mob at the funeral of the spy Roger Cly in chapter 14, small scale though it is, foreshadows the far greater fury of the Paris mob in chapters 22 and 23. In the same way, Darnay's trial at the Old Bailey, and Carton's part in it, parallels the savage mockery of a trial before the Paris Tribunal.

Of this Dickens says:

> Before that unjust tribunal, there was little or no order of procedure ensuring to any accused person any reasonable hearing. There could have been no Revolution, if all laws, forms and ceremonies had not

first been so monstrously abused, that the suicidal vengeance of the Revolution was to scatter them all to the winds.

Lack of justice in society, Dickens is saying, if prolonged past endurance, will not only lead to people seeking revenge, it will also lead to the disappearance of justice of any kind. Here Dickens is speaking not just in general terms of the lack of fairness in society: he is speaking specifically of the actual system of justice, the 'laws, forms and ceremonies' which can evolve or be designed to ensure, as he says, that any accused person has any reasonable hearing. Only if this can be done, he implies, can the duties and rights necessary to a fair and free society be enforced and upheld.

In *The Pickwick Papers,* Dickens shows the law as largely oppressive, against whose thick plating we can batter ourselves in vain.

In *Bleak House,* Dickens makes another excoriating attack on the legal system. Through the character of Skimpole, he also explores the question of accountability. Could society function if there is no accountability, if we were all to avoid paying for what we eat, drink and wear, or return armchairs in a damaged state? John Jarndyce concludes that Mr Neckett, of Coavinses, is a 'necessary man'.

In *A Tale of Two Cities,* that oddly matched pair of lawyers, Carton and Stryver, illustrate different aspects of the law. Stryver is self-important, aggressive, unmannerly and apparently successful. Carton is strangely passive, entirely unambitious, often drunk, and held back by feelings of worthlessness and impotence.

It is Carton, nevertheless, who is the real lawyer. It is only after receiving Carton's help in analysing the legal issues in a case and marshalling the arguments that Stryver can perform on the day in Court. As we see when he removes his wig at Darnay's Old Bailey trial, Carton also has that gift for the dramatic which can, when used with intelligence and integrity, produce the most effective advocacy.

We see from his addresses to Lucy that the aggressive and talentless Stryver is without any real human sympathy. He is also a defender of the old regime, not only in England but in France.

It may not be fanciful to believe that Dickens sees in the figure of Sydney Carton, unrecognised and suppressed, operating fitfully and without optimism, something of the true spirit of the English common law - something which, like Carton himself, is almost lost, or perhaps like Manette, buried, but is alive still, and having at least the potential to become an engine of justice, at once subtle and robust, which can hold governments to account and achieve that balance of rights and duties, and of freedom and accountability, which is necessary to any just society.

Dickens is a resourceful and creative novelist, but he is also an unashamedly campaigning writer, and when we consider him as such I think we may also have a greater understanding of his creativity.

In the last chapter, Dickens tells us what Carton's last thoughts would have been at the point when, having selflessly changed places with Darnay in the prison, he meets his end on the scaffold. They would have included these:

> I see a beautiful city and a brilliant people rising from the abyss, and, in their struggles to be truly free ... I see the evil of this time and of the previous time ... wearing out.
>
> I see that child who lay upon her bosom and who bore my name, a man winning his way up in that path of life that once was mine. I see him winning it so well that my name is made illustrious by the light of his. ... I see him the foremost of just judges and honoured men... .

In all this, we may perhaps see a little more clearly how Dickens who, as a young man in 1838, expressed so strongly the sense of powerlessness and indignation he felt in his encounters with the law, and became the man who gave enthusiastic encouragement to his own son when he set out to study law at Trinity Hall, Cambridge exactly thirty years later.

11.
GREAT EXPECTATIONS

Illusions and Evidence

Though not so closely autobiographical as *David Copperfield*, *Great Expectations* is a novel concerned with a young man's progression from childhood to early adulthood in the *Bildungsroman* manner. While the early scenes are observed with a child's objectivity and intensity, the subsequent chapters depict the yearnings and self-critical embarrassments of youth and early manhood.

Pip's first dramatic encounter with the convict Magwitch takes place in the churchyard:

> 'Hold your noise!' cried a terrible voice, as a man started up from among the graves at the side of the church porch. 'Keep still, you little devil, or I'll cut your throat!' ...
>
> The man, after looking at me for a moment, turned me upside down, and emptied my pockets. There was nothing in them but a piece of bread. When the church came to itself – for he was so sudden and so strong that he made it go head over heels before me, and I saw the steeple under my feet – when the church came to itself, I say, I was seated on a high tombstone, trembling, while he ate the bread ravenously.

Seeing the church go head over heels, with its steeple under his feet, was only the first of the deeply disorientating and subverting experiences Pip was to undergo, and each was, in one way or another, to test his moral integrity.

Terrifying though his encounter with the convict Magwitch is, this first disruption of Pip's innocent life awakens feelings of compassion as well as fear. The second disruption, his visit to Miss Havisham's house and his meeting with Estella, makes him ashamed of his coarse hands and thick boots, and Pip becomes only too aware of the 'long chain of iron or gold, or of thorns and flowers' which binds him from that day forward.

Pip's pre-Estella life did have, along with his sister's fierce ministrations and Pumlechook's bullying, times of real happiness and contentment. Close to where he encounters Magwitch by the churchyard is the Battery where, as Pip says:

> I had been down there on a Sunday with Joe, and Joe, sitting on the old gun, had told me that when I was 'prentice to him, regularly bound, we would have such Larks there.

Even after the last of his regular visits to Satis House, when Miss Havisham had paid a handsome premium for him to be bound as an apprentice blacksmith to Joe, Pip's conversation with Biddy about his wish to become a gentleman takes place where they:

> ... were out on the marshes in lovely summer weather, and began to see the sails of ships as they sailed on.

Nevertheless, the effect of Pip's visits to Miss Havisham, of being called a 'common labouring boy' and being allowed to kiss Estella, had been to render as nothing such charms as his village life had held.

As Pip tells it in chapter 14:

> Home had never been a very pleasant place to me, because of my sister's temper, but Joe had sanctified it. I had believed in the best

> parlour as a most elegant saloon; I had believed in the front door, as a mysterious portal of the Temple of State whose solemn opening was attended by the sacrifice of roast fowls; I had believed in the kitchen as a chaste though not magnificent apartment; I had believed in the forge as the glowing road to manhood and independence. Within a single year all this was changed. Now, it was all coarse and common, and I would not see Miss Havisham or Estella see it on any account.

The third disruption of his life takes place after four years of apprenticeship. Mr Jaggers makes his sudden and dramatic appearance as 'a lawyer from London' in the familiarly companionable location of the Three Jolly Bargemen. The effect of his arrival is twofold. Jaggers magically brings with him the realisation of Pips' dream of becoming a gentleman and he then also appears to personify, in quick succession, two profoundly different aspects of the law as a social institution.

Jaggers first appears when Wopsle and his fellow wiseacres in the Three Jolly Bargemen have been reading a murder report in the local paper, with Wopsle exercising his talents in dramatic representation of the scene. Jaggers asks the company whether they believe the man to be guilty. When they say they do, Jaggers, biting his finger and effortlessly dominating the little group, points out to Wopsle's profound discomfiture that none of the witnesses have been cross-examined and that the prisoner has reserved his defence. He reminds the company of that great legal principle, the presumption of innocence, and asks what they would say about the conscience of someone who would condemn a fellow creature unheard.

Later the same evening, after publicly expounding on the law's role in defending an individual's right to fair trial, Jaggers demonstrates an entirely different face of the law – the arrogant and oppressive aspect it can display in its dealings with ordinary people. Jaggers asks Joe for a private conference at Joe's home at the forge and, apparently automatically, deploys lawyer's techniques for putting his interlocutor in a bad light:

'Now, Joseph Gargery, I am the bearer of an offer to relieve you of this young fellow, your apprentice. You would not object to cancel his indentures at his request and for his good? You would want nothing for so doing?'

'Lord forbid that I should want anything for not standing in Pip's way,' said Joe, staring.

'Lord forbidding is pious, but not to the purpose,' returned Mr Jaggers. 'The question is, would you want anything? Do you want anything?'

'The answer is,' returned Joe sternly, 'No.'

I thought Mr Jaggers glanced at Joe, as if he considered him a fool for his disinterestedness. But I was too much bewildered between breathless curiosity and surprise to be sure of it.

'Very well,' said Mr Jaggers. 'Recollect the admission you have made, and don't try to go back on it presently.'

'Who's a-going to try?' retorted Joe.

'I don't say anybody is. Do you keep a dog?'

'Yes, I do keep a dog.'

'Bear in mind, then, that Brag is a good dog, but Holdfast is a better. Bear that in mind, will you?' repeated Mr Jaggers, shutting his eyes and nodding his head at Joe, as if he were forgiving him something.

The worlds of Jaggers' adversarial legalism and Joe's profound human affections finally collide. Jaggers persists in getting Joe to confirm that he won't accept compensation for the loss of Pip as his apprentice, at which point Joe indignantly begins to square up to Jaggers with 'every demonstration of a fell pugilistic purpose' and the lawyer, at a loss for once, backs away.

This encounter is essentially in the same spirit as that between Mr Pickwick and Mr Dodgson in the office of Dodgson and Fogg, though on that occasion Sam Weller has to lead Pickwick away from a potential altercation with that lawyer. A similar exchange occurs between Mr Brownlow and the magistrate Fang in *Oliver Twist*. Pickwick, Brownlow and Joe Gargery expect the representatives of the law to act according to the rules of ordinary civility and they discover to their indignation that there can be a considerable divergence between the decencies of ordinary life and some modes of conduct prevailing in the legal system.

This tension underlies Pip's relationship with Jaggers and only resolves as the relationship develops.

As Dickens wrote to his friend John Forster when planning *Great Expectations*:

> '... you will find the hero to be a boy-child, like David ... To be quite sure I had fallen into no unconscious repetitions, I read David Copperfield again the other day, and was affected by it to a degree you can scarcely believe'.[1]

The narrative of the book is personal only to a degree, but it is a significant degree. Dickens could have written a powerful novel concentrating on the relationships between Pip and Joe, Estella, Miss Havisham, Biddy and Magwitch, leaving Jaggers as a simple legal nonentity responsible for paying out Magwitch's money to Pip. Instead, he makes Jaggers into one of the most significant characters in the book – significant in being, with Joe and Magwitch, one of the three quite different men who stand in some way as a father-figure to Pip, but also significant in that role as being a lawyer.

Pip's reaction to the invitations to Satis House and the apparent realisation of his dream of social transformation is, predictably, unqualified acceptance and a yearning for the status which would enable him to associate with Estella. It tests his loving relationship with Joe and Biddy to breaking point. On his first clumsy attempt to reconcile the two worlds by persuading Biddy to educate Joe, Pip cannot understand Biddy's quiet observation that Joe, too, may have his pride. A year or so later things have changed but only a little: on answering

Miss Havisham's call to visit her and Estella at Satis House, one part of Pip knows he should stay overnight with Joe and Biddy but soon:

> ... I was not by any means convinced on the last point, and began to invent reasons and make excuses for putting up at the Blue Boar.

In parallel to this stage of Pip's development is his changing relationship with Jaggers.

When Pip comes to London in chapter 20 his point of contact with his new guardian is Jaggers' office in Little Britain. Suitable quarters have been arranged for Pip in Barnard's Inn – another of the old Inns of Chancery – which he shares with Herbert Pocket, the boy he fought with in the garden of Satis House. Pip's gentlemanly education begins – initially through Herbert Pocket's kind counselling – but he is also introduced to the lawyer's world.

Even the cabman who takes Pip to his office is afraid of Jaggers' fearsome reputation and declines to take more than the standard shilling fare. Pip is then asked to wait in Jaggers' room while an unprepossessing figure – 'Mike' – is bundled out of the way. Pip sits in the client's chair, behind which the wall is greasy with the marks of many shoulders. He looks up at two forbidding death masks of Williams and Bishop, who had been convicted of the murder of 'the Italian Boy', a street entertainer, in 1831 and across at the lawyer's forbidding black horsehair seat and decides that the outside air might be a little fresher. He goes for a stroll:

> So I came to Smithfield, and the shameful place, being all asmear with filth and fat and blood and foam, seemed to stick to me. So I rubbed it off with all possible speed by turning into a street where I saw the great black dome of St Paul's bulging at me from behind a grim stone building which a bystander said was Newgate Prison. Following the wall of the jail, I found the roadway covered with straw to deaden the noise of passing vehicles, and from this, and the quantity of people standing about, smelling strongly of spirits and beer, I inferred that the trials were on.

Pip's personal life continues to be our main concern but the focus on Jaggers' practice in *Great Expectations* moves our attention from a concern for integrity of accounting such as emerges in the depiction of Harold Skimpole, Wilkins Micawber and William Dorrit, to the injustice in the criminal law created by the crude and undiscriminating methods of prosecution, and the problematical nature of evidence in trials.

In his first walk in the vicinity of Little Britain and Newgate Pip having, as a kind of preparation, passed by the 'shameful place' of Smithfield, comes upon:

> Two men of secret appearance lounging in Bartholemew Close, and thoughtfully fitting their feet into the cracks in the pavement as they talked together, one of whom said to the other when they first passed me, 'Jaggers would do it if it was to be done'.

Jaggers then appears. He puts his hand on Pip's shoulder and walks him along by his side without saying anything to him. He speaks to the two secret men, however:

> 'Now I have nothing to say to you,' said Mr Jaggers, biting his finger at them. 'I want to know no more than I know. As to the result, it's a toss-up. I told you from the first it was a toss-up. Have you paid Wemmick?'
>
> 'We made the money up this morning, sir,' said one of them submissively, while the other perused Mr Jaggers' face.
>
> 'I don't ask you when you made it up, of where, or whether you made it up at all. Has Wemmick got it?'
>
> 'Yes, sir,' said both men together.
>
> 'Very well; then you may go. Now, I won't have it!' said Mr Jaggers, waving is hand at them to put them behind him. 'If you say a word to me, I'll throw up the case.'

Later, Wemmick brings in the hapless Mike, who claims to have found a witness who 'in a general way', will swear 'to anything'. When Jaggers, infuriated, asks how he dares to tell him that, Wemmick softly intervenes:

> 'Spooney!' said the clerk, in a soft voice, giving him a stir with is elbow.
> 'Soft Head! Need you say it to his face?'

Mike then produces another answer, saying that the witness is prepared to swear 'ayther as to character, or to have been in 'is company and never left him all the night in question'. Jaggers clearly believes that Mike's first answer is more likely – unfortunately – to be true, but accepts the second on face value.

We see what sort of lawyer Jaggers is, and how he operates. His fundamental concerns are first, the need to exclude anything that is not relevant to the issue and second, in light of his duty not to mislead the court, his need not to be aware of anything that would unequivocally compromise his client's case.

A powerful lawyer, feared in many quarters, keeper of secrets and socially knowledgeable, Jaggers could be seen as similar in many ways to Mr Tulkinghorn, the solicitor in *Bleak House*, though the two lawyers could not be more different:

> Mr Tulkinghorn, sitting in the twilight by the open window, enjoys his wine. As if it whispers to him of its fifty years of silence and seclusion, it shuts him up the closer. More impenetrable than ever, he sits, and drinks, and mellows as it were in secrecy; pondering, at the twilight hour, of all the mysteries he knows, associated with the darkening woods in the country, and the vast, blank shut-up houses in town.[2]

Jaggers knows all too well that his clients are almost always compromised in one way or another and that he is working in an erratic legal system where the odds are in any case stacked against them. His constant hand washing – indeed the first thing the child Pip was aware of when meeting Jaggers on the stairs at Satis House was the smell of scented soap – is both a physical and symbolic method of dissociating himself not only from the lifestyle of his clients but also from the legal system in which he has to work.

Jaggers' forensic skills are those which he displays constantly in his conversations with Pip; the ability to separate the relevant evidence from irrelevant matters and identify precisely what evidence is necessary to support his client's case and to undermine the prosecution. Pip's appreciation of his guardian develops as he understands his eagerness for the evidence by which, when handled with sufficient skill, justice might sometimes be achieved. As Pip himself becomes more confident he begins to understand these techniques and on rare occasions to use them. At one stage Wemmick says admiringly of Pip that he was 'quite a cross-examiner'. Later, when Wemmick is about to take Pip into Newgate in chapter 32 Pip asks:

> 'Did your client commit the robbery?'
>
> 'Bless your soul and body, no,' answered Wemmick, very drily. 'But he is accused of it. So might you or I be. Either of us might be accused of it, you know.'
>
> 'But neither of us is,' I remarked.
>
> 'Yah!' said Mr Wemmick, touching me on the breast with is forefinger; 'you're a deep one, Mr Pip.'

Jaggers' commanding presence and practised style of questioning might suggest he is a barrister but his unpretentious office close to Newgate and his direct dealing with clients at that time make it clear that he is not. In fact, he is described later in the book as Miss Havisham's 'solicitor and man of business'.

As well as preparing cases for barristers, solicitors were able to represent clients in the lower courts and Jaggers very effectively acts for defendants before the stipendiary magistrates in the relatively new 'police courts'. In chapter 24, shortly before Pip's first visit to Wemmick's home at Walworth, Wemmick takes Pip to a police court in the City, to 'see Mr Jaggers at it':

> We dived into the City, and came up in a crowded police court where a blood relation (in the murderous sense) of the deceased with a fanciful taste in brooches was standing at the bar, uncomfortably chewing something; while my guardian had a woman under examination or cross-examination – I don't know which – and was striking her, and the bench, and everybody with awe. If anybody, of whatever degree, said a word he didn't approve of, he instantly required to have it 'taken down'. If anybody made an admission, he said, 'Now I have got you!' The magistrates shivered under a single bite of his finger. Thieves and thief-takers hung in dread rapture on his words, and shrank when a hair of his eyebrows turned in their direction. Which side he was on, I couldn't make out, for he seemed to be grinding the whole place in a mill ...

The 'crowded police court' Pip visits here was almost certainly one of those set up following the Middlesex Justices Act of 1792 – the same kind of court as that over which Mr Fang presides in *Oliver Twist*. An encounter between Jaggers and Mr Fang would certainly have been a memorable one.

In contrast with Pip's almost broken relationships with Joe and Biddy, the relationships which he now forms in his new life in London – apart from his strangely formal understanding with Estella – seem warm and rewarding. Pip has a real friendship with Herbert Pocket and Mr Jaggers has asked him to dine with him at his house in Gerrard Street on two occasions. The first is in chapter 26 where Pip is invited to bring his friends Startop and Drummle and Jaggers draws attention to Molly's wrists. Jaggers, in a confidential way, asks Pip about Drummle – 'Who's the spider?' and is interested to 'screw discourse out of him'. Just before Pip leaves he apologises to Jaggers for Drummle's argumentative manner and Jaggers in a perfectly friendly way dismisses the matter and agrees with Pip that he should keep clear of Drummle as much as he can, but says that he likes Drummle as 'one of the true sort', even though later, at chapter 48, he says he 'either beats or cringes'.

In chapter 36, when Pip had just come of age and been told he was to have an income of £500 a year, Jaggers asks Pip where is going to dine and Pip has the confidence to invite him to dine with Herbert and himself in their chambers. Pip is also making arrangements with Wemmick about helping Herbert to a partnership. He knows that Estella is to marry Drummle, and is taking this deep disappointment well enough to be able to warn Estella against marrying such an unfeeling man. Although the break of faith and affections with Joe and Biddy remains unresolved, Pip is nevertheless living confidently and showing genuine kindness and responsibility for Herbert in the new social environment.

If the book has one key chapter it is chapter 39. Pip is twenty three and no longer lives in Barnard's Inn or with Matthew Pocket, but shares book-lined rooms in the Middle Temple with Herbert. Nowhere else in Dickens's novels seems to realise more closely the author's own boyhood hope of 'growing up to be a learned and distinguished man' of which he speaks in the 'biographical fragment.'

The autobiographical element in the book is quite strong here. Barnard's Inn and Furnival's Inn were two of the old Chancery Inns which, by letting out sets of rooms, survived in a largely moribund form until the late nineteenth century. Dickens himself occupied rooms in Furnival's Inn, Holborn, on leaving his family home in 1834 and Pip in his quarters in Barnard's Inn lives in a similar way.

This binding together of real life and creative fiction seems to reflect both Dickens' interest in the law as a social institution and his attraction to the societies such as the Inns of Court and Chancery. In November of that year Dickens had written, as we have noted, to the Steward of New Inn, another of the ancient Chancery Inns, enquiring about accommodation there and expressing an intention to proceed to the Bar. This was the only Inn of Chancery specifically associated with the Middle Temple, and it was to the Middle Temple that New Inn students, after a period of study, normally progressed.

It is in chapter 39 that a great wind, blowing from the east into the Temple on that crucial night, did not just extinguish the lamps and attack the physical buildings of the Temple but also carried news that blew the whole structure of Pip's social position into fragments:

> Day after day, a vast heavy veil had been driving over London from the East and it drove still, as if in the East there were an eternity of cloud and wind. So furious had been the gusts, that high buildings in town had had the lead stripped off their roofs; and in the country, trees had been torn up and the sails of windmills carried away; and gloomy accounts had come in from the coast, of shipwreck and death. Violent blasts of rain had accompanied these rages of wind, and the day just closed as I sat down to read had been the worst of all.
>
> Alterations have been made in that part of the Temple since that time, and it has not so lonely a character as it has now, nor is it so exposed to the river. We lived at the top of the last house, and the wind rushing up the river shook the house that night like discharges of cannon or the breaking of the sea. When the rain came with it and dashed against the windows, I thought, raising my eyes to them as they rocked, that I might have fancied myself in a storm-beaten light-house.

Magwitch, the returning convict, now appears at the door of Pip's Temple chambers as if the wind had brought him from New South Wales, which in a sense of course it had. He also comes in darkness. Pip finds the lamps on the staircase had been blown out, as had the lamps in the court. Even the coal fires burning on the barges on the river were being carried away by the wind 'like red-hot splashes in the rain'. He also comes when Pip is alone, reading. It is not casual reading but a regular, methodical activity:

> I read with my watch upon the table, purposing to close my book at eleven o'clock.

It is as if Pip is actually realising Charles's boyhood hope of becoming 'a learned and distinguished man', rather than embodying Magwitch's own conception of his London gentleman as a rich, profligate young man-about-town.

Pip recognises him suddenly, after challenging his right to question him:

> ... I knew him! Even yet I could not recall a single feature, but I knew him! If the wind and the rain had driven away the intervening years, had scattered all the intervening objects, had swept us to the churchyard where we had first stood face to face on such different levels, I could not have known my convict more distinctly than I knew him now, as he sat in the chair before the fire.

The revelation that his present income and gentlemanly status depends not upon Miss Havisham' favour but on a source at the lowest, most wretched level of society is inevitably the most profound shock for Pip, particularly as it carries with it the knowledge that there is, after all, no plan linking him in any way to Estella. The sharpest pain of all, as Pip expresses it, is that it was for this that he had 'deserted Joe'.

Pip's earlier unhesitating embrace of his opportunity to move away from the honest and innocent way of life of his childhood might suggest that his new life was in some essential way false and hypocritical in nature. His reaction to Magwitch's revelations confirms our long-forming impression that this is not the case. His dealings with Jaggers – whom, as we will see, he actually shocks by his discovery that Magwitch was Estella's father – with Wemmick, and with Estella herself have been entirely honest, direct and respectful, and to Herbert Pocket he has been a thoughtful and generous friend.

We learn more about Jaggers, and about Pip's developing relationship to him, in the later stages of the book. In chapter 48, after Pip, Startop, Drummle and Wemmick have dined at Jaggers' house and seen the powerful wrists of his servant Molly, Wemmick describes how hard Jaggers worked to win an acquittal for Molly at her trial for murder:

'Mr Jaggers was for her,' pursued Wemmick, with a look full of meaning, 'and worked the case in a way quite astonishing ... He worked it himself at the police-office, day after day for many days, contending against even a committal: and at the trial where he couldn't work it himself, sat under counsel and – everyone knew – put in all the salt and pepper.'

Wemmick then explains the bold but entirely logical argument by which Jaggers succeeded in the case. The question at issue was the cause of certain scratches on the backs of Molly's hands. The prosecution argued that Molly was exceedingly jealous of her female victim's relationship with a certain man, and as evidence of this jealousy they put in evidence that she was suspected of destroying her child by this man.

This evidence almost certainly would not be admitted now. Even if it could be said to be to any extent relevant, the prejudicial effect of this 'strong' but unproven suspicion against Molly's character in the eyes of the jury would outweigh its value as actual evidence. However, Jaggers allowed the evidence to be admitted. He then turned it to his client's advantage by saying that if the prosecution wished the jury to believe that Molly had destroyed the alleged victim's child they would have to accept the possibility that the scratches on the back of Molly's hands could have been made by the child.

He argued, in effect, that the prosecution had themselves introduced an alternative explanation for the scratches which could only weaken their original argument that the scratches had been made by Molly's adult victim. He made the point that they were not prosecuting Molly for destroying the child. He then argued that by introducing evidence that the child might have caused the scratches, the prosecution itself had shown they did not have confidence in their own argument. They therefore could not expect the jury to have confidence in that argument either. This was the kind of 'salt and pepper' Jaggers put into Molly's case as he 'sat under counsel'.

The misleading power of appearances and the importance of relying only on what can be ascertained as evidence is of course the hard lesson Pip has to learn with regard to the roles in his own life of Miss Havisham and Magwitch. When, immediately after Magwitch has revealed himself, Pip goes to Jaggers to verify Magwitch's story, Jaggers points out that he is not responsible for Pip's assuming that Miss Havisham was his benefactor:

> 'And yet it looked like it, sir,' I pleaded with downcast heart.
>
> 'Not a particle of evidence, Pip,' said Mr Jaggers, shaking his head and gathering up his skirts. 'Take nothing on its looks; take everything on evidence. There's no better rule.'

Much later in the book, in chapter 51, we see the somehow more mature and confident Pip for once put the impressive Jaggers off his stride when, having pieced together, from what he had learned from Wemmick and from what Magwitch had disclosed to Herbert, the true facts of Estella's parentage – Molly being her mother and Magwitch her father – he makes Estella's father's identity known to Jaggers:

> 'Perhaps I know more of Estella's history than even you do,' said I. 'I know her father, too.'
>
> A certain stop that Mr Jaggers came to in his manner – he was too self-possessed to change his manner, but he could not help its being brought to an indefinably attentive stop – assured me that he did not know who her father was. ...
>
> 'Yes,' I replied, 'and is name is Provis – from New South Wales.'
>
> Even Mr Jaggers started when I said those words. It was the slightest start that could escape a man, the most carefully repressed and the sooner checked, but he did start, though he made it part of the action of taking out his pocket-handkerchief. ...
>
> 'And on what evidence, Pip,' asked Mr Jaggers, very coolly, as he paused with his handkerchief half-way to his nose, 'does Provis make this claim?'

'He does not make it,' said I, 'and has never made it, and has no knowledge or belief that his daughter is in existence.'

For once, the pocket-handkerchief failed. My reply was so unexpected that Mr Jaggers put his handkerchief back into his pocket without completing the usual performance, folded his arms, and looked with stern attention at me, though with an immovable face.

Pip then appeals to Jaggers to tell him of the circumstances of Estella's adoption. Jaggers, in effect, ignores this request until Pip appeals to Wemmick, who, he says, he knows to have a gentle heart and a pleasant home where he cares for his old father.

This is so contrary to the grim and unfeeling persona that Wemmick maintains at the office that Jaggers and Wemmick suddenly look oddly at each other, Jaggers relaxes into something of a smile and Wemmick becomes bolder:

'Pip,' said Mr Jaggers, laying his hand upon my arm and smiling openly, 'this man must be the most cunning imposter in all London.'

'Not a bit of it,' said Wemmick, growing bolder and bolder, 'I think you're another.'

Jaggers then reveals not only the circumstances of Estella's adoption but the degraded nature of the environment in which he worked, and his motive for saving one child from it:

'Put the case that he lived in an atmosphere of evil, and that all he saw of children was, their being generated for certain destruction. Put the case that he often saw children solemnly tried at the criminal bar, where they were held up to be seen; put the case that he habitually knew of their being imprisoned, whipped, transported, neglected, cast out, qualified in all ways for the hangman, and growing up to be hanged. Put the case that pretty nigh all the children he saw in his daily business life, he had reason to look upon as so much spawn, to develop into fish that were to come to his net – to be prosecuted, defended, forsworn, made orphans, bedevilled somehow'.

'I follow you, sir.'

'Put the case that here was one pretty child who could be saved ...'

The conditions which Estella had been born in are echoed by by that described by her father, Magwitch, of his own childhood, in chapter 42:

> 'I've been carted here and carted there, and put out of this town and put out of that town, and stuck in the stock, and whipped and worried and drove. I've no more notion of where I was born than you have – if that much. I first became aware of myself, down in Essex, stealing turnips for my living. Summon had run away from me – a man – a tinker – and he'd took the fire with him, and left me very cold. ... This was the way it was, that when I was a ragged little creature as much to be pitied as ever I see, I got the name of being hardened. 'This is a terrible hardened one,' they says to prison visitors, picking out me. 'May be said to live in jails, this boy.'

It is this crude, oppressive legal system in which Jaggers practises. As a compassionate man, the only way he can continue to work is by washing his hands at every opportunity, symbolically as well as physically cleansing himself of the contamination of his working environment, and by surrounding himself – and of course Wemmick – with a protective plating of legal rigour. He works with compromised materials but he knows that sometimes, if the lawyer is skilful enough, the crude machinery of the law can be made to work, as it did so successfully with his defence of Molly.

Jaggers and Wemmick together initially present the impenetrable, rigorous and often harsh face of the law. As Pip comes to know them as human beings – Jaggers as a father figure, Wemmick as a friend – he begins also to understand something of the discipline and skill of legal practice which can sometimes achieve justice.

Pip's more positive view of the law's power perhaps reflects the evolving views of Dickens himself. The legal skill which Jaggers deploys so effectively to save Molly is far more impressive than the opportunistic tricks and complacent bungling of Sergeants Buzfuz and Snubbin, the two advocates in *Bardell v Pickwick*.

Pip can also be said to pass the severe test set by the ruin of his expectations. He decides he can no longer accept the benefit of Magwitch's wealth and, with Herbert, buries himself in the business of protecting his benefactor and arranging for him to leave the country before he can be denounced as a returned convict. The back windows of the house in Essex Street where Pip and Herbert shelter Magwitch still overlook the Temple courts. The great wind which had carried Magwitch to the Temple, battering the building in which Pip had been reading and bringing an end to his expectations, did not demolish Pip's ability to act in the essentially thoughtful and responsible way.

The matter of his relationship with Joe and Biddy nevertheless remains unresolved until, following the death of Magwitch, Pip at last gives way under the strain of caring for his benefactor and passes into the unconsciousness of a profound fever in which the tensions and contradictions of that relationship seem to be purged away.

Pip awakens to find himself humbly grateful for Joe's tender care. They cannot return to their early ways of innocence, however. The purging illness does not and cannot restore Pip's relationship with Joe and Biddy on its original basis. When taking a convalescent walk with Joe – still, perhaps significantly, in the Temple gardens – Pip realises this as Joe's manner towards him changes, becoming more distant and 'respectful' as Pip's strength returns. Joe realises before Pip does that, although their newly re-established friendship will remain – 'ever the best of friends' – each of them can properly live only in the respective ways of life that they have adopted – Pip in his Clarriker's clerkship and Joe back at his forge and married to Biddy.

The River Stair of the Temple in the early nineteenth century, before the construction of the London Embankment. The southern buildings of the Temple were more exposed to the river at that date

12.
OUR MUTUAL FRIEND

A Lawyer Learns to Love

Dickens' satiric voice can still be heard clearly in *Our Mutual Friend*, but as the novel progresses, his concerns coalesce into larger and sadder themes. The first instalment or 'number' of the book appeared in May 1864, some five years after the publication of Darwin's *Origin of Species* in 1859, and the novel seems to reflect a new perspective on the subject of change and natural history.

London in the 1860s was a larger metropolis than it had been in the 1820s, when Dickens had begun to write, though the author moves around it with his usual confidence. The book opens with Gaffer Hexam and his loyal daughter Lizzie searching for dead bodies in the filthy water of the Thames; moves to west London, to the 'bran new' establishment of the Veneerings, newly arrived on the social scene and hosting substantial dinners for any presentable people they can persuade to come; then to Holloway, a mile or so north of St Pancras station and the home of the Wilfers and their two daughters Bella and Lavinia, struggling to maintain a sort of gentility on 'Rumty' Wilfer's pay as a clerk in the city office of Veneering, Chickweed and Stobbles.

We also see Silas Wegg's balladmonger's stall on the pavement of Cavendish Square, W1. Mr Nicodemus Boffin, now known as the 'Golden Dustman' because he is the legatee of his old employer the refuse magnate John Harmon, engages Wegg as his personal reader and leads him to Boffin's Bower, otherwise known as Harmony Jail, where 'certain dark tall mounds rose high against the sky' and the way is shown by 'two lines of broken crockery set in ashes', probably in the area between Somers Town and Pentonville, behind King's Cross Station, where there was a notorious dust heap at Belle Isle.

The plot largely turns on the unusual will of John Harmon senior which leaves his estate to his son John Harmon Junior on the condition that he married Bella Wilfer, leaving the money otherwise to his foreman Nicodemus Boffin as the residuary legatee. When John Junior returns to England he is attacked and robbed by the ship's third mate, who himself drowns while John survives. The attacker resembles John and so it is John Harmon who is believed drowned. Thus free of his old identity, John decides to adopt the name Rokesmith and to test Bella by seeing if she will marry him without his money. The plot is complicated by the discovery, in Old Harmon's dust mounds, of two later wills, one leaving the estate to the Crown, and an even later one which leaves it to Nicodemus Boffin, who benevolently gives most of the property over to John Harmon junior, simply retaining the 'mounds'. The scheming Wegg, finding the first of the two later wills, tries to use it for blackmail but he is defeated, and justice is achieved, without any legal help or even a legal presence, through the actions of Boffin himself, assisted by Mr Venus.

Two young lawyers, Lightwood and Wrayburn, begin to link up the key locations of the book. Mortimer Lightwood is a solicitor with very little practice, Eugene Wrayburn a barrister with no practice at all, and they share a set of rooms in the Temple. They are dining at the Veneerings when a messenger appears – it is Charlie Hexam, sent by his father who has pulled a body from the river with papers naming Lightwood as its solicitor, and the two men accompany the boy in a cab back to Gaffer's riverside dwelling:

> The wheels rolled on, and rolled down by the Monument and by the Tower, and by the Docks; down by Ratcliffe, and by Rotherhithe; down

by where accumulated scum of humanity seemed to be washed from higher ground, like so much moral sewage, and to be pausing until its own weight forced it over the bank and into the river. In and out among vessels that seemed to have got ashore, and houses that seemed to have got afloat – among, bowsprits staring into windows and windows staring into ships – the wheels rolled on until they stopped at a dark corner, river washed and otherwise not washed at all, where the boy alighted and opened the door.

'You must walk the rest, sir; it's not many yards.' He spoke in the singular number, to the express exclusion of Eugene.

Despite this implied exclusion, Wrayburn accompanies his friend to Gaffer's home and from there to the police station. Lizzie's father declares the honest nature of his livelihood:

'I do everything regular. I've giv' notice to the police and the police have took possession of it.'

says Gaffer, maintaining his claim to uprightness amid his dubious surroundings.

Wrayburn's lack of any significant participation in the evening's events presages his subsequent role. Though he is often present, he does virtually nothing in the book except fall in love with Lizzie Hexam, and even then he manages to enrage his rival for Lizzie's affections, Bradley Headstone, the schoolmaster of Lizzie's young brother Charlie, simply by indicating several times that he has absolutely no interest in him.

In chapter 12 the two lawyers have a visitor to their Temple chambers. Rogue Riderhood wants to swear an affidavit saying that he suspects Gaffer Hexam of murdering John Harmon. All three then travel to the Police Office close to Hexam's home and a watch for Hexam is kept, during which Wrayburn first sees Lizzie, through the window of her home:

> She had no other light than the light of the fire. The unkindled lamp stood on the table. She sat on the ground, looking at the brazier, with her face leaning on her hand. There was a kind of film or flicker on her face light; but on a second look, he saw that she was weeping. A sad, solitary spectacle, as shown him by the rising and falling of the fire.

In chapter six of Book the Second Bradley Headstone brings Charlie to see Wrayburn in the Temple, ostensibly to allow the boy to object to Wrayburn's paying for some education for Lizzie but in fact in order that Headstone can confront his rival.

Lightwood and Wrayburn are at leisure in their Temple chambers, smoking before the fire, Lightwood mildly teasing his friend about their new fittings and asking whether he has any feelings for Lizzie, while Wrayburn avoids any commitment on the point. Wrayburn becomes aware of walkers in the court below – 'Two belated wanderers in the mazes of the law' – and begins to throw bits of soil from a flowerpot on to the wanderers.

The visitors shelter in a doorway which is at the foot of the friends' staircase and subsequently come up and knock at their door. Charlie Hexam then begins to recount how often Wrayburn has been in contact with his sister. Wrayburn responds only by speaking to Headstone:

> 'Was this worth while, schoolmaster?' murmured Eugene, with the air of a disinterested adviser. 'So much trouble for nothing? You should know best, but I think not.'
>
> 'I don't know, Mr Wrayburn, ' answered Bradley, with is passion rising, 'why you address me -'
>
> 'Don't you? Then I won't'.

Wrayburn's attitude of non-engagement so enrages Headstone that he later attempts to murder him, following which Wrayburn is rescued from the river by Lizzie.

Apart from his falling for Lizzie, Wrayburn's role remains entirely passive. He seems content to be called to the bar and occupy barristers' chambers for the satisfaction of his family but has no impulse to involve himself in the law as a profession, or indeed to have anything to do with it. It is not antipathy, but it is profound indifference, as if he does not see the law as having any significant function in society.

There are two love stories in the novel – that between Rokesmith/Harmon and Bella Wilfer and that between Eugene Wrayburn and Lizzie Hexam. Rokesmith is an entirely virtuous figure, not wishing to take advantage of his father's will to compel Bella to marry him with the promise of wealth, but wanting to see if Bella really can take him without the prospect of it. Wrayburn is a figure in suspension, apparently without vices but without virtues either.

He behaves decently towards Lizzie but a relationship leading to marriage seems to Lizzie unachievable because of the judgement of society. What is seen as the social gulf between them would make marriage impossible. The social gap between Lizzie and Wrayburn is very great: Lizzie's father, Gaffer Hexam, earns his living where lawful activity can quickly shade off into criminality, and Lizzie of course has a loyalty to her father which compares with that of Amy Dorrit to her father and brother.

Wrayburn is a barrister on the margins of the legal system and in that respect resembles Sydney Carton and Tom Traddles, but unlike them he doesn't care about the law at all. His inaction seems a kind of sympathetic reaction to the condition of the world he finds around him.

Little Dorrit was about political and administrative stasis and subsequently about financial corruption, the central concern being that of financial accountability, both personal and corporate. *Our Mutual Friend* is concerned not so much with politics or finance as with the greater natural processes of decay, death and rebirth, apparent death and transformation.

Gaffer Hexam lives by recovering corpses from the river, is accused of murder where no murder has taken place, and is drowned in the very waters from which he gained his livelihood. By his death he defeats Rogue Riderhood's attempt to claim the reward offered for identifying him as young John Harmon's murderer. Riderhood escapes one drowning when run down by a steamer, comes to believe he cannot be drowned but then does drown while struggling with Bradley Headstone because Headstone had disguised himself as Riderhood when attempting to kill his rival Wrayburn. Wrayburn survives, rescued from the water by Hexam's daughter Lizzie

Old John Harmon made his living by collecting the refuse cast off by society, becomes rich in doing so, and seeks to exercise control over his son and prospective daughter-in-law from beyond the grave. His son young John Harmon seems to die but re-emerges to defy the dispositions of his father.

Noddy Boffin becomes apparently very wealthy as John Harmon's residuary legatee and loses this status on the recovery of a later will from the decaying mounds of refuse, but not before going through an apparent transformation into miserhood and re-emerging as his old benevolent self. John Rokesmith, the 'mutual friend' of the title, presenting as a much-needed lodger to the Wilfers and a potential secretary to Mr Boffin, emerges as neither, but the son and heir of Old John Harmon, to displace Mr Boffin as legatee.

Disguises used to test loyalty, the discovery of wills and the ensuing changes of fortune, attempted murder and the recovery of the victim and actual murder and the recovery of the victim's corpse are the commonplace staple of fiction. When these events are as numerous and complex as they become in *Our Mutual Friend*, however, they become a theme rather than a plot device. When set against the physical examples of natural decay, death and rebirth, loss and re-use and the apparent dissolving of the barriers between life and death, they contribute to a sense of impermanence in which we can see the events of human life as part of the natural processes of decay and regeneration in which our own attempts at moral judgement have less and less relevance.

Hamilton Veneering's career has some resemblance, though on a much smaller scale, to that of *Little Dorrit*'s Mr Merdle. Veneering's firm, 'Chicksey, Veneering and Stobbles', has its office in Mincing Lane,

EC3, where many druggists and herbalists were based, suggesting that his quickly-gained riches derive from the adulteration of foodstuffs – hence the scorn of his analytical-chemist butler – and his rapid rise to membership of the House of Commons is equally quickly followed by descent into bankruptcy.

Instead of the stock market speculation of *Little Dorrit*, we have the allegedly speculative market in orphans. When the Rev Mr Milvey and his wife go searching for an orphan for the Boffins to adopt:

> For the instant it became known that anybody wanted an orphan, upstarted some affectionate relative of the orphan who put a price on the orphan's head. The suddenness of the orphan's rise in the market was not to be paralleled in the maddest records of the Stock Exchange. He would be at five thousand percent discount out at nurse making a mud pie in the morning, and, being enquired for, would go up five thousand percent premium before noon.

In the background of course we have Mr Venus' taxidermist's shop near the church in Clerkenwell, where Wegg sees:

> A pretty little dead bird lying on the counter, with its head drooping on one side against the rim of Mr Venus' saucer, and a long stiff wire piercing its breast. As if it were Cock Robin, the hero of the ballad, and Mr Venus were the sparrow with his bow and arrow and Mr Wegg were the fly with its little eye.

> Mr Venus dives and produces another muffin, yet untoasted; taking the arrow out of the breast of Cock Robin he proceeds to toast it on the end of that cruel instrument.

What had been an arrow returns to its role as a toasting fork. The bird's once-living body is replaced by a muffin. Amidst these bizarre transformations, reality itself becomes something of a jumble. Mr Venus describes a reconstructed body he has just sent to a school of art:

> '... a perfect beauty ... One leg Belgian, one leg English, and the pickings of eight other people in it.'

There is even the possibility of buying and selling human body parts:

> 'You can't buy human flesh and blood in this country, sir; not alive, you can't,' said Mr Wegg, shaking his head. 'Then query, bone?'
>
> 'As a legal point?' asks Venus.

The blurring of boundaries is further exemplified by Silas Wegg's endless reading of Gibbon's *Decline and Fall of the Roman Empire,* in which centuries of human strife and ambition can be seen as part of a natural process of decline and fall, change and decay, and again by Wegg's continual mangling and regurgitation of poems and ballads familiar at least to Dickens' first readers.

The situations which call for our moral judgement, such as that of Veneerings or of Molly Higden, are ranged with those which simply involve natural or apparent processes of change and rebirth, such as the Harmon-Hansford-Rokesmith-Harmon transformation process or the survival and subsequent death of Riderhood, or Gaffer Hexham's trade of recovering corpses from the river or the contents of Mr Venus' shop or decay, such as the dust heaps of Harmon's jail and the ooze and filth of the river itself. Judgement of individual actions and the role of the law itself comes into question as the boundaries between these aspects of our existence become increasingly blurred.

Eugene Wrayburn is a decent man, however. From the first time he sees Lizzie Hexam she remains in his mind, and on his second visit to the Limehouse Police Station, when they are waiting for Gaffer Hexam to return, he climbs from their hiding place under a boat to Hexam's home. He looks through the window at Lizzie waiting for her father by the fire and sees she is weeping. When Lightwood later suggests they go up and 'take a peep through the window'.

'No, don't!' Eugene caught him by the arm. 'Best not to make a show of her.'

He is still showing the same sensitivity and restraint in book four chapter 6 when he visits Lizzie at the riverside village where she works in the paper mill. Lizzie firmly declines to accept his attentions. The social distance between them means that they cannot marry, and if she becomes his lover without marriage she becomes a disgraced woman in society's eyes. To her, and to Wrayburn when he thinks about it, there is no way forward and Wrayburn ultimately accepts that their relationship, such as it is, must end:

> The purity with which in these words she expressed something of her own love, made a deep impression on him for the passing time. He held her, almost as if she were sanctified to him by death, and kissed her, once, almost as if he might have kissed the dead.
>
> 'I promised that I would not accompany you, not follow you. Shall I keep you in view? You have been agitated, and it is growing dark.' ...
>
> 'There is but one means, Mr Wrayburn, of sparing yourself and of sparing me, every way. Leave this neighbourhood tomorrow morning.'
>
> 'I will try'.

A little later, walking alone by the river, Eugene states the problem which, according to the rules of society, seems to afford no solution:

> 'Out of the question to marry her,' said Eugene, 'and out of the question to leave her. The crisis!'

A moment later, however:

> In an instant, with a dreadful crash, the reflected night turned crooked, flames shot jaggedly across the air, and the moon and stars came bursting from the sky.

Bradley Headstone's sudden attack breaks into Eugene's ordered life, not only seriously injuring him but also smashing into the social rules by which Eugene believed himself bound.

Even after his rescue, it takes a long illness and a slow recovery for him to realise what is his proper course of action, just as was the case with Pip and with Dick Swiveller. Eugene, so long unmotivated by the law, eventually finds a motive for action in his love and admiration for Lizzie.

Lizzie's self-denying loyalty to her father and brother is similar to Amy Dorrit's devotion to her family, but there is a significant difference. The difficulty Lizzie has to face is not the one Amy Dorrit faced – that of her father's lack of financial rectitude and moral responsibility which occupied Dickens for so long. More simply perhaps, it is the difficulty of dealing with the poverty and social opprobrium associated with her father's way of life. The question of accurate account-keeping is no longer so important.

Just as Little Dorrit's was by Arthur Clennam's offer to her, Lizzie's loyalty is tested. She has the opportunity of a better life. Miss Abbey Potterson offers to take her under her wing in that warm, competent and honest establishment The Three Jolly Fellowship Porters if she would leave her father, but Lizzie does not give way.

There are two love stories in the book, and one of loyalty, all concerned with people breaking through the barriers constructed by others. In John Harmon's case, the barriers were constructed by his father's strange testamentary conditions, in Eugene Wrayburn's case by society as a whole, so ably represented by the arrogant Podsnap and his companions at the Veneerings' table and in Lizzie Hexam's case, by the community's suspicion of her father. All three are successful in overcoming these barriers because of the strength and sincerity of their love. While in these conditions society's legal framework seems to diminish in importance, both Eugene Wrayburn and John Harmon discover that love has the power to give direction and purpose to individual human lives.

NOTES

Chapterisation varies slightly between editions. Where a passage is not found as cited it will usually be located in the chapter immediately before or after the chapter referred to.

Introduction
1. Gesta Henrici Secundi (RS 1867) 1 P 207
2. Magna Carta 1214, Chapter 17.
3. Letter to Steward of New Inn 13/11/1834. Pilgrim Edition Letters.
4. Letter to Edward Chapman 27/12/1839. Pilgrim Edition Letters.
5. The Uncommercial Traveller No XIV: 'Chambers'. 'Members of the Inns dine in Hall at long tables, but every two facing pairs of diners is formed into a set of four people. Conversation is expected to take place within the set of four so that everyone can participate.
6. Fielding K T. Speeches of Charles Dickens. Oxford: Clarendon Press, 1960.
7. Fitzgerald P. Bozland. Dickens Places and People. London: Downey & Co, 1895: p 237
8. Simpson AW. 'The Common Law and Legal Theory'. Oxford Essays in Jurisprudence, 1960.
9. Hale, Sir Matthew: Reflections on Hobbes's Dialogues on the Law. In Sir William Houldsworth, History of English Law Vol V p 505.

1. The Pickwick Papers

1. In the Tugges sketch the young lawyer arriving from the Temple is received with great respect and speedily introduced to Mr Tugg's daughter.
2. This restriction was removed in stages from 1843 onwards, being totally removed by the Evidence Act of 1851.

3. Nicholas Nickleby

1. Here Dickens is again recording a feature of the legal scene shortly before it disappears. In 1839 a Company could be incorporated only by Royal charter or by an Act of Parliament. The two MP's are on the platform to reassure potential shareholders that Parliamentary approval would be achieved. In 1844 the Joint Stock Companies Act enabled corporate status to be conferred on payment of fees of £10. Under the Limited Liability Act of 1855 Limited liability could be gained without an Act of Parliament.

4. The Old Curiosity Shop

1. MacKenzie, Norman and Jeanne. Dickens: A Life. Oxford: Oxford University Press, 1979.
2. The profession of attorney is by far the older of the two, dating from the 13th century when an attornatus had the authority to act on behalf of their clients and to prepare their cases but did not speak on their behalf in court. They were usually trained in one of the Inns of Chancery but practised in the common law courts. The profession of solicitor emerged in the 16th century and solicitors were recognised as officers of the Court of Chancery by the 17th Century. By the Judicature Act of 1873 all attorneys, proctors and solicitors became solicitors of the Supreme Court.

5. Barnaby Rudge

1. The First Book of Kings, 19. 11. The still small voice was the calm voice of conscience in which, after the fire and the earthquake, God spoke to the prophet Elijah.
2. Coke, Sir Edward: Preface to the Eighth Reports 1611. In George Garnett. Magna Carta - History and Context. University of London Press, 2018.
3. Tambling, Jeremy. Dickens' Novels as Poetry, Allegory and the Literature of the City. London: Routledge, 2015.
4. Elofson, Woods and Todd, eds. The Writings and Speeches of Edmund Burke. Oxford: OUP, 1997 Vol III.
5. Sonnet III.
6. A Tale of Two Cities, Book the Third chapter 12.

6. American Notes and Martin Chuzzlewit

1. R v Desmond and Barratt. Times 28/04/1868. The doctrine of intent in murder remains the subject of discussion in English law, including consideration of whether the victim's death or serious bodily harm was part of the principal purpose of the relevant act.

7. David Copperfield

1. For instance in Emmanuel Kant's 'Observations on the Feeling of the Beautiful and the Sublime', 2.217. In Anthropology, History and Education. Eds Zoller G and Loudon RB, CUP 2007: 'One can bring about that noble attitude that is the beauty of virtue' when a person *'subordinates their particular inclination to such an enlarged sense of the beauty and dignity of human nature'*. (my italics)
2. Hale, Sir Matthew: Reflections on Hobbes's Dialogue of the Laws. Houldsworth, Sir William: History of English Law, 7th Edition, London 1956 p 502.

8. Bleak House
1. The Earl of Oxford's Case 1615. 1 Rep Ch 1.
2. Dickens met a similar old lady 'of weird gentility' in St Luke's Hospital for the Insane in 1851.
3. Blackstone, Sir William: Commentaries on the Laws of England. II Co 51. Allen, Jesse. 'Law and Artifice in Blackstone's Commentaries'. University of Pittsburgh School of Law. 2014.
4. A Tale of Two Cities, Book 3 chapter 14.
5. Symonds Inn, though not in the usual lists of Inns of Chancery, certainly existed. In Boyle's View of London 1799 the Clerk of the Errors Office of the Court of Common Pleas was to be found there at Master Pepys Chambers and the Clerk of the Papers Office of the King's Bench was at No 6.

9. Little Dorrit
1. 'Number accurately' ie keep an accurate account. The motto of the Institute of Chartered Accountants.
2. Bentham, Jeremy. Writings on the Poor Laws. Oxford: Clarendon Press, 2001.
3. Malthus, Thomas Robert. An Essay on the Principle of Population. London: J Johnson, 1798.

11. Great Expectations
1. Forster, John. The Life of Charles Dickens. London: Everyman's Library, 1969. Vol I Book 1 ch 4, 3 Book 2 ch 1,2.
2. Bleak House, chapter 22

MICHAEL LYNCH

Michael Lynch was born in Manchester and read English Language and Literature at Oxford University. He taught English for several years in schools and colleges and was subsequently called to the Bar at the Middle Temple, specialising as a consultant in Employment Law. He is married with two grown-up children and for many years lived in Staffordshire where he served as a County Councillor. Now retired, he lives in the Cambridge area and teaches courses on Dickens, Jane Austen and George Eliot at the University of the Third Age in Cambridge. He is a member of the Dickens Fellowship and a member of the Royal Society of Literature. He is currently working on a book of limericks.

Mike was drawn to write this book partly by the fact that Dickens himself had been a member of the Middle Temple for fifteen years between 1839 and 1855.

From Canbury Press

Under the Wig
A Lawyer's Stories of Murder, Guilt and Innocence
William Clegg
ISBN: 9781912454082
Hardback – £22.00

'This is a gripping memoir from one of our country's greatest jury advocates, offering a fascinating, no-holds-barred tour behind the scenes of some of the most famous criminal cases of modern times.'
The Secret Barrister

Contact us: contact@acropolispublishing.co.uk

acropolispublishing.co.uk

www.ingramcontent.com/pod-product-compliance
Lightning Source LLC
Chambersburg PA
CBHW032125160426
43197CB00008B/523